Psychot
Warneford Hospital
Oxford OX3 7JX

Rewriting Family Scripts

THE GUILFORD FAMILY THERAPY SERIES
Michael P. Nichols, *Series Editor*
Alan S. Gurman, *Founding Editor*

Recent Volumes

REWRITING FAMILY SCRIPTS

Improvisation and Systems Change

JOHN BYNG-HALL

Foreword by Frank S. Pittman III

The Guilford Press
New York London

To my wife, Sue,
and sons,
Andrew, Peter, and Stephen

© 1995 The Guilford Press
A Division of Guilford Publications
72 Spring Street, New York, NY 10012

Printed in the United States of America

This book is printed on acid-free paper.

Last digit is print number: 9   8   7   6   5   4   3   2   1

Library of Congress Cataloging-in-Publication Data
Byng-Hall, John.
    Rewriting family scripts : improvisation and systems
  change / by John Byng-Hall.
       p.   cm — (The Guilford family therapy series)
  Includes bibliographical references and index.
  ISBN 0-89862-876-8
      1. Family psychotherapy. 2. Family—Psychological aspects.
  3. Attachment behavior. 4. Schemas (Psychology) I. Title.
  II. Series.
  RC488.5.B95   1995
  616.89′156—dc20   95-16208
                                                    CIP

Foreword

We humans are not just the sum of our experiences or the sum of our relationships, we are even more the sum of our stories. Undeniably, the story itself is more powerful than the events it has been created to reveal and explain.

Much that therapists do involves changing the stories people tell about themselves and one another and their relationships. Different schools of family therapy champion different techniques for rewriting family history, and even different philosophies about it.

"Politically correct" therapists, out to protect people from guilt by making them aware of the ways in which they have been abused or disenfranchised, like to rewrite family stories in such a way that people who are doing undesirable things are seen as so powerless that they cannot help themselves: What they do is not their fault, but is the fault of their abusers, perhaps their parents or the society. This leaves the patients disempowered.

"Therapeutically correct" therapists, out to empower people and make them aware of the control they do have over their lives, like to rewrite family stories in such a way that the seemingly powerless member gains the power to change something and bring about desirable change. Either approach is systemic, connecting with the family feedback mechanisms for enhancing and diminishing behaviors and emotions, but one sees the symptomatic family member as a victim of the system and the other sees the symptom bearer as a powerful player in the system.

Some of us try to go beyond therapeutic correctness into what might be considered "dramatic correctness," rewriting family stories to make them comedies rather than tragedies. In a tragedy, people helplessly, stubbornly, or suicidally fail to change when they have the chance, and instead proceed determinedly down a predictable path toward an inexorable disaster. In a comedy, someone changes, breaks out of step with the familiar family script, just at the right moment to ensure a favorable outcome. Therapy must change life from a tragedy into a comedy. And it might as well be fun.

There are few more compelling story tellers in family therapy than John Byng-Hall, and none I can think of who make therapy and the rewriting of family stories, scripts, myths, and legends so lively, so full of surprises, so playful, so full of fun. Byng-Hall seems incapable of a sense of tragedy: The inescapable doom of those unaccustomed to adaptation and change is quite foreign to his nature, and as his own story unfolds it becomes clear why he has had to grow so strong. Byng-Hall is unshakably therapeutically correct and empowering; he never permits anyone to feel helpless and powerless in his presence. And, at every moment, even the most painful ones, he loves life and wants to lead others into it.

Byng-Hall's scholarly book is informed by Bowlby's theories and research about *attachment* and the connection between secure or insecure attachment to parents and subsequent attachment anxieties in later life. He examines the incoherent scripts insecure people follow to maintain some form of attachment in a life in which their stories do not help them feel either empathic or secure. One's childhood does not have to be ideal, but the stories about it have to be coherent.

Byng-Hall explores the recursive cycle between changing family stories, changing family scripts, and changing family relationships. He says that therapy is not over until his clients have rewritten their stories in a way that makes their lives *coherent, empathic,* and thus *secure.* Then they can create new scripts for themselves and, as they change old patterns and do things differently, they can begin to improvise: to take the risk of doing things based on the new situations rather than on the old myths.

I had never looked at families, stories, and change in quite these ways before reading *Rewriting Family Scripts,* and so far I like the effect this perspective has had on me. It really does add a logic to some of the flying-by-the-seat-of-my-pants therapy I have been doing. I do not recall another theoretical frame work that feels so right to me. The book makes me exhilarated about being a family therapist. As Byng-Hall describes dozens of rich and lively stories of people achieving that level of empowerment and liberation, of learning to improvise, the joy for them, for Byng-Hall, and for us as observers is palpable.

When I first read some of Byng-Hall's work I was delighted with his flexibility, his imagination, his security in intermingling techniques, in fumbling around, without feeling any need to be in total control, or to know where he was going and how he was going to get there. I had already written about the "desperately resourceful therapist" who might as well have been Byng-Hall, never at the mercy of his theories or limited by the bag of tricks he brought with him, always alert to an opening into the family, a tool they were giving him to use to prod them along. He was just so downright human. And perhaps the thing I loved most about Byng-Hall as a therapist was his unwavering banner of optimism about the human condition and people's capacity for change.

I met Byng-Hall about 20 years ago, at a meeting of the Editorial Advisors to *Family Process* in the Yucatan Peninsula of Mexico. I tell a story about it, which is absolutely true—except, of course, for the details, the cast of characters, and the sequence of events. I had rented a Volkswagen beetle to explore the wonders of the jungle there, and somehow ended up with 8 or 10 passengers. I forget who was in the car with us, perhaps (why not?) Virginia Satir, Jay Haley, Salvador Minuchin, Lyman Wynne, Margaret Singer, Carl Whitaker, and Murray Bowen.

Without a map or compass, I got us lost, and the more desperate the family therapists got, the more sure they were they had the right techniques for getting me back on track. They sculpted us, double binded us, single binded us, moved us around in our seats, encouraged us to leave home or go home again, and even went crazy in front of us. None of them had an accurate map of this foreign territory, but their own disorientation did not stop them from championing their favorite solution to it.

I went from sheepish to sullen to testy in no time. In fact I was seriously considering abandoning family therapy right there in the jungle. I swore that if one more brilliant family therapist gave me a magical answer to a problem he or she did not fully understand yet, I would dump them all right there in a pool of crocodiles.

At that point John spoke for the first time, informing us cheerfully that the situation brought to mind a bit of family legend involving a great-great-whatever uncle, Admiral Byng, who during the Seven Years War in 1757 could not find the French he was supposed to fight. He did not know quite what to do, did not know which of his experts to trust, so he did nothing. He merely abandoned his fort in Minorca to the French and was subsequently shot for doing so. He survives only as a symbol of incompetence in high places.

This seemed a graceful way of telling me that I was driving, and that I had to do something, even if it were wrong. I could not abandon family therapy to the vines and reptiles of the Mexican jungle. I suddenly saw what had gone wrong with family therapy: Some therapists had come to believe that they or their heroes knew the simple answer even if they did not know the complex question. So rather than ask the family therapists for more magical solutions, I stopped at a filling station and asked a local for directions.

Byng-Hall, by telling a good humored story, converted tragedy to comedy, saved family therapy from the crocodiles, and, unlike his uncle, must forever be remembered in glory. *Rewriting Family Scripts* confirms what I already have learned from Byng-Hall: that a good story is worth more than a car load of magic, and a good theory may be worth even more.

—FRANK S. PITTMAN III

Preface

My mother always seemed to know what my father would do next. I can remember marvelling at this. How could she know? Could she listen to his thoughts? When I realized much later that both my parents would go into familiar routines together this idea was less surprising. It is easy, after all, to predict events that happen again and again. But how could they manage to repeat their daily routines in the first place? That is the interesting question. The complex collaborative mechanisms involved are among the wonders of human nature. How can all the members of a family predict each other's actions so well that they seem to be following a script—each coming in on cue as the plot unfolds? And why do some families repeat the same old self destructive performance again and again, following the same old futile plot down to its grisly denouement? And how can we help them to try something else? These are some of the questions that family therapists have asked over the years. This book attempts to answer them in a fresh way.

Actors usually follow a written script. If they want to rewrite the script—as they may be encouraged to do in experimental theater—they improvise until a new plot emerges that they then adopt for future performances. The actors thus become authors of their own new script. Rewriting family scripts involves a similar process. The main thesis of this book is that families are more likely to be able to alter old patterns if they feel secure enough with each other to risk improvising with fresh ways of relating. Feeling unsure about how other family members will use, or misuse, any new initiative will encourage individuals to resort to old, well-worn predictable pathways. Rigid scripting is often the result of putting safety before exploration.

I have used script theory to explain how patterns are repeated.

Many workers have used the concept of script; these include developmentalists (Stern, 1994; Nelson, 1981), cognitive psychologists (Schank & Abelson, 1977; Tomkins, 1979), transactional analysts (Steiner, 1974), psychoanalysts (McDougall, 1986), attachment theorists (Bretherton, 1985), sex therapists, (McCormick, 1987), social scientists (Cronen et al., 1982) and others such as psychodramatists and some sociologists. Most of these ideas center on how the individual develops a script for what to do in certain circumstances. There has been less emphasis on how these personal scripts are linked into a system of relationships. This extrapolation is relatively simple because a shared script is one that is in each member's mind and then enacted in family scenarios. A family script thus provides a way of articulating "inner" and "outer" family dramas.

I use attachment theory (Bowlby, 1988; Ainsworth 1991; and see Holmes, 1993, and Karen, 1994, for recent reviews) to think about how family attachments can provide a secure family base (Byng-Hall, 1995) from which it is safe enough to explore new ways of relating. I can feel reasonably confident that attachment theory is a "good story" because much of the theory has been validated by high-quality research. This research has also discovered that the sort of narrative that individuals use in describing their past attachments can predict what sort of attachments they are observed to have with their children (Main et al., 1985). At last here is a research link between "inner" mental representation and "outer" dramatization of a family scene. Family therapists' current interest in narrative (White & Epston, 1989) makes this a particularly rewarding piece of research.

Postmodernism has helped us to see that all stories have their own particular validity, and that there is no one truth. This enables us to respect our clients' stories, and to stop seeing our own perceptions as objective truth. Clients, however, come to us because their stories are no longer helpful. They do not want any old story to replace it, wisely they want one most likely to help them to solve their problems. We need to search for the best possible story that works for us with our own clients. Attachment theory is par excellence a modernist project exploring the underlying mechanism for the survival of homo sapiens. I like Pocock's suggestion (1995) that harnessing both modern and postmodern positions in family therapy can create a "better story."

I have been fascinated by the myths that we in the family therapy movement have built up around ourselves (Byng-Hall, 1988). We have a long long tradition of being pioneers. We believe that we have found the truth (modernism?) where others have failed, especially those with ideas about the individual. As this form of self idealization nears its half-century perhaps we should increasingly challenge this piece of self deception. It cuts us off from many important advances in the exploration of human experience. In order to protect our idealized superior position from which we can look down on"them," we have turned instead to ideas from less relevant fields such as philosophy and biology. This book has been written against the background of disillusionment with the abstract nature of some of the theorizing within the field. People can simply disappear. We need to repopulate the theories. Luckily there is a healthy move toward an interest in the interface between the family system and the intrapsychic system. Any systemic theory that fails to include an understanding of its main sub-system is a very impoverished theory—indeed it is unsystemic. For my practice anyway, there is no adequate and coherent systemic theory of family relationships currently available in the literature. This book provides a conceptual framework that I have found to be useful in helping families to explore new ways of relating.

The reader needs to know how my ideas have been influenced by my past. I have included pieces of information about my family and childhood in various parts of the book where it seemed relevant to the issues being discussed. In my child psychiatry training I was schooled in object relations theory at the Tavistock Clinic (Dicks, 1967, for marital work; Box et al., 1981, for psychoanalytic family therapy). This theory attempts to explain how the family becomes represented as "objects" in each member's mind, but says less about the consequences of being an"object"in other people's minds. I then espoused systems theory in the early 1970s, which deals with mutual influences between all family members, but says less about the mind. I was exposed to ideas about attachment theory from early in my training, and subsequently I was appointed to the post left vacant when John Bowlby retired in 1973, and so experienced the mixed blessing of being scripted to follow a famous figure. Since Bowlby had a long and productive retirement spent at the Tavistock, I got to know him and his ideas well.

I never had a family therapy training because there was no train-ing in England at the end of the 1960s and early 1970s when I started working with families. However many of the world's family therapy pioneers, representing all the major schools of family therapy, have come through London over the years. From them I have learned a great deal. I have improvised with many ideas and tailored them to fit my own style. As with anyone who has been theorizing for a long time I have had the curious experience of having ideas that I touched on earlier being"pioneered"later. In 1973 I wrote about family myths in terms that were not dissimilar to social constructionism, but I discovered that Ferreira had already done so in 1963. Such are the unwitting leapfrogging advances in knowledge. I also wrote about family stories: Other writers have recently gone much further. In this book I have chosen, at risk of seeming to be dated, to maintain the language in which my original ideas were proposed because it provides a different slant.

This book is primarily written for practicing family therapists, but will also be suitable for students. It covers most of the central issues of family therapy practice, and it can provide an introduction to how to conduct therapy. The book will also be of interest to attachment theorists, family theorists, and developmentalists who are looking for a family systems framework in which children's development can be seen as a process mutually influenced by all family members. I have tried to write with a minimum of jargon with the belief that if an idea cannot be put into plain words then it is probably muddled. In other words, my ideas can also be understood by those who are interested in families whether or not they are therapists.

The clinical material is mostly illustrated by describing particular families in some depth and length. I think this is valuable when attempting to demonstrate how ideas are integrated into a whole. As families often have overlapping issues, some of the same themes may be revisited. Although repetition may at times seem irritating or redundant, I believe that being exposed to many variations on a theme can be a good way of fully understanding an issue. I have thus tried to improvise around each theme in a way that is congruent with the message of the book.

Those readers who like to approach ideas from clinical illustrations may chose to read Chapter 5—which is a full case study—either first or after Chapter 1.

Acknowledgments

Families come first. The reader will see how much I owe to both my own family and client families for teaching me how families survive and thrive. In addition, my family graciously, on the whole, put up with loosing an enormous amount of 'home time', and emotional energy that I poured into this book. Special thanks go to the families who read drafts and generously made helpful comments on my story of their therapy.

There are a host of colleagues, too numerous to mention all, who have contributed to the ideas in this book. I give John Bowlby a posthumous thank you. Peter Bruggen provided a powerful training experience and also helped me with the text. Members of the Systems group at the Tavistock Clinic have provided inspiration: A special thanks must go to Rosemary Whiffen who was my co-chairperson in setting up the group in the early 1970s; also to Jenny Altschuler, Charlotte Burck, Barbara Dale, David Campbell, Emilia Dowling, Stephen Frosh, Gill Gorell Barnes, Judy Hildebrand, Sebastian Kraemer, Caroline Lindsey, and Renos Papadopoulos. In addition, Rosemary Whiffen has helped with the text, as has Gill Gorell Barnes who also helped in the whole development of the book and gave important advice. Joan Stevenson-Hinde and Juliet Hopkins made invaluable suggestions about my use of attachment theory, and Sophie Freud made very useful suggestions about scripts and helped me to get going initially. Maggie Dennis helped with the language. My analyst, Pearl King, gave me invaluable insights into family life as well as helping me to feel at ease with my past. Bernice Slagel and Melissa Balfour devoted energy and enthusiasm to putting it all down on paper. Guilford Publications has helped to nurture the book through its long gestation period. Seymour Weingarten taught me the meaning of the term "dead line"; they die—but are incidental to the live product. Sharon Panulla encouraged me when lagging, while Jodi Creditor skillfully improved my English American style. Final thanks must go to my wife, Sue, who read and reread the text and helped to make it as clear as possible.

Contents

FROM SCRIPTS TO IMPROVISATIONS

O·N·E

Secure Enough to Improvise

There is an apparent paradox at the core of family life. Repetition provides the launching pad for change. We may feel secure enough to explore if we can predict that support will be readily available if and when it is needed, especially if new ventures run into trouble or if potentially dangerous situations arise. Difficulties that lead to consultations with a family therapist often arise out of conflict within the family's own relationships. This book proposes a model of change in which the therapist helps the family to feel secure enough to risk improvising in those relationships. They can then explore how to create a more secure family situation in which solutions to present and future problems can be worked out.

There are other advantages to the tenacious predictability of family life. The family roles that are reliably fulfilled allow for a degree of collaboration that is quite extraordinary. The family script can provide routines for family life which can be followed almost automatically. Imagine having to negotiate every action without familiar pathways—we would never get beyond breakfast! This capacity to go onto automatic pilot frees the family's energy to be focused on what is novel. Repetition becomes the background against which change is the foreground; that which is new becomes the focus of attention. In contrast, chaos obscures potentially significant change, unless the new behavior facilitates consistency, in which case that new pattern becomes the foreground, thus becoming the new center of attention. Either way, it is the interplay between repetition and flux that is the basis for growth. Rewriting family scripts follows the sequence of a scripted pattern giving way to some improvisation followed by the establishment of a new pattern.

FAMILY SCRIPTS AND SCENARIOS

Family scripts can be defined as *the family's shared expectations of how family roles are to be performed within various contexts.* The term "expectations" implies anticipation of what is to be said and done within family relationships, as well as family pressures to perform the roles as expected. If one member fails to perform in the prescribed way, another member of the family may be recruited to take up that role instead. In other words, the plot is "scripted" while the cast can change. However, individuals can become typecast. Family members can identify themselves with particular roles, as well as become identified by others as characteristically occupying those roles. The term "shared" does not mean that everyone has the same view of what is, or should be, going on. Often family members see things differently and vary in their wishes to change the pattern, either now or in the next generation. For example, children can vow to themselves to follow different patterns when they become parents. No one, however, acts in a way that successfully breaks the current pattern. Hence, family expectations of what will happen remain the same.

The term "family script" is best reserved for relationships that involve more than one generation. Marital or couple scripts are subscripts of the family script and warrant a book of their own. These scripts will be mentioned in this book mainly in the way that they affect other generations. Parenting scripts are, however, more clearly central to family scripts.

Family scripts are revealed when repeating patterns of family interaction are either observed or described. When an episode is acknowledged by the family as being typical of what happens in that particular situation, it can be seen as a scenario that represents the family script for that particular context. The same scenario is expected the next time the situation arises. I am using the term "scenario" to imply an encounter of which it can be said that something significant happens within family relationships. The nature of relationships is illustrated by the way in which the decisive moments are handled during the scenario. The roles that each plays in family relationship will also be clarified. This episode can be enacted over a few minutes, a few days, or even longer.

The basic elements of a family scenario include a *context* in which family members engage with each other, say around a particular task; a *plot* in which family members "motives" become clear as the scenario unfolds; and an *outcome* in which the consequences of the encounter are revealed. As the usual outcome can be anticipated in the early phases of a scenario, the image of where things are heading can motivate each person to try to either change the direction in which things usually go, or to collaborate in the reenactment. If a particular outcome has been particularly unpleasant in the past or is especially feared, all members of the family may be motivated to avoid it happening again whatever the immediate cost. This can help to explain the curious phenomenon of members of a family joining in a family scene knowing full well that it will inevitably lead to tears. Each person may, however, feel compelled to act to prevent what he or she fears might be an even worse disaster. The solution has now become the problem.

Individual enactments may be remembered by the family. The way that stories are told is discussed further in Chapter 8. The attitude toward what happened is conveyed in the telling. It can become a parable or moral tale that encodes the rules of family relationships. Some aspects of the story convey what should be avoided; others what should be emulated. Retelling helps to ensure that the image becomes shared. Between the moment of the enactment of a scenario and the telling of the story there is, of course, extensive editing and shortening. A videotape of the whole episode would, no doubt, reveal interaction of incredible complexity that could be interpreted in countless ways. The distillation process of editing is one way that the family generalizes its images to guide its members in what to do and say when, where, how, and why. The perception discerns within this complexity a plot and an outcome. This organizing, or punctuation, of the story provides meaning to what is going on.

The expected scenarios for each particular family situation thread together to create an overall script for how all family relationships are expected to be conducted in general. This is the complete family script. If, however, one scenario is generally agreed by the family to be typical of all contexts, this can then be used to represent the family script for the family's relationships in general: an "exemplar family script."

The therapist, however, is usually interested in scenarios in which the complained of behavior is enacted. Instead of calling these "problem scenarios," I prefer to see them as attempted solution scenarios. This helps us to focus attention on how each person tries to solve the problem. It also recognizes that the behavior that is experienced now as problematic may have started out as an attempted solution to an earlier problem. The scenarios that emerge in therapy are coconstructed between the family and the therapist who is interested in particular themes.

Vignettes of what happened between sessions can be discussed. The systems therapist is likely to ask questions that paint a wider picture: "Where was Dad while this was going on?" . . . "How did you show what you felt about it when he went off to the pub during all this?" . . . "Did Jane notice your anger?" The coconstructed story may then become part of the family beliefs about what to expect of itself. For this reason when a family is reporting an episode that happened at home, I ask what was the old way of doing things and what was new about it; there are always some fresh moves, however small, leading to unexpected consequences. This focuses the therapy on how the family can do things differently. Family members come to believe that they can change things for themselves. Some scenarios are enacted within the session, which allows the therapist to be involved in some of the fresh moves.

VIGNETTE FROM A FIRST FAMILY
THERAPY SESSION

To help to illustrate some of the main ideas in the book, I will describe aspects of the first session of work with the Morton family. Further material from the work with this family will also be used later in the book.

The Mortons came from a close-knit farming community. Frank, the father, worked in an apple orchard; Annabel, the mother, looked after the children. Jason, aged 5, was out of control and was hitting his younger brother William, aged 2. Annabel was afraid of battering Jason when she reached the end of her tether. By the middle of the first session the two boys were rampaging round my office. Annabel and Frank were trying to reason with them to sit down. Not surprisingly, this had no effect. Frank eventually slid down onto the floor and started to play with them, and the boys settled quite quickly. When playing together, father and sons reminded me of a group of siblings. Annabel used the space provided to talk to me. She told me how desperately she wanted to get back to work and have some adult company again. She told me how she would lose her temper with Jason, especially when he hit his little brother William. She told me that sometimes she had to call her husband to come in from the orchard. He could always settle the boys by playing with them.

I noticed during this conversation that Frank had set up a game of trains, putting three chairs in a line, one behind the other. Then Frank did something odd. He rearranged the seats so that the front two seats were put side by side instead of one behind the other. He put Jason on one of these seats and then sat himself on the other, while William was placed behind. Frank and Jason then became completely engrossed with each other. This intrigued me. I tried to connect this game with the information that Frank had given me earlier in the session, that he was one of identical twins. I suddenly realized that this might have been what he was now re-creating with Jason. At this moment Annabel noticed my increasing preoccupation with the game, and that I was not listening to her. She stopped talking to me and turned away abruptly. I felt guilty about my wavering attention. She then saw William—who was also feeling left out—give Jason a shove in the back. Jason, furious, turned around and took a swipe at William, but he missed and fell off his chair. Annabel exploded, "Jason! You horrible boy! Don't bully your baby brother." This outburst disrupted the play, and Jason's behavior went out of control again.

The above vignette was clearly unique because it occurred in the context of the first family therapy session. The setting and my presence will have influenced what happened. It is also only my version of what happened. However, the enactment as I perceived it showed some similarity to what they told me happened at home when problems arose: Jason was unruly; mother could not manage him; her temper erupted when Jason attacked his brother; and father was often called home to settle him, which he did by playing with him. When stories about problematic episodes that occurred before therapy or between sessions follow similar pathways to those seen in the session, it adds some support to the notion that this behavior is scripted.

IMPROVISING A NEW SOLUTION TO THE PROBLEM

Improvising implies abandoning the set script and extemporizing instead. This may happen when the old script does not fit the current situation, or when those involved are in search of something different. Sketching out the basic elements of a new scenario can create a situation in which the improvisation becomes necessary.

The therapist can help to create a new coconstructed scenario by suggesting a goal (Minuchin & Fishman, 1981) which the family then achieves in their own way. If the therapist only sketches in the basic ground rules of a new scenario, then the family can improvise ways of relating within that scenario. If the therapist defines too much of how it should be enacted, they will feel that they are following his script, not rewriting their own. In the session Jason's behavior deteriorated following his mother's angry outburst. I helped the family to regain control of Jason's behavior using modified structural family therapy techniques (Minuchin, 1974; Minuchin & Fishman, 1981). I generally use this structural approach only when children are out of control—I find it invaluable. I usually suggest a scenario in which it becomes necessary for the family to improvise. I ask the parents to settle the children when it is clear things cannot go on as they are. The basic guideline (in those families in which there are two parents) is that they should plan each strategy together. I also try to block each move that has not worked in the past.

I suggested to Frank and Annabel that they had to work as a team to settle the children, otherwise we could not continue. We had already discussed how reasoning with the boys did not seem to help, so whenever they tried this I commented on it. Father tried using play once more, but that quickly deteriorated into chaos. They were now thrown onto their own resources. They had to improvise a new solution. I suggested time and time again that they consult each other to make a shared plan. When either parent acted unilaterally I pointed it out. Eventually they were able to agree that Frank should hold Jason until he settled down. He did this by sitting Jason on his knee but holding him very loosely. Frank explained that he was terrified of hurting Jason, who echoed this idea by complaining that his father was strangling him. Small wonder Frank had avoided disciplinary confrontations in the past. Jason continued to wriggle and fight, complaining loudly. I suggested that Frank and Annabel discuss with one another how to settle Jason down. After another 5 minutes of struggle they began to do so in a way that showed that they were collaborating as parents. Up to then they had talked about Jason as if he was their sibling. When they talked as parents, Jason relaxed, put his thumb in his mouth, snuggled down into his father's arms, and shut his eyes. He was suddenly a secure, relaxed little boy. I congratulated them. Both parents were surprised and delighted.

Because I had given no instructions other than using a simple guideline about sharing, and blocking previously failed solutions, they had to find their own way. They were then able to accept that it was their own achievement. As they walked out at the end of the session, Frank said that it was the most constructive thing he had done. A new script was emerging which, if it became established, would include a change of family structure from a pseudosibling family organization to that of parents and children. Next session they reported that Jason had been well behaved for a week. He then, however, started getting a little more difficult again, especially with his mother. More work was, of course, needed. Father was still scripted as the one who could manage Jason. In a later session Annabel was able to control Jason in her own way (described in Chapter 4).

I find that unraveling some of the origins of the scripted scenarios frees families to explore new pathways. Work on the present and the past can reinforce each other.

TRANSGENERATIONAL CONTINUITY AND DISCONTINUITY: REPLICATIVE, CORRECTIVE, AND IMPROVISED SCRIPTS

Family life is a rehearsal for the next generation. Each parent has scenarios from childhood which if repeated in this generation can be called "replicative scripts." Some childhood experiences will have been uncomfortable and attempts may be made by parents to avoid these with their own children. This choice of the opposite style of parenting can be called "corrective scripts." There are also parenting styles that are improvised, or are influenced by observing other families. These, if repeated over time, will become scripted as part of family life. These can be called "improvised scripts." When comparing past and present, it is often possible to see elements of all three types of script in any scenario. Thus, current family scripts emerge out of an interweaving of these scripts. Episodes in each parent's past that occurred at the age or stage that the children are now entering are particularly likely to be echoed in what is going on now.

Repetition of Scenarios from the Previous Generations

Over the next few sessions with the Mortons, I built up a picture of both parents' pasts. I could then see what each parent had brought from childhood to the vignette in the first session.

Frank's Background

I drew the genogram in the fourth session (see Figure 1.1). When Frank and his twin brother were nearly 2 (the same age as William), their father had been killed trying to repair the electric cooker. Frank's mother went into a state of profound shock and withdrawal. To make things worse, Frank's paternal grandfather, the local publican, became convinced that his daughter-in-law had caused his son's death, and started to persecute her with threatening letters. The twins turned more and more to each other for comfort, and became inseparable. When the twins were aged 4 (Jason's age now), Frank's mother married Jim, who tried to protect her from her ex-in-laws by prohibiting them from having any contact with the family, and hence stopped

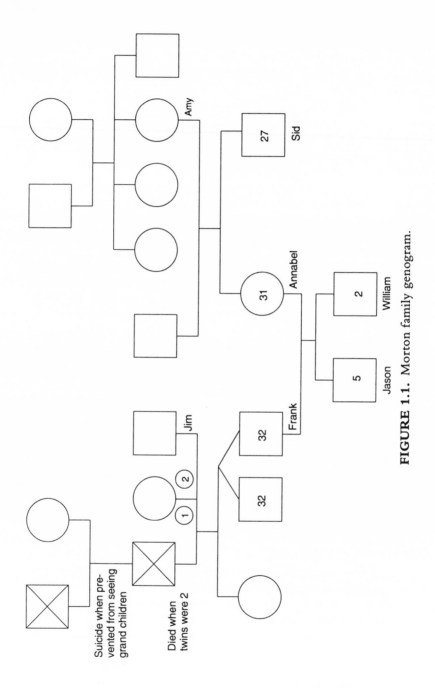

FIGURE 1.1. Morton family genogram.

Suicide when pre-
vented from seeing
grand children

Died when
twins were 2

Jim

Frank

Annabel

Sid

Amy

Jason

William

10

them seeing their grandchildren. Unfortunately, this did not end the family's woes. Frank's grandfather then proceeded to shoot himself and left a suicide note saying that he killed himself because he had been barred from his grandchildren. Frank's mother and Jim dealt with this by trying to expunge the first husband and his family from their memory—as if they had never existed. They attempted to create a myth of an intact nuclear family with Jim as the birth father.

Seen in this light, Frank's twinning with Jason in the first session can be seen as repeating aspects of his time when he, Frank, was a small child of 2 and had turned to his twin as a solution to his mother's withdrawal when his father died (the mother's withdrawal was represented at this moment in the therapy scenario by Annabel). A new man, Jim (now represented by the therapist), had then come in to rescue his mother when Frank was 4 (which is close to Jason's age now). These elements were part of Frank's replicative script. His corrective script was largely expressed through being determined to be there for his boys, unlike his own experience of losing his father.

Annabel's Background

Annabel's mother, Amy, had been in conflict over whether she had wanted a girl or a boy. This was not surprising considering the circumstances of her own birth. Amy had been the third girl in a family desperate to have a boy. There was a family legend about this told as a joke, but whose message was deadly serious. When Amy was born her father was said to have taken one look at her and seeing that she was a girl he ordered a bath to drown her, and then sent for a lawyer to start divorce proceedings. When Amy's mother was pregnant for the fourth time, she was sent to the Lake District so that she could drown the baby if it was another girl. This baby turned out to be a boy who was worshiped at the expense of the girls. Unfortunately Amy replicated this pattern in the next generation. When she had a son, Sid, 3 years after Annabel was born, she proceeded to dote on him but withdrew from Annabel, whose life was turned upside down by her little brother's arrival. Annabel was said to have beaten Sid "black and blue" out of jealousy, but she could not remember any of that. Now that Annabel had two children herself, she was trying to correct this jealous reaction by protecting her "baby" son, William, from the expected black-and- blue beating by the jealous older sibling. Hence her anger with Jason when he tried to hit William in the session. However, she also came frighteningly close to replicating the black-and-blue beating in her rages with Jason. Jason reminded Annabel of her brother Sid whenever Frank gave all his attention to him, thereby excluding her.

The Therapist's Family Script

The therapist's background also plays a part in shaping scenarios in therapy. Why did I engage with Annabel in a separate conversation—something I usually try to avoid in a session, while I was secretly more interested in the train game? Looking back I am reminded of a time when my own mother was upset. I was aware that I was very special to her. She was lonely and isolated on a huge ranch in East Africa. Since my father was out most of the time, I often felt that I should be with her more to relieve her loneliness. But I longed to be with him, and it was wonderful when I was. I have an image of playing on the lawn with him, riding on his back as he crawled. The images of the train and the riding games resonate, as do the images of mothers who are left out by men who are elsewhere.

Positive Framing of Replicative, Corrective, and Improvised Scripts

This technique is discussed in detail in Chapter 11 but is introduced here. Positive labeling can be given to replicative scripts by labeling them as being loyal to the family of origin. I pointed out to Frank that he was being loyal to his family's old solutions by leaving space for me to care for Annabel while he was getting, and giving, comfort to Jason.

Corrective scripts can be given a positive frame by pointing out to parents that they are struggling to provide a better experience for their children than their parents were able to provide for them. I pointed out that Frank was determined to be there for his children because his father had not been there for him, and Annabel, while determined to prevent her youngest child from being beaten black and blue by his elder sibling, was also struggling to stop herself from beating her son who reminded her of her brother.

Improvised scripts, unlike the historical replicative and corrective scripts, are written in response to current situations. They are improvised either out of necessity—as in the situation where Jason had to be controlled in the session—or driven by curiosity and a wish to explore new ways of relating. A stimulus for improvisation is a degree of uncertainty about what to do next so that interaction must be played off the cuff. Positive comments can be made about how much the family is exploring unknown territory. I remarked on how Frank was being an inventive pioneer in the way he was being a father in this family.

ATTACHMENTS AND SECURITY

The context in which uncertainty is experienced by family members provides a crucial variable in determining how the uncertainty is used. Is the setting secure in the knowledge of mutual trust and support? This makes it easier to take a risk and do something differently. Or is it experienced as insecure? In which case the relationship itself might be felt to be threatened by any new turn of events.

Security can be thought about within the framework of attachment theory (Bowlby, 1969, 1973, 1980, 1988), which is based on ethology, and explores the evolution of behaviors that ensure the survival of the species. Attachment behavior is defined as the behavior of a person seeking proximity to his or her attachment figure in a potentially dangerous situation (Bowlby, 1969). This is a mechanism that protects children—or adults—when vulnerable. It helps them to survive. The specific affectionate bonds established between family members can last throughout life, and so contribute to a continuing sense of security, and provide a source of ongoing care and concern.

Although the reader is probably familiar with the theory, I will briefly describe attachments as a way of delineating the principles that I will use in the book. A typical attachment behavior scenario can be observed in a park. This incidentally was also the setting that provided some of the early research (Anderson, 1972). It can be described in the following way:

> A toddler is playing in the park with his parent who is sitting reading on a bench. The child wanders away to explore something he or she has found in the grass. Every now and then the child comes back to the parent for a brief interaction: sharing discoveries, exchanging a few words, or getting a cuddle. The child then wanders off again to explore, but never going beyond a certain distance. If, say, a dog or something threatening appears, the child is likely to rapidly abandon play and run to the parent, arms outstretched to be picked up. The parent may notice the threat first and call the child. The child stays with the parent until danger passes, whereupon he or she gets off the parent's lap and wanders off to explore again, safe in the knowledge that he or she will be protected by the parent if need be.

In short, the child uses the parent as a safe base from which to explore, and parent and child stay in contact to ensure that they can get together in the presence of any potential danger. Within the attachment behavior scenario, the context is one of potential danger; the plot is of getting together as quickly as possible; and the motive for the child is to feel safe again, while the parent's motive is to protect the child.

This also illustrates the general principle of how in situations of potential threat the child stops exploring the outside world and seeks proximity to the parent or, in the absence of a parent, another attachment figure. The principle is safety first and exploration later. In terms of script theory a potentially threatening situation evokes tightly scripted behavior in which parent and child predictably got together. Exploration, however, allows for more improvisation.

An attachment figure needs to either tackle any potential danger successfully or move out of the danger zone. If, for instance, the dog stays in the vicinity and looks aggressive, the parent may move to another seat. It is this capacity of an attachment figure to deal with potential threats that gives those attached to him or her a continuing sense of security.

The therapist, in turn, can become a temporary attachment figure to the family. The family comes to him or her in a crisis. Each family member can quickly become attached to the therapist in this situation and can build some trust. The therapist can thus provide a temporary secure base from which the family members can explore their own solutions. However, if the family therapist is to establish him- or herself as a temporary attachment figure for the family, he or she has to be seen to be aware of the factors that threaten the family's relationship. Few families would trust a therapist who seems unable to see or acknowledge any dangers, or is unable to help them to attempt to tackle them. In families the potential threat may be coming from within the family itself, as in the Morton family where it turned out that both parents were afraid of hurting Jason.

The Mortons were able to begin to trust me when they found that I could help them to take charge of Jason, and so prevent the possibility of hurting him. This established the base from which they could later trust me sufficiently to explore the underlying fears about the tensions in their own relationship.

Effect of Security on Uncertainty: Either to Explore a Novelty, or to Avoid Strangeness

When a child is confronted with a situation of uncertainty there are potentially two contrasting responses. Which of these responses is evoked depends on the sense of security. If a young child is feeling secure with a parent, who is also available and keeping an eye on things, the child is likely to perceive a new object, whose nature is uncertain to the child, as being a novelty. This arouses the child's curiosity. For instance, a discarded package found in the grass of the park might arouse curiosity, in which case the child is likely to go to explore it. If, however, the child is feeling insecure, either because there is no trusting relationship with the caretaker, or the context is potentially threatening (e.g., when it is dark), a newly found object is more likely to be seen as strange and potentially dangerous. The child will usually then keep away from it. In other words, from a position of perceived protected safety new objects are seen as novel and will be explored. From a position of unprotected potential danger the same new object might be seen as strange and will be avoided. This differential response to uncertainty has obvious advantages for survival.

Similarly, any new behavior of uncertain origin emerging in a relationship (e.g., unexplained impatience) might be seen as either strange and treated as potentially dangerous, or novel and will arouse curiosity. If it is perceived as strange, attempts may be made to avoid reprovoking the impatience, returning to old familiar ways instead. If the impatience arouses curiosity, then it will probably lead to trying to discover what it is all about, and to improvise ways of dealing with it. If, however, it becomes clear that the impatience poses a problem and something has to be done about it, new solutions may be improvised out of the necessity to sort things out. For instance, the impatience may signal that the impatient person cannot go on relating any longer in the same old way. In this situation individuals are more likely to feel safe enough to launch out into the unknown of improvisation if the relationship itself is secure. A secure relationship can be expected to weather any storms that might blow up as a result of confronting the underlying causes of the irritation. Also, in a secure relationship each new move that is made by one person is likely to be experienced by the other person as novel, thus evoking further exploration and inviting mutual improvisation. New, previously unknown, vistas may then open up. Improvisation is also encouraged when reliable support from other family members, or a therapist, is available should any new interactions create difficulties.

In summary, there are two main forms of improvisation in family relationships. First, there is improvisation that comes out of *necessity*: Something has to be done when old solutions are not working. This is analogous to the "potential danger" phase of attachment organization. Second, there is improvising out of *curiosity* or fun when it feels safe to try something new, even if it is uncertain where it will lead. This is analogous to the "exploratory" phase. A secure relationship supports the possibility of improvisation in either of these situations. A therapist who is trusted by the family can make the risks involved in improvisation feel less frightening, even when family relationships are insecure.

Secure and Insecure Attachment Patterns

Parent and Child Attachment Patterns

A brief introduction to attachment patterns will be given here. A more detailed description, including research findings, will be given in Chapter 6.

Children's responses to separations from parents (Bowlby, 1973; Robertson, 1952) reveal some of the ways in which they cope with threats to their attachments. In prolonged separations in which small children are placed in strange environments such as hospitals, the children's behavior is likely to go through a series of transitions. First, the child protests, calling for the parent and searching for him or her. In other words attachment behavior is continuously aroused. After a while the child becomes despairing and goes into what appears to be a state of mourning. But, on the parents' return, the child will turn away and appear disinterested. In other words, attachment behavior toward the parent eventually becomes switched off and the child becomes detached.

When the child and parent are once again reunited, this journey can often be reversed. There may be a period of distance from the parent, but the child may then begin to cling and become demanding, never allowing the parent out of sight—the attachment behavior has become continuously switched on again. Eventually the child may start leaving the parents' side to explore the outside world again. In other words, attachment behavior resumes its normal place in the child's relationship to the parent, and is only switched on again at appropriate times. The child is then free to explore autonomously while maintaining contact with the parent.

What is significant, however, is that this return journey may not go smoothly. The circumstances of the separation (e.g., the child has a serious operation) can influence what happens. However, it also depends in part on the parental responses to the child's unfamiliar behavior. The child's turning away on reunion is often very upsetting for the parent. It can invite a reciprocal distancing response from the parent. If for some reason the parent cools his or her emotions toward the child or rejects the child, then attachment behavior might remain switched off. The relationship may, however, progress back to the next phase, where attachment behavior is switched on permanently. The parent, in this trying situation, may find the clinging and demanding behavior of the child so exasperating that at times he or she wants to escape. This is likely to provoke the child to even greater clinging. Parent and child may then become engaged in a mutually reinforcing cycle, which maintains the permanent arousal of attachment behavior even in situations that are otherwise safe. They become "over close." It appears from this that it is the mutually reinforcing interaction patterns within relationships that can establish long-term attachment patterns. Those patterns then become mutually "scripted."

I was working with a family whose 3-year-old daughter had to go into hospital. Her mother stayed with her. Her grandmother, to whom she was very attached, could only visit occasionally. In the hospital she became clingy toward her mother, as would be expected in this threatening situation. But the girl turned away from her grandmother whenever she appeared. This pattern persisted when she went home. The grandmother was devastated and started to distance herself. I helped her to see that this was her granddaughter's way of trying to avoid being hurt by reengaging with someone who was so special, but who, she has discovered, might disappear. Following this, grandmother felt less rejected and stopped keeping out of the way, but made cautious but persistent approaches to her granddaughter instead. Their relationship soon improved. Because the girls' clinging behavior was understandable to her mother, she did not feel trapped by her child, and mutually reinforcing patterns were not established. The little girl eventually returned to secure attachments to both mother and grandmother.

Ainsworth (1967) explored what happened between normal mothers and infants at home, first in Uganda, and later in the United States (Ainsworth et al., 1978). Following brief separations in a laboratory setting, she found patterns of attachment similar to those seen during prolonged separation. Two groups of children seemed to be insecurely attached. A small minority of the samples were clingy and demanding, like the child protesting about a separation, while a sizable minority were more detached. The majority of ordinary children had secure attachments to their mothers, similar to those that existed prior to separation. The children would protest when left by mother, but on her return they could be readily comforted and then would explore autonomously.

Ainsworth's laboratory test, designed to evoke attachment behavior, is called the Strange Situation (SS) procedure (Ainsworth et al., 1978) (see Chapter 6 for a detailed discussion). Very brief vignettes are presented here. *Securely attached* (Pattern B) children's attachment behavior is switched on by the separation. They may protest and want to go with the parent. On reunion they settle quickly, attachment behavior is switched off, and they start exploring again. *Insecure/avoidant* (Pattern A) children do not seem concerned when the parent leaves; they may play with toys in an unimaginative way, and even turn away from the parent on his or her return. Their attachment behavior is minimal. *Insecure/ambivalent* (Pattern C) children cling to the parent, protest strongly on separation, and are inconsolable by the parent on return. They may remain clingy to the parent and fail to explore. Their attachment behavior is maximal. *Insecure/disoriented* (Pattern D) children do not have a coherent strategy, but they may show evidence of approach–avoidance conflicts. A high percentage of maltreated children are insecure/disoriented which makes sense of any approach–avoidance conflict. Attachment behavior is aroused and so they approach the parent, but the parent is also a source of danger and so they may veer away or stop dead in their tracks. This is a complex but important group of potentially disturbed children that has fairly recently been discovered and is still in the process of being elucidated.

The parent's side of the story is provided through an interview about his or her childhood experiences of attachments, the Adult Attachment Interview (AAI; Main et al., 1985). This indicates a parent's current working model, analogous to a personal script of attachment relationships. The categories of the parents' AAI could predict in 75–80% of cases the pattern of a child's attachment to the parent (Main et al., 1985), even when the AAI was administered during pregnancy (Fonagy et al., 1991).

The attitude that the parent has toward attachment helps to explain his or her child's behavior. Parents of securely attached (Pattern B) children are categorized or *autonomous/free* (F). They are able to give a coherent account of childhood, in which they can remember how it felt to be a child with all of its joy and miseries, and could also empathize with the difficulties their own parents must have had. These adults can tune into their own children's experiences and respond appropriately to their needs, for instance, going to them when distressed, but giving them autonomy when they want to explore.

Parents of insecurely attached children give an incoherent account of attachments, but the distortion of the story fits the type of insecurity the child demonstrates. Parents of insecure/avoidant (Pattern A) children are categorized as *dismissive* (D). They dismiss the importance of attachments, denying any hurt or upset feelings about potentially upsetting episodes in their past. They also forget large parts of their childhood. It is as if they block painful feelings, and so cannot empathize with their children's distress. The children soon learn that going to the parent for comfort leads to a rebuff. Thus the children, in turn, learn to cut out upset feelings so that they no longer want to turn to the parent. Attachment behavior diminishes. In contrast, parents of insecure/ambivalent (Pattern C) children are categorized as *preoccupied/entangled* (E). They are so tuned into painful childhood experiences that they are preoccupied by the past and with other unresolved issues. The children then find that they can only get the parent's attention by working at it. They are likely to become demanding and clinging in an attempt to force the parent to notice and care for them. The parent responds ambivalently, responding at times, resenting the pressure at others, and making his or her own demands on the children when feeling upset.

Marvin and Stewart (1990) noted that disengaged styles of transacting were similar to insecure/avoidant (Pattern A) attachment relationships, while enmeshed styles of transacting were similar to insecure/ambivalent (Pattern C) relationships. Although this parallel is far from exact, it helps family therapists to place the phenomenon of attachment relationships within familiar categories.

The Family's Attachment Patterns

I use the concept of a secure family base (Byng-Hall, 1995) to provide a systemic framework for understanding the pattern of family's attachments, in which the mutual influences between each attachment can be thought about. The secure family base provides a reliable network of care that gives every member, of whatever age, a sufficient sense of security to explore and develop. Members know that "the family" will be there for them if and when needed. This shared sense of security and belonging can be undermined if, for instance, competition for care leaves some members excluded. All will think, "If it happened to him it might happen to me." Or if the family has power battles, adverse social situations, or losses, it may reduce the availability of care. The nature of a secure family base is considered in greater detail in Chapter 6.

The family therapist has a unique opportunity to observe the current household's attachment pattern. This may be immediately apparent on entry of the family into the strange situation of the therapist's room, at which point attachment behavior is likely to be aroused.

In the Morton family's first session, Jason came into the room first but stayed close to his father, and Annabel followed with William. Frank sat down and put Jason on his knee, and Annabel sat next to Frank and put William on her knee. But Frank then made an overture to William who quickly left his mother to come to him. Thus, the pattern of Frank playing with the two children while Annabel was sitting on her own was established within a few seconds of coming into the room. It was also clear that William's transfer to his father was initiated by Frank but agreed upon by his mother who let him go, and by William who was happy to move over to his father. In other words, there was some consensus as to the distance pattern.

Additional information about the attachment pattern can be gained from the Family Separation Test (Byng-Hall, 1995), a procedure I designed for families with young children. This test is easy to carry out during therapy. Before the session the parents are asked if they would collaborate in a simple test. They are then given written instructions. The children are thus not warned of what will happen— just as in the SS procedure—so they assume that it is their parents who are making the decisions. The parents are instructed to leave the room at a given signal from the therapist, leaving the children with the therapist. They are then asked to return to the room after 6 minutes, to enter the door together, and to stand side by side for 5 seconds before reacting naturally. This procedure reveals (1) difficulties in separating, (2) any attachment behavior, or caregiving between the siblings during the separation, and (3) attachment behavior to the therapist. It also (4) demonstrates which parent is the preferred attachment figure for each child on reunion and (5) gives clues as to the nature of each of the attachments.

In the Family Separation Test, William was very upset at the departure of his parents. He called for his father first but eventually cried for both parents. Jason comforted William by hugging him. After 3 minutes William settled and they came to play with the therapist, whom they had known for 2 months. On reunion, Jason avoided eye contact with his mother, went to his father, and sat on his lap. William went to his mother first, but only to fetch his comfort cloth. He then went over to his father.

Thus, in these two family scenarios both children end up with their father. Mother is left on her own. This pattern was repeated many times early in the therapy. It suggested that both boys had insecure attachments to mother, with avoidant feature for Jason, and ambivalent for William, while both were more secure with father. In a SS procedure with mother this was confirmed. Jason was found to be insecure/avoidant (Pattern A), while William was insecure/ambivalent (Pattern C).[1] Both were securely attached to their father. This would suggest that the patterns seen on entry to the first session, together with the Family Separation Test and the overall pattern in the sessions, might provide adequate information about attachment patterns for therapeutic purposes in families with young children (Cotgrove, 1993).

---

[1]Classification made by Joan Stevenson-Hinde and Ann Shouldice.

The Morton family illustrates another research finding: A child's pattern of attachment behavior with one parent does not predict the type of attachment with the other. One may be secure, the other insecure. Both the Morton children were insecure with mother but secure with father. It has been shown that the adverse effects of an insecure relationship with one parent can be ameliorated to some extent by a secure relationship with the other. No doubt, in the long run, Jason and William will benefit from their good relationship with their father. Or to put it another way, their situation might have been much more serious if they had also been insecure with their father. In terms of family attachment patterns, however, the presence of asymmetry in the security of attachment with each parent can cause problems. The more one relationship is preferred, the more the other may be neglected or undermined. This was especially true of the Mortons, where Annabel felt left out by the children preferring to go to their father.

Family attachment patterns can be understood if the meanings behind either being included or left out are elucidated. Some members may feel abandoned if left out; others feel invaded if relationships become too close and intense. This originates in the way that family scenarios are now, or have been enacted in the past. A normal family's struggle to establish some family interaction in which everyone is included and no one is excluded is explored in some detail in Chapter 12.

Improvising When Feeling More Secure

As we have seen, the potential danger in the Morton family came from within the family when Annabel was anxious about hurting Jason, and Frank was also fearful about disciplining him. This triggered an attempted solution scenario which was tightly scripted, and led to Frank coming home and settling the children through play. But although this reduced the sense of danger, it still provoked a sense of insecurity because now Annabel was reminded of the enraging experience of her parents' giving preferential treatment to her brother. Her tension meant that the boys' attachment behavior remained aroused, and focused on their father. This, of course, brought Jason and father even closer together. This maintained Annabel's fear, and little exploring or improvising on her part or anyone else's could happen in this situation.

As the therapist I had started to provide a secure base in which Frank had been able to control Jason. As we have seen earlier I had, however, for my own reasons, been recruited into being more interested in what was happening between Jason and his father. This left Annabel feeling left out once again. It was not until I became aware that I was replicating that childhood experience for Annabel after drawing her genogram that I was able to set about redressing the balance. Annabel also helped me to escape that trap when she pointed out that the original problem they came with was her difficulty in coping with Jason when her husband could not be there. She needed some help with that. Once I had helped Annabel with this problem the whole family could relax and improvise, and Annabel could also take charge of Jason. My failure early on to engage adequately with Annabel probably slowed the therapy. This still showed at follow up when Annabel rated her relationship with the therapist as neutral, whereas Frank rated it strongly positive. After reading this chapter Annabel found it helpful that her sense of not being properly listened to had been validated. She appreciated my explanation of why I had reacted in that way. If I had understood it at the time, and had shared it with the family, it might have helped.

The factors that enable a therapist to provide a temporary secure base for a family are discussed in more detail in Chapter 6. From the experience with the Mortons, it can be seen that it ideally includes establishing a roughly symmetrical relationship with each person in the family so that no one feels left out. It also involves identifying the core difficulties, and then helping the family to deal with them. The therapist also needs to be aware of his or her own participation in the therapy–family attachment patterns.

The Nature of Scripts

SCRIPTS: A SHARED METAPHOR

For me the most compelling reason for using the term "script" is that families understand it immediately. If they complain about how the same situation arises again and again, we are soon likely to find ourselves talking about scripts. Although I will probably have introduced the actual term "script," it may soon be forgotten and a shared set of metaphors emerges in the discussion: old scripts, writing new scripts, and improvising, etc. The metaphor of script is, of course, universal in our culture through theater, film, and, above all, television: "All the world's a stage, and all the men and women merely players" (Shakespeare, *As You Like It*). Because script theory also forms the basis for my thinking, it provides a link between my theory and the family's experience. This then does not leave me stranded by having knowledge that is locked into esoteric theory. I can tell them what I know in a form that they can use, and I learn something from them which adds directly to my knowledge.

Family therapists have used various metaphors to describe shared representation. These metaphors include family maps, family choreography (Papp, 1976), family paradigms (Reiss, 1981), and family models. None of these terms however can represent the full drama of family life—with all its action and discussion—in the way that family scripts can.

Object relations theory (Scharff & Scharff, 1987) offers a way of looking at the individual's mental representation of the family, his or her internal objects. The theory has also been used to explore some of the ways in which individual members, "inner families" connect with each other. However, the connections are usually seen as linear cause-and-effect processes in which one person has an effect on another. One example is *projective identification*, in which one member

23

induces another member to enact a role that he or she has disowned. This leads to a series of crisscrossing mutual projections within the family, each member playing disowned roles for the other. In other words, family object relations is built up out of multiple linear cause-and-effect assumptions in which conflict is seen to arise from a person's psychopathology and extends to influence another's behavior. This idea does address one aspect of family process in that each member's behavior does affect others, but it does not address how conflict can be created by the interactions between everyone involved. Also, projections tend to be visualized as traveling from one person to one other person rather than contributing to the whole family drama. The concept of family script posits that everyone has the whole family drama encoded in their minds but identifies more with certain roles, and, in turn, is identified by others as playing particular roles.

Family scripts can thus account for how individual members may disown responsibility for what happens and attribute blame to someone else in the family. But scripts do not imply that each person has to take back the bad "projection" and see it as belonging to themselves. Instead, change in script terms is seen as stemming from a recognition that everyone has a potential role in creating the scenarios, and that finding other more fruitful ways of interacting is both possible and can solve the problem. The "bad" bits do not have to be reowned and worked through as a prerequisite of change. This different approach suggested by the concept of family script does not mean, however, that some of the valuable insights of object relations theory about how individuals function have to be jettisoned. It is possible to translate some object relations concepts into family script terms (Byng-Hall, 1986). This allows for the integration of some of object relations ideas but places them in a more systemic frame.

FAMILY SCRIPTS, RITUALS, MYTHS, STORIES, AND LEGENDS: HOW THEY RELATE TO EACH OTHER

The concept of family scripts (Byng-Hall, 1985b) needs to be differentiated from various related phenomena with which they can become confused. *Family rituals* are a subcategory of family script. They represent shared expectations of how the family will interact on particular occasions. They are symbolic enactments celebrating particular functions, often at points-of-life transitions such as weddings, funerals, bar mitzvahs, graduation ceremonies (Imber-Black et al., 1988), or annual celebrations such as Christmas. In some families there are daily rituals such as saying grace before meals. The way in which the ritual is prepared for, enacted, and then the pertinence reflected upon reaffirms family roles and family values. Rituals also provide opportunities for change. For instance, the moment that the next generation takes over hosting the ritual, say, Christmas celebrations, marks an important shift in the life cycle. Family scripts have wider applications than rituals, as they are potentially at work throughout all family interactions, although they are reaffirmed by rituals.

Family myths (Ferreira, 1963; Byng-Hall, 1973, 1979; Bagarozzi & Anderson, 1989) are used to describe sets of beliefs that the family has about itself (discussed further in Chapter 8). Ferreira considered that family myths were essential for every family as they provided guidelines for action. A family script is similar to Ferreira's guidelines for action. In other words, scripts define what you do about beliefs. They are not the beliefs themselves. Family scripts also have to be differentiated from narrative. *Family stories* that families tell about themselves are clearly different from scripts. Scripts prescribe the action to be taken now and in the future, whereas the stories give an account of the action that was taken in the past.

The general structure of a *family legend,* which is a family story told frequently because it has implications for how the family should conduct itself now (Byng-Hall, 1982a, 1988; and see Chapter 8 for further discussion), is, however, very similar to that of a script. In both legend and script, family members play roles in an unfolding drama. Individual members of the family may identify themselves or be identified with particular roles within the drama's plot. The plot gives meaning to the family interaction, and indicates where the drama, or story, is leading. This is often revealed through the sequence of interactions: one action follows another along a familiar track. The way in which stories and scripts interweave with each other can be thought about in the following way. A family predicament is resolved in a way that is remembered. A story is then told about this, which helps to establish it as a model for future solutions of that predicament. This solution becomes fully scripted after it has been reenacted several times, and is then perceived as a normal part of the family's repertoire.

SCRIPT THEORY: SOME THEORETICAL ISSUES

Development of Scripts in Childhood

Stern (1985) studied how preverbal infants came to be able to respond appropriately to the routine events in their lives, such as feeding time or bath time. Given that every episode is slightly different, the infant builds up a generalized mental representation of all similar episodes. This mental representation takes the form of a prototype to represent all similar events. Stern called this a representation of interaction that is generalized (RIG), which is "something that has never happened before exactly that way yet it takes into account nothing that did not actually happen once" (p. 110). Stern described how a specific action, say, fetching a bottle of milk, may act as a retrieval cue for the mental representation of these contexts which brings into the baby's mind what he called the "evoked companion." The usual feeding routine would then be compared with what was currently happening.

Stern (1985) also describes selective attunement in which the child becomes molded to fit the parent's fantasies about the child. The parent responds selectively to one of the infant's emotions or behaviors while ignoring others, so that the child himself comes to emphasize these aspects of his experience. An example would be an enthusiastic response to the baby's happy moments while ignoring the baby's upset moments, which are then not validated or clarified through attunement. This may cause problems for dealing with upsets later. Selective attunement can also teach a child which emotions are acceptable and which ones are not. In one family, for instance, the parents responded with great interest to their son's dressing up in female attire. He was eventually referred to me for cross-dressing (his treatment will be described in more detail in Chapter 3).

Nelson (1988) discusses how children learn to put scripts for particular events into words. Three- or 4-year-olds can give a general description of what happens during a typical event such as a meal time. Memories of specific episodes, however, are retained only briefly and soon merge with the general script for the event and the details are lost. Particularly unusual aspects of an event are stored as autobiography, such as when a problem is resolved in a new way. Schank (1982) described how features that differ from the norm may, if repeated, lead to the formation of a new script; for instance, they may differentiate a meal from a snack. Nelson (1981) also explored how children can learn to share scripts through language. She found that children between 3 and 8 years, who did not know each other and were given a shared task, say buying a snack together, would spend a considerable amount of time finding out what each other's scripts for snacks were. They would chatter away about meals and snacks, reminiscing about past outings and what they had had to eat. Once each knew what the other meant by the word "snack," they would run off and buy one together. A feature of this creation of a shared meaning was that the children try to find something that is also shared culturally. A child who does not develop a script which is shared with his peers behaves in an increasingly egocentric manner and becomes isolated. It is easy to see, then, how members of the family would learn the shared meanings within the family, and how unless this also links to cultural scripts the family may become isolated.

Cramer (1992) describes how an infant is like a new actor in an old script; that is, he plays a role in his parents' scripts that come from their past. He discusses how this molds the child's sense of himself. Cramer calls the parents casting directors and discusses how the child may represent figures from the past such as grandparents, and how this creates problems both in the parent–infant relationship and for the emerging identity of the child.

Children Learning Roles in the Family Script

Script theorists have said less about how children develop scripts for family life. Put simply, this is how I see it:

When the metaphor of the theater is used, several perspectives can be identified, both on stage and in the audience. Children spend a lot of time intently observing what happens in the family. From their position in the audience, they are seeing what happens between those family members currently on stage. Equally important, by using social referencing, they observe how other members of the family view what is going on. Children often glance at their parents for cues about how to interpret what's happening—for example, "Is mother pleased or worried about father getting cross with my brother?"This is how the family's attitudes toward what happens in interaction are absorbed. When observing what is going on "on stage," children can put themselves in the shoes of either the person perceived as taking action or the person acted upon, and imagine what it is like to be in that role at that particular moment. Switching from one perspective to another, the child comes to understand some of the motives behind interaction by seeing it from each person's point of view.

On-stage experiences include being acted upon and taking action. And, again just as important, observing what observers think of what is happening. This piece of social referencing includes paying attention to how others in the "audience" react to what has happened. Children are especially interested if parents discuss together what he or she has done. Siblings are also an important source of ideas and observations on the adult world. In time the child builds a "theory of mind" (Baron-Cohen et al., 1993) in which the child appreciates that other people can have different thoughts and feelings from themselves. He or she learns how to anticipate other people's characteristic responses by observing how each reacts in family scenarios. The child can also gain a sense of congruence between the experience of self and others' expectations: "This is my special way of doing things. Everyone expects me to do it that way. So do I."

Social referencing also helps to establish what are the significant moments in family interaction. When a particular family transaction occurs, children may note a heightened interest shown by others. This puts that event center stage. Subsequent discussion in which further judgment is added then helps to imprint the nature of the unfolding event in the collective memory. Any subsequent stories about it may help to retain the theme central to the family preoccupations.

The child eventually learns to be an actor on the stage and becomes capable of reflecting on the event and its meaning to both him- or herself, and others. Motives behind each person's actions become clear. This provides the basis for recognizing the script that he or she might be drawn into. The capacity to stay in the role of observer provides the possibility of not joining in.

The Programming Function of Scripts

Schank and Abelson (1977), cognitive scientists, approached the problem of how scripts were built up by simulating scripts on computer programs. This threw some interesting light on the programming and sequential aspects of scripts. Schank and Abelson's ideas, although interesting, are rather limited, in that they describe stylized, everyday situations in which programming of behavior is not subject to much change. The computer also provides a deterministic world in which nothing outside of what was programmed in can be retrieved (chaos theory and viruses aside!). Interactional experiences, however, follow emergent processes, in which every aspect of experience, even memories (Rosenfield, 1988), is created anew through the way that all the factors involved at that moment in time influence what emerges. In this sense, every living event is a new creation in some way or another. Despite this, however, the inevitability of the computer program provides a useful metaphor. Members of families sometimes come to feel as if they are being programmed to behave in certain ways by the family, hence the famous cry, "Now look what you have made me do!" Nelson (1981) described an ideal script as one that can include all the reliable and predictable events, but is open and leaves room to incorporate all the possible and acceptable actions compatible with the script. This allows for improvisation within broad guidelines in order to achieve the goals of the script. The script can build up a rich repertoire, and leave space for further variations in the future.

Sequence is usually an important aspect of scripts. Scripts often prescribe a set sequence en route to a particular goal. This happens in many family tasks or rituals, such as a formal meal. A predictable sequence in any interaction carries the enormous advantage that everyone knows what comes next, each participant can come in on cue, and the whole interaction can go into an automatic enactment, thus saving a great deal of energy in routine situations. In other scripts the order is less important, but a particular range of behaviors may be required instead. A script for a relationship is typical of this. A daughter's script for her relationship with her father may include a range of behaviors depending on his mood. For instance, he must be humored by being supported when he is upset, complimented when he is dejected, and placated when he is angry. Although relationship scripts are context sensitive, there will be periods of time when they become sequential as well, This is seen in face-to-face situations in which each person's behavior is the other's context, and there is a routine task, say, in greetings or farewells. Family rituals also often follow a sequence. Sexual intercourse is a classic example of a sequential script that unfolds in a particular way for the couple. Sex therapists find the concept of script particularly useful for this reason (McCormick, 1987).

Schank and Abelson (1977) describe how scripts have goals and subgoals, while plans and subplans are needed in order to reach those objectives. When this concept is applied to families, it is apparent that family tasks have obvious purposes, whereas family relationships have less well defined goals. The overall goal of family relationships is that of being there for each other at the end of the day, so that if problems arise you can call on your relatives for support. The plans must include how to maintain adequate emotional and physical contact, with subplans of how to pledge and seek loyalty; how to kindle affection so that your relative will want to support you when the time comes; and how to apologize and forgive when unfortunate things are done, etc.

Attachment behavior is a biologically programmed behavior which can be conceptualized in terms of scripts (Bretherton, 1985, Byng-Hall, 1990, 1991b). Bowlby (1969) used control theory to explain how the approaching couple "steer" toward each other so that they finally meet. The cybernetics of the control system include feedback of information about how the direction each is taking is aligned toward the goal. For instance, if the child when wanting to reach the parent starts deviating from a course set toward the parent, he or she is likely to receive negative feedback which acts to correct the deviation—for example, "Don't go that way." Any movement in the right direction is given positive feedback, which encourages further change of direction—for example, "That's better!" Bowlby calls this the "goal-directed system," or, when two or more people have the same aims, a "shared goal-directed system." This illustrates one way in which scripts can lead to collaboration in achieving a task.

Motivation for Enacting Scripts

The anticipated outcome provides the motivation to initiate an enactment of a script. Tomkins (1979), a cognitive psychologist, explored how script enactments are driven along by affect. Individuals are often stimulated into action by feelings, and those actions may also provoke emotions in others, thus setting up interactions. He divided the affects into positive ones, such as joy or pride, which reward behavior; negative ones, such as fear or shame, which produce avoidant behavior; and surprise, which he linked to reevaluation of a situation. It has been argued that attachment behavior is motivated by the overall goal of achieving "felt security," or feeling less insecure. In families, the affect of "here we go again" is associated with feeling drawn inevitably into yet another reenactment of a scenario. This usually has a contradictory aspect: The individual is reluctant to act because of the experience that it leads nowhere, but at the same time, the individual feels impelled to do so.

Boszormenyi-Nagy and Ulrich (1981) have some interesting ideas about what drives family members to do what they do in relationships, especially in terms of caring for each other. They conceived of a family ledger with debits and credits. Individuals build up a sense of entitlement, in which it is felt that someone owes them something—for example, a child sensing that he is owed some caring that his parents did not give him. Others may come to feel that they owe someone else something, because of what they themselves received. A well-balanced ledger across a life cycle would be one in which parents build up entitlement through devoted care of their children, while the children are happy to pay it back when their parents grow old and need to be looked after themselves. A particularly interesting idea is that the individual may be motivated to collect the debt from someone other than the person who owed him or her something in the first place. The classic situation is the deprived child who grows up demanding care from everyone in order to make up for what was not received as a child. This, of course, usually fails and leads to ideas of having a baby who will at last provide him or her with the yearned-for love. Needless to say, things go wrong when the child demands attention instead. The child is, in turn, deprived by the deprived parent and is likely to grow up determined to extract what care was due from the next generation (or from others in the community, including therapists). The cycle of deprivation is thus completed through replicative scripts. I like this way of thinking because it rings true, and families understand the notion quickly. It also points to a different solution, that of forgiveness of parents, as a way of canceling the debt and thus breaking the intergenerational transmission of problems. Psychotherapy may unfortunately sometimes open up anger with parents instead. This gives people a sense of justifiable grievance, which only adds to this problem. The way to avoid this is to help parents understand their parents' dilemmas, and to see that they struggled as best they could in the circumstances. Genogram work should then go back at least as far as understanding the grandparents' upbringing.

Self-Fulfilling Prophecies

Scripts are also orientated toward the future, and generate predictions about what will happen next. Some of these predictions are made for the more distant future; a grandmother may say of a grandchild, "He will go far," or, "She will end up in trouble." Watzlawick et al. (1967) and Watzlawick (1984) discuss how some assumptions can create self-fulfilling prophecies. The assumption can create the event. An example is the news item that mistakenly announced a gasoline shortage. This led to everyone filling their tanks, and, consequently, there was a shortage. If a parent makes predictions for a child's future based not on what he knows of that particular child's personality and capability but rather based on his experience of a past member of the family, this creates a situation close to the classic self-fulfilling prophecy in which the prophecy itself produces the end result. This may happen, for instance, when a child is cast as a replacement for a lost relative, and the parents expect certain behavior that is characteristic of the dead person. As mentioned previously, Stern (1985) describes how the child is attuned to fit the parents' expectations. This causes problems because, of course, no one can be someone else. Also, not infrequently the unwelcome aspects of the dead person are reproduced instead of the wished-for characteristics. It must however be remembered that optimistic predictions can also act as a helpful self-fulfilling prophecy, so long as the child or family has the capacity to respond to the prediction. Unrealistic expectations spell disaster. Therapists often talk about "when you resolve this problem" as a way of predicting success. As most families do have the capacity to change, which is being rediscovered in therapy, this statement sometimes carries sufficient conviction to seed expectations of success.

In cybernetic theory, when a goal is based on an anticipated outcome derived from an inner model of the world (Rosen, 1979), there may be a *feedforward loop*, in which information from the process of traveling toward the goal is not used to correct the direction—for example, driving somewhere without any map of how to get there. There is *no feedback loop* to tell the driver when he deviates from the route. This situation may arise when someone else sets your goal with a prophecy—for example, "You will come to no good," without specifying the pathway that would lead to this. You cannot then take evasive action to choose to avoid it happening. Some predictions, of course, are intended as warnings of disaster with messages about how to avoid disaster spelled out; for example, "If you do not do your school work, you will end up unemployed." Even so, the prediction can act as a self-fulfilling prophecy as it tells the individual that the prophesier has an image of potential disaster awaiting him or her.

A tragic script is one in which the assumption is that, despite every attempt, all will be lost. This sense of inevitable disaster may be more important than the content of what is to happen. Every action has a lead weight tied around its neck. An individual may take over this mantle from someone in the previous generation. He or she may, however, attract the tragic role perhaps as the child who is always expected to fail or make a mess or be ill, or whatever the family's feared theme is. Here the prediction is made about function and process and not about the final destination. The subject of these predictions is dogged continually by the expectations behind this label. It is remarkably difficult for a child to avoid this fate, unless he or she discovers that they are based on an expectation from the past. A child's assumption is that he or she earned the label, which after a while may become true. Targets of prophecies may be particular relationships (e.g., "that marriage will not last"). Or, the whole family may have a tragic label. Optimistic predictions and expectations can also influence the course of the script, so long as they are also realistic.

Types of Family Scripts

Family life is too varied and complex to classify all possible scripts. However, it is worth considering how significant scripts can be identified. They can be categorized by their function, their plot, or the relationships involved. The relationship referred to is usually self-evident—for example, the whole family or a subsystem such as father–son, couple, sibling, grandmother–granddaughter. Interactions between generations involve "intergenerational scripts," whereas patterns from previous generations that are transferred to current interaction are "transgenerational scripts," the best known of which are "replicative" or "corrective scripts." Function can be added. The family script may include problem solving, attachments, meal-times, authority, parenting, etc. These functions may be further specified as belonging to a particular relationship (e.g., mother–daughter attachment). Particular function may also be specified for transgenerational scripts, especially those which are to do with the family life cycle (e.g., leaving-home script), which are events that parents have usually been through themselves, so one might refer to mother's replicative leaving-home script, father's grieving script, and so on.

The plot of particular scripts may be identified either through the family's expectation of the general direction in which things are likely to go (e.g., tragic, optimistic, successful, supportive, pioneering scripts). Or, scripts may be identified through the main strategy employed—for example, avoidant (attachment); authoritarian (discipline); and replacement (grieving script), in which the sense of loss is reduced by replacing the dead person with another member of the family.

Problem-solving or conflict-resolving scripts are of particular importance to family therapists. It is these that usually need to be rewritten. They can often be identified by their main strategy, such as triangulation, in which problems between dyads are resolved by bringing others in; conflict avoidance; coercion or oppression; blaming and scapegoating; cooperation and collaboration; negotiation; etc.

JOINING IN FAMILY SCENARIOS, OR STAYING OUT

Recruiting Family Members into Roles in Scenarios

The ways in which family members are recruited into the family script are numerous and complex. Chapter 12 discusses how newborn babies are inducted into family scripts, and Chapter 3 discusses how identities within the script are passed from generation to generation. Roles within family scripts are necessary to family functioning. The family has to find ways to ensure that vacant roles are fulfilled. Families in which roles are readily exchangeable find few problems with this. Even the children may have been rehearsed in the role by being asked to take over briefly when a parent is absent or ill; cooking, shopping, and caring for a sick parent are all examples. Where roles are more clearly allocated to specific people, absence creates a vacuum.

Mechanisms by which individuals are recruited into vacant or poorly performed roles include the following:

Emotional Pressure

If some role is not being performed adequately, intense emotions may be aroused (e.g., indignation, fury, or anxiety), especially if the role was important for the family. This will lead to all-round pressure, often using shaming or guilt-arousing techniques, on the person who usually fulfilled the role to get on with the job. Failing this, others will be drawn in to take up the role. For instance, the family pressure put on Frank to settle the "out of control" children was intense. Annabel persuaded him to do so because of her own anxiety about what she would do if he did not. The children also wanted him to be involved with them for their own reasons.

The Inclination to Step into the Role

This may come from replicative or corrective scripts for parents, as did Frank's desperate wish to provide his children with a father in the face of a depressed, irritable mother. Certain contexts that used to evoke old childhood scenarios may trigger the parent into action.

Outside Replacements

If the person recruited starts to default despite pressure to continue, an outsider may be brought in if the vacant role is important enough. Frank, because of his work commitments, eventually could no longer be relied upon to relieve what felt like a dangerous situation at home. When Annabel reached the end of her tether, I was recruited to help.

Reflecting on What Is Going on Rather than Enacting Scripts: Containment within the Family

The capacity to refrain from taking inappropriate action is as crucial as acting when it is needed. This involves using the capacity to reflect on what is going on rather than being drawn into the interaction. The "reflecting self" (Fonagy et al., 1991) functions like a theater of the mind (McDougall, 1986), in which the "audience self" is observer not only to the outside drama but also to the inner drama of past memories that are evoked by what is going on. It is then possible to make sense of what is happening and then take appropriate action. So when a family member, especially a child, is out of control and goes beyond acceptable behavior, the emotions that are aroused in those around him or her are not acted upon but reflected on instead. When some sense can be made of why this has happened, the child can also be helped to understand it. Object relations theorists (Winnicott, 1960) call this whole process "containment." In this way the child develops a coherent story about how and why emotions arise and action is taken. The child also identifies with the parents' way of reflecting on what is going on. Thus the child starts to make sense of intense emotions and learns to contain feelings by reflecting on them rather than acting on them. It is interesting that Main et al. (1985) found that securely attached children at 6 years of age are more able to be self-reflective (i.e., they can reflect on their own mental processes) than insecure children can. Mothers of secure children are also more likely to be able to be self-reflective (Fonagy et al., 1991). This would suggest that the parent modeling the capacity for self-reflection may play an important part in helping the child to establish secure relationships.

Often there are several people who act as a team to contain a child acting on impulse, perhaps both parents, or a parent and a grandparent, or elder siblings. In this case the disturbance can create potential problems within the "containing" relationship. For instance, a child's difficulties in accepting his parents' relationship, from which he feels excluded, can do this. The child may try to get in between parents. The same principle of containment holds. What is going on must not be acted upon but understood. It is not uncommon to hear parents say, "He seems to be trying to drive a wedge between us," and then to discuss why this happens and what to do about it. Parents can also contain each other's troubled experiences. If, however, they are not able to contain each other's upset emotions these may then spill over to incorporate the child, who thus becomes part of their marital drama. It is harder for a child, but it is not unknown, however, for him or her to contain it and pass the conflict back by saying, "You are only getting at me because you're cross with each other." In therapy it is sometimes possible to tell from observing when the children go off and start playing in the middle of their parents' arguments that a qualitative change has occurred in the parents' argument. The child often knows when his or her parents are containing the difficulties within their relationship so that it will not spill out to involve him. This may be when the parents have stopped scoring points and blaming each other, and show signs of finally getting down to trying to solve their problems. Children know the difference, even when the intensity of the argument may actually increase.

In the absence of ways of containing families, upset emotions and impulses, various dramas will be put into action. This will often affect outsiders who may, in turn, be used as containers.

How Do Therapists Avoid Being Recruited into the Family Script?

Once a family therapist becomes a player in the family script, he or she will not be in a position to change anything. On the other hand, the therapist's knowledge of what it is like to be in the family can also be invaluable. The therapist can join in the family interaction, know it from inside and then step back. This distancing process, however, needs either support of others or particular skill. The pressure to join the family or to be organized into taking some role within it, such as a peacekeeper or problem solver, can be very powerful. The power of the family to recruit is probably due to several factors. If several family members share a similar set of expectations of what the therapist should do, it is often more organizing than if just one person does so. The family may leave a vacant role for the therapist. It is hard, for instance, not to fill the vacant role of rescuer if someone in the family is being unfairly attacked and no one is doing the defending. Intense interaction is also more geared to trigger immediate action on the part of the therapist than it is to set him or her thinking. The therapist then gets caught up in the process. The therapist's own family scripts may also become triggered, because the person is familiar with being drawn into his or her own family dramas, as I was in the Morton's first session in which I became Annabel's reluctant supporter.

There are several strategies for dealing with these situations: Some are to do with counteracting the mechanism of the recruitment process, and some are to do with containing the emotional pressure. The strategies for counteracting recruitment processes include the following.

1. *Using a team.* The team can generate a therapeutic belief system which commands more loyalty from the therapist than does the family's script. I do not, however, believe that a team is essential for family therapy; working on one's own is often highly effective. Working some of the week with a team or being able to take the family occasionally to a team for consultation is, however, very helpful. I try to do this.

2. *Using a one-way screen.* This can allow for a group behind the screen to remain as an audience—meta to the therapeutic system. The therapist can also regain the meta position during consultations behind the screen. The observers can intervene directly during the session either through the telephone or earphone (Byng-Hall, 1982c) to help keep the therapist on a therapeutic track. A reflecting team in which the observers and the therapist discuss what they have observed, while the family watches, offers the greatest opportunity for the

therapist to reestablish his or her role as therapist. The reflecting team also allows the family to be meta to the discussion, and hence less likely to feel they have either to recruit the therapist back into their own view of things or to repudiate what he or she stands for.

3. *A clear therapeutic procedure.* This helps to ensure that the therapeutic script survives.

4. *Circular questioning* (Palazzoli et al., 1980). This consists of asking a series of questions about how each member sees other relationships in the family. It has three main effects on the recruiting process. First, it keeps the therapist in charge as the role of questioner is very powerful and centralizing; second, it reduces the amount of interaction between family members who are all listening to what is going on; third, it asks families to process information through beliefs and not by communication through interaction. I use circular questioning to regain my meta position when I feel myself slipping into taking a particular role.

Techniques for containing the emotional impact include the following.

1. *Reflecting on the process.* Understanding what is going on can provide a pause between the family's action and plunging into a response that could merely represent another move within their family script. If I start to feel like acting in response to feelings, especially if I am angry, or I am drawn to take sides, I know that I need to understand why. If I do not understand, then I am liable to become a "member" of the family. It is easier to resist responding to what at first sight appears to be an appalling piece of behavior if it is possible to understand the function that the behavior has within the family's scenario. Time spent in breaks during the session, either on one's own or preferably with colleagues, is very valuable in arriving at a systemic formulation.

2. *Seeing emotion as valuable information.* When emotion is valued as a useful cue as to what is going on, it is more likely that emotion will not just be acted upon immediately, but it will also be reflected upon. If there is a team, and the therapist shares his or her emotional reactions immediately on arriving back in the observation room, it has two effects: First, it provides information; second, it quickly reduces the affect that was potentially driving the therapist into action while he or she was with the family. The observation group then contains the emotion instead.

A great deal can also be learned from exploring the various emotions aroused within the team. At times, the feelings of the therapist are at variance with those of the observing group. This can be because the therapist refuses the invitation to fill a vacant family role, say, of confronting someone. The group then experiences the vacuum instead and experiences the pull toward action. This can provoke intense frustration as they can do nothing and the therapist is not taking action on their behalf.

3. *Differentiating the therapist's script from that of the family.* This has implications for training. I work on the genograms of my trainees, looking at their scripts which drew them into the professional caring role. The supervision group explores possible trigger situations with client families, that might recruit the supervisor into particular responses. We explore whether they are likely to trigger replicative or corrective responses. I conceptualize the supervision group as providing a secure base from which therapists can explore family therapy skills, but also to understand some of their own responses to families. The amount of time devoted to this is, however, only the minimum sufficient for the job. The group is a work group and not a therapeutic group. Those who want to explore their own responses further are encouraged to find an appropriate therapeutic context. A few do this. I had a personal analysis in the early 1970s, which I have found useful in helping me to understanding trigger situations.

4. *The therapist's sharing his or her emotional experience with the family.* I find that this is an effective way of halting a feeling of having to do something without quite knowing why. I often use this when not working with a team. The family then becomes my team. I say that I have found myself feeling sad, confused, upset, etc., in the session. I ask whether any other members feel the same way. This often leads to an opening up of a discussion about how this is experienced by many members of the family. Quite commonly it is the identified patient who feels similar to how I feel. This then leads to an exploration of what happens to provoke this feeling in the family. Together we can contain our own disturbing emotions by understanding them and doing something about them. This is an important piece of sharing.

At times I use all the above techniques. My style is quiet and reflective, rather than active and controlling. Students observing my work remark that they find it hard to understand how I avoid getting angry, or how I keep going despite all this. This is probably because I do contain the emotions even more than I realize. The students sometimes say that they start to feel angry themselves with the family, and they long to be able to confront them. Or, they feel irritated with me for not confronting the family. This is an interesting example of the effect of leaving a role vacant, and the emotional pressure that this can generate.

Interactional Awareness

Interactional awareness (Byng-Hall, 1986) enables families to monitor what is happening while they interact. It is the way they track their own processes. This may show in the way they give each other knowing smiles; or glances to see how someone has taken something that has been said; or nods, fleeting frowns, or slight turning away in disagreement, as well as other metacommunications that enable family members to let each other know what each is feeling and whether they feel understood, and whether they have, in turn, understood what the others are going through. Interactional awareness helps families to collaborate in a way that is adaptable to each person's needs. It involves keeping an eye on both how interactions are unfolding, and what these interactions may mean to all those involved. This enables them to change direction if it is necessary. In short, interactional awareness is an essential part of the mechanism for providing positive and negative feedback during interaction.

Interactional awareness is a group phenomenon because although each person is involved in monitoring, in their own particular way, what is important is how perceptions interweave, or complement each other. For instance, a mother keeps an eye on the children, while the children social reference father's attitude to the therapist. Interactional awareness includes very rapid review/preview operations as people think about what has just happened and guess about what is about to happen next.

Interactional awareness consists, ideally, of the potential for:

1. Awareness of the *consequences of interaction* which enables the individual to guess what the results of particular actions might be, and how these will affect everyone.
2. *Self-awareness,* that is, having some idea about why one is acting in a particular way, and how this relates to past and present experience.
3. *Empathic awareness* of what may underlie other members' motives and how they feel about what is happening.
4. *Understanding of the meaning of interactions,* which involves being aware of what is being transacted, and why, and where it may be heading. Each person's motives can be assessed, and whether they are shared or in conflict.

At a group level, adequate family interactive awareness creates:

5. *A shared coherent perception* of what is happening between those involved, based on compatible internal models of the rela-

tionships. Each individual's views and attitudes may well differ, but his or her perceptions are not totally contradictory. Each member can then construct a coherent story out of what is happening that can be shared with the others. Paradoxically, this means that it is easier to improvise and take off on a new track. Everyone can soon make sense of the new direction and follow suit by adding his or her own fresh response. A new coherent story line can then emerge.

T·H·R·E·E

Identification Across
the Generations

Family life is a rehearsal for future generations. During the rehearsal the child is an understudy to the parent, identifying with aspects of their parents' parenting while disapproving of others. The child is writing his or her life scripts. These influence the sort of person he or she is going to be in the future, and the type of family that he or she will help to create. This can be called the "script for future family life," which differentiates it from the "family script," which is the current shared script. When the child grows up, he or she is likely to establish long-term relationships with a view to creating a family with someone who has shown some capacity to play some of the roles in his or her script for family life, and vice versa. The desire to know what a new partner's upbringing was like is common when deciding to begin a family. The way the story is told will reveal the attitude that he or she may take toward any future children, and his or her potential parenting styles. In this way a new shared family script can be written, with echoes from the past.

IDENTITY AND IDENTIFICATION
PROCESSES IN SCRIPTS

Before considering the complex role of identity as it threads across generations, it is worth discussing some of the basic components of identity and identification. A sense of identity has two main dimensions. First, it is the perception of the self being an entity that is distinguishable from all others. Second, identity is the feeling of being someone who, despite changing circumstances, physical states, and relationships, remains constant—in other words, it exhibits continuity and coherence (Simon et al., 1985). Identity thus has a future orientation. You come to expect that you will behave in the future as you have in the past. But there is also a self as you intend to be in the future, for instance, envisaging playing a role in a corrective script. The internal images of oneself enacting a role in various scenarios, past or future, can be enormously varied, such is the richness of the imagination. Some of these roles may be sensed as "not really me," others are accepted as representing various aspects of oneself—having a continuity with past experience of how one has been. Attitudes to these different selves vary: the person one would ideally like to be, the acceptable self; or the unacceptable shameful part of one's being.

Identity is also influenced by how others see you because you are cast in other people's scripts. There may be a discrepancy between how others see you and how you feel about yourself. The image enacted for outside consumption may be a "false self," a context-bound chameleon self. The contradictions between these different aspects of one's self-image may threaten the sense of coherence and continuity of being. When core identity is threatened, various strategies may be used to resolve what can be a disturbing experience. The acceptable self may, for instance, have to be sustained by another member of the family representing the disowned self, enabling one to play a counterpart role, say, "strong and independent," to the other's "weak and dependent" role. Sometimes what is needed is affirmation of the acceptable self by other family members. This can be achieved through a family myth which represents those images that are mutually accepted by all family members as representing each person. This agreed set of identities can provide each member with a sense of continuity across time. Family myths are discussed further in Chapter 8.

Identification is the process of basing one's own identity on aspects of someone else. The identification can be with what that person does, with aspects of that person's own sense of self, or with the status of that person—for example, a son identifying with his father because he senses that he will also be a father one day. Identification is, however, often a reciprocal and systemic process as the person that is used as an identity model may also see the identifier as being similar to him- or herself. An example would be the parent who sees a child as a chip off the old block. It is against this complex background that we need to consider identification between generations.

REPLICATIVE AND CORRECTIVE
PARENTING SCRIPTS

As described in Chapter 1, children will inevitably take some of their family experiences and re-create them in the next generation as replicative scripts. With other experiences, which may have been uncomfortable or even intolerable, children will often attempt to do the opposite when they bring up their own families. They will develop corrective scripts. There is always a tension between these two scripts as many parents will recognize.

I came to understand this tension when our children were small. My wife had bought a portable video camera to film families in therapy. She decided to practice on our family, so she set it up to film breakfast. Watching the tape afterward I observed a wonderful, sensitive father, responding to each child's needs, discussing their plans for the day, and so on. I was impressed and somewhat surprised. Then I saw the newspaper come up, shutting out the children. Chaos reigned. Food was grabbed across the table, arguments started, and the father was totally oblivious behind the paper. I suddenly recognized my own father. He would read so intensely that nothing my sister and I could do would gain his attention. It was quite an unpleasant shock to realize just how much I replicated that behavior. Later I discovered that my wife had left the camera running when she left the room. At that moment I had stopped the "performance" and reverted to type!

Another example of the tension between replicative and corrective scripts is the parent who was oppressively disciplined as a child, and has vowed not to discipline his or her children in the same way. This may indeed produce a new, permissive form of discipline as in the superreasonable style of the Mortons. But under moments of stress, he or she may replicate exactly the same form of ferocious discipline, sometimes saying and doing precisely the same things as his or her parent did, in what can be a very precisely scripted scenario. Annabel recognized her mother's tone of voice when she suddenly slipped out of her polite reasoning style into a rage with Jason when he was hitting William.

Choosing a partner with whom to start a family usually involves the opportunity to reenact both replicative and corrective scripts, in ways that repeat the best of both parents' experience. Alternatively the choice may allow each to adopt a counterpart role to a disowned identity. A favorite maneuver is to find someone who can replicate the uncomfortable parenting roles, perhaps by selecting a potential disciplinarian who matches one's own overly strict parent. This can free oneself to take on the more acceptable corrective role, by playing a counterpart permissive role to the disciplinarian parent. The strict partner may, in turn, be making up for a frightening lack of control or discipline in his or her own childhood, so that he or she can play a counterpart role to chaotic lax discipline. The result is a contrasting complementary style of parenting in which each criticizes the other. A further possibility is that the discipline roles will be played out within the marriage itself. This is when one parent takes a controlling parental role vis-à-vis the other, who is then placed in a child role. One partner may suddenly find him or herself back in the unwelcome role of chastised child. In contrast there is an opportunity for each parent to own both sides of the split that existed in their upbringing, and to integrate the two aspects. Instead of one parent being permissive and the other authoritarian, each can be both firm and forgiving at the appropriate moment.

The choice of partner along oedipal lines, that is, on the basis that the partner is like the parent of the opposite sex, is so well known that it tends to obscure the often considerable impact of siblings on mate choice (Toman, 1961).

For example, the marriage of the Mortons (introduced in Chapter 1) had many features of a sibling relationship. It is easy to see why Frank as a twin should use twinning as a model for his apparent closeness to his wife. He often behaved in a pseudomutual way with Annabel, as if she already knew exactly what was happening to him, in the way that identical twins can relate. But for Annabel to choose a sibling type of relationship needs further explanation. Having been devastatingly jealous of her brother when he was young, Annabel found that her relationship to her brother was transformed when he became adolescent. After a period when they had been separated for several months, while she traveled, the relationship suddenly became very close. This was because now older he started to care for her—something that she had always longed for. He behaved like an older brother who, for instance, selected suitable boyfriends for her. This finally provided her with an experience that was both warm and close, in contrast to her father who was frequently unavailable. She instantly recognized Frank's ability to provide this sort of sibling-type relationship. Unfortunately she found herself displaced by Jason as her husband's "sibling."

IDENTITY AND IMPROVISATION

Reciprocal identification processes occur between generations. The older generation is scripting the next one, while the younger generation is identifying with the previous one. Within this interplay a reedited family script is coconstructed. The interesting questions are, how much space is permitted for improvising new ways of doing things, and how much do the old family scripts put a constraint on what happens? Parents can, if they choose, allow their children freedom to play within broadly set limits, while children can also choose their own identity, but which may not match their parents' script for them. Once a child can say to himself, "I am not exactly like what mummy thinks I am," he or she is able to nurture a self-definition. This self-definition may not be played out immediately but becomes part of the projected future in which the child chooses or vows to be a particular sort of person. Characteristically this happens again and again at different ages so the child builds up a repertoire of potential images of the future. Children can also make their own mark on current family identities, which then can redefine the parents who may come to see themselves in a different way: "I am a parent of a scholar/ delinquent/dancer, etc."

Family life can provide a stage on which various ways of relating can be tried out. The context marker of "play" means that the family accepts that there is a pretend element to what is going on. This gives everybody permission to experiment within certain limits without risking being stuck with a reputation acquired through their new behavior. This can be called a "transitional script," with which the family can partially identify, but not yet fully. If, however, what happens suits everybody and is repeated, it will, in time, become incorporated as the pattern of behavior that is typical of the family, and hence is accepted as a new script. This happens repeatedly throughout the life cycle, with the potential to expand and extend the family's expectations of how they can relate to each other.

IDENTIFICATION WITHIN FAMILY SCENARIOS

The influence of family scenarios on the identity of the child is important. During everyday family interaction the child is likely to be identifying with each parent's behavior and will tend to replicate that behavior as an adult. However, when the situation becomes stressful, either of two things can happen. First, when the situation becomes uncomfortable, the child, although upset, can still remain aware of the experience. In that situation a counteridentity might emerge in which the child makes a conscious resolution to be very different from the parent who is causing the pain. This happens most often when there is a sense that what is happening is unfair. This is made more likely when the other parent or other family members disapprove of what is being done. Individuals can often trace these corrective scripts back to conscious intentions in childhood.

The second situation is when the interaction becomes characterized by intolerable emotional or physical pain, say, in an abusive interaction. The child may then momentarily distance himself from the terrifying position of being a victim, and escape into a dissociated state. The child may, for instance, experience him- or herself as floating above the scenario as a disembodied spectator. This gives the freedom to identify with either the aggressor or the victim or both. The whole episode, or aspects of it, may, however, be repressed and hence remain unavailable for review. In this case the identification with either the aggressor or the victim is hidden from awareness. The child may then become involved in similar abusive contexts in the future, either as the abuser or victim or both, at different times. However, not all victims become abusers. They may identify with a rescuer or a comforter who either has been longed for and conjured up in the imagination, or is based on some person who did comfort them at some point. Alternatively, the identification adopted may be as someone who would not get into any sort of relationship in which he or she could become abusive or be abused. This could lead to a more isolated existence. Both the identifications, with the rescuer and with the recluse, represent corrective scripts, but frequently without conscious choice, so the individual often remains unaware why he or she takes on that role.

So we can see that some of the scenarios for future enactment will be held accessible to awareness in memory; others will only make themselves apparent when triggered into action. The identities adopted, conscious and unconscious, may, however, color the individual's approach to relationships. However, one style of relating may be overt and predominant, while the other remains covert or occasional. The overt style may show in either the corrective or replicative parenting script. Frequently several strands of identity acquired from each parent, or parental figure, are woven together into each individual's identity.

SCRIPTING THE NEXT GENERATION

Clearly the family can influence which way the child's main identification goes. On the one hand, if the child has a good relationship with the parent, who is content with his or her own identity and which is also valued by the rest of the family, then the child is very likely to comfortably adopt a replicative identification. The parent is also likely to hope that his or her offspring will follow, broadly speaking, in the same way of life. If, on the other hand, the parents' overt facade is a "false self," while the hidden aspect of the parent represents the frustrated, or thwarted, ambitions which he or she may then wish the child to express vicariously. The child may then be identified with, and identify him- or herself with, the covert aspects of the parent. If a child is unable to fulfill parental ambitions, then the grandchildren in the next generation may be delegated to do so instead.

Another powerful transgenerational scripting can come through replacement scripts in which the child is identified with a lost and unmourned member of the family. The unmourned member may be a grandparent who may have died near the time of the birth of the child. Or it might be one of their own siblings, or a stillbirth which preceded them. Probably the most common form of replacement scripts, however, is to carry the identity of a separated parent, so that relationships with that parent can be continued in absentia. The child often bears some resemblance to the lost partner, because of the genetic makeup and also through his or her identification with the other parent, thus behaving in a similar manner. This, of course, can be very unfortunate for the child when the breakup of the relationship left bitterness and anger toward the departed partner.

CASE ILLUSTRATION: THE GRANT FAMILY

The Grant family was referred to me because the parents were worried that their eldest son, Sebastian, aged 8, was too effeminate and was dressing up in girls' clothing. Sebastian and his younger brother, Paul, aged 5, had been in the habit of enacting little playlets. Their parents, Dawn and James, were both interested in the theater. They had recently realized, however, that Sebastian always chose the female parts and that he was now being teased at school for behaving like a girl. Indeed, the situation had reached a serious level because the older boys were beginning to pinch his bottom and touch his penis. Although cross-dressing is an unusual symptom, I have chosen this family because the intergenerational attitudes to the children's gender is very clear-cut and, hence, it illustrates the issues. The nature of effeminate behavior in boys and its prognosis is a highly complex topic (Zucker & Green, 1992), and it is not appropriate to discuss the details here.

Family History (see Figure 3.1)

When I asked the parents whether they had wanted a boy or a girl, when expecting Sebastian, they said they had not minded, but added that both grandmothers had very much wanted a girl. The maternal grandmother, Julietta, was the eldest in her family. Hers was a Spanish Jewish family, and they had been very disappointed to have a girl first and paid a great deal more attention to the boys when they came later. This made Julietta very angry, but secretly she wished she had been a boy. One story the family told was that Julietta had been out gardening one day, when she looked up and saw her father walking purposefully past her on his way to her brother's house which was down the street. Although he was only a few feet away, he never looked up. This told her that her father was not at all interested in her, only her brother. She became increasingly bitter and estranged from her family. When Julietta got married she wanted to have a son first; thus, she replicated her parents' pattern. When she did produce a son first she was triumphant, as she had succeeded where her own mother had not. However, later, she wanted her own children to have girls first—a corrective script. Julietta kept some of her childhood dresses to give to the anticipated granddaughters. Her son had two sons and so she was very hopeful that her daughter, Dawn, would produce a granddaughter. When the last two grandchildren turned out to be boys as well, Julietta finally gave away her dresses to a charity in disgust. Dawn, Sebastian's mother, had wanted to be a boy when she was a child, thus identifying with her mother's wish to have been a boy, but as she grew up she ambivalently came to terms with being a woman. When Sebastian was a little boy, she gave him dresses to wear during his playlets. This followed her mother's unfulfilled wishes.

Sebastian's father, James, was Scottish. His father, Hamish, Sebastian's grandfather, was a hefty Scottish farmer, whose main claim to fame was that he had a won a tossing-the-caber competition at a Highland Games. James's mother, Janet, had been brought up in Edinburgh and was interested in cultural things. To Janet's dismay, when her mother-in-law died, her father-in-law and his other son, who was of limited intelligence and had never left home, came to live with the family. Since she had two sons herself, she found herself living in a household with five males. Janet desperately missed someone to share her more feminine and cultured interests in life, especially because her husband was determinedly "hypermasculine." James grew up to be overtly very masculine in a rather rigid way, identifying with his father while secretly he yearned for the discussions about

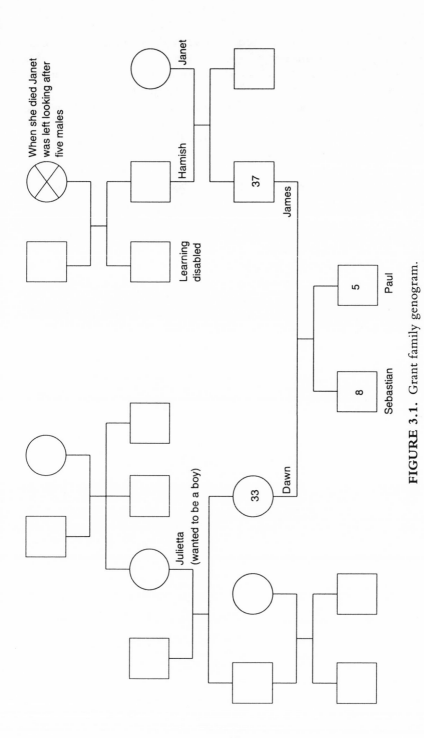

FIGURE 3.1. Grant family genogram.

49

art and the theater that he used to have with his mother, covertly identifying with his mother.

When James and Dawn met, they found that they shared an interest in the theater, which somehow managed to counter their families' preoccupation with undemonstrative masculinity. James was a statistician working in an insurance company, while Dawn worked part-time in a shoe shop. Neither felt fulfilled; both were mildly depressed. Their main energy was provided by their two sons, who soon discovered that their parents reacted miraculously with an increase in interest to their pretend play, which evolved, with considerable encouragement from the parents, into little playlets with costumes and scenery changes and so on. Sebastian had been a beautiful baby and was often mistaken for a girl by passersby, which Dawn enjoyed. In addition, Dawn would wander around the house naked, and James noticed that Sebastian was particularly fascinated by her body. She seemed to value her female aspects by showing her body to her son and by giving him dresses to wear. She was delighted when other people identified him as being a girl; she encouraged him to copy her feminine side and not enjoy her rather unglamorous tomboy self. It was also clear to Sebastian that his father came to life whenever feminine things were being discussed, or displayed, and that he was really dissatisfied with his dry, boring masculinity with which Sebastian was, as a result, discouraged from identifying. Paul was different. He was boisterous from a very young age, and both parents responded to his aggressive, active style; he became a "hypermasculine" little boy. Each parent thus had an uneasy split between the masculine and feminine aspects of themselves, but dealt with this vicariously through scripting their two sons into very opposite male and female roles. Everybody in the family seemed to enjoy this arrangement until it dawned on them that their eldest son could become a homosexual. Mother's reactions, in particular, swung from being delighted with him to being disgusted. In the meantime the threat of sexual abuse of Sebastian was mounting.

Therapy

I will focus my description of the therapy on the vicarious wishes being expressed across the generations. I was struck by how quickly I was inducted into being a fascinated member of the adult audience to the performances of these two entertaining little boys. I pointed this out and we discussed how hard it was not to encourage either Sebastian's feminine behavior or Paul being a miniature "Rambo." Sebastian drew some figures with beautiful flowing garments. He was highly creative. He could not understand what the fuss was about when his parents brought him into the clinic. However, it soon dawned on him that his parents were very anxious about his interest in dressing up and doing anything girlish. His drawings became more and more restricted and dull, until one picture had a solitary bulldog staring out balefully at the viewer, while a child in a cloak was walking out of the picture. I suddenly realized he was taking on the dull, restrictive, and angry aspects of his father's personality, while his creativity was making an exit. This was not the identification that anybody, least of all Sebastian, really seemed to want. I then defined the purpose of therapy as being to try to help the family not to become typecast in their roles. All of them seemed to be in danger of being trapped in unwanted roles. We discussed how both parents felt restricted and displeased about their lives. They would love to be more varied in what they did, and even Paul was becoming an increasing problem, as he was so actively aggressive. I suggested that the family should help Sebastian to choose what sort of person he wanted to be. What he was complaining about most was being teased and bullied at school. The task for his father was to help him to be an ordinary boy at school so that he was no longer teased. In the meantime I suggested Sebastian might dress up in some male clothing which was also interesting. He got himself some wizard's clothes and brought them to one of the sessions. He put the garments on and asked if he could cast a spell. His mother encouraged him to do this. He stood up in front of the family and quoted the witches' curse from Shakespeare's *Macbeth*: "Double, double, toil and trouble. . . . " He suddenly realized that this was a female role and asked his mother if this was okay, and she nodded approvingly. Afterward his father was very proud of the fact that he had been able to quote it all correctly. I had noticed that Sebastian's social referencing was almost always to his mother, looking at her to see whether she approved or not of what he was doing.

I invited Sebastian and his father to the next session, leaving the other two out. The task was to help Sebastian behave in a way that would seem normal for a boy. I told Sebastian, since he had been only very recently aware that he was being teased about certain behaviors, we could use the one-way mirror for him to see what that particular behavior looked like. His father could help to point it out to him. They chose two pieces of behavior that seemed to provoke ridicule. The first was when he bowed after a performance in the school play— he did it with a tremendous flourish. I asked him to show me, while he watched himself in the mirror. He stood up and bowed to the mirror. I then asked him to repeat it several times, each time making the flourish more extreme. I pointed out that repeating the behavior would reveal more clearly what it is that gets him teased. At first it was fun; I must have appeared to be like the parent who was encouraging him to perform. However, by persisting to the point where he looked ridiculous, he started to be reluctant to go on. Stern (1985) discusses how children of depressed parents may learn to regulate upward the excitement in interaction in order to try to lift their parent's spirits. However, these children do not then learn how to lower their own excitement. They do not know when to stop. In this exercise I regulated upward to a ludicrous level so that Sebastian in response started to set his own top threshold. His father who was watching also began to feel that it was overdone and, therefore, was no longer escalating the behavior, but helped Sebastian to slow it down as well. I then asked James to show Sebastian how to bow in a way that would be acceptable and not attract teasing. His father did this with quiet, restrained dignity, and Sebastian was able to imitate him. I was encouraging Sebastian to identify with his father, but in the context in which his father was alive and interesting, and not that of his boring work context.

I then repeated the same exercise with the second activity that attracted teasing: his stereotyped effeminate walking. I encouraged him to walk the way he imagined a girl walked and to watch himself. Again, I escalated this to the point where he was reluctant to go on, and I noticed that his father looked increasingly uncomfortable. I then asked him to walk like an 8-year-old boy, which he proceeded to do. For the first time there was no sign whatsoever of the stereotypical walk that I had seen him using before. I gave Sebastian and his father the video to take home so that they could work further on this issue. I suggested that they should do this without either mother or Paul present, but then to decide together what to tell her about what had happened. In this package of interventions I aimed to reduce what might be seen as effeminate behavior; to encourage Sebastian to identify with his father; and to put a masculinity boundary around his father and himself in which his mother was not an immediate part. He began behaving less and less like a girl; the teasing at school lessened; and Sebastian and his father started to do things together, such as going skiing. This sport provided a blend of masculine athleticism with the aesthetic, graceful, flowing movement. Both males could enjoy these elements together.

I had a number of sessions with the parents on their own, working on mutual interests and helping them to think about how they might make their own lives more interesting. This put themselves at center stage instead of the boys' behavior. Each acted as audience to the other's new and interesting ideas about new options at work. Later they became increasingly concerned about Paul who was becoming more and more difficult. I suggested that they should become increasingly bored by both Paul's aggressively masculine "Rambo" antics, and any of Sebastian's residual effeminate behavior. Paul's behavior abated, and Sebastian's public cross-dressing disappeared. However, Dawn found some scarves hidden away in his bedroom, and he admitted that he had been using them. I had a private session with Sebastian and he showed me just how sensitive he was to scripting by the adults by giving me many answers he thought I wanted to hear. He told me how he was now an ordinary little boy. However, the session went on long enough for him to finally tell me that when he did dress up as a girl he felt that he actually was a girl. Sebastian was now creating his own self-perpetuating cycle, through his secret cross-dressing. This self-maintaining behavior is one of the criteria that I use when considering individual psychotherapy for children. Sebastian saw a child psychotherapist for 2 years.

In the last family session I suggested that the parents had to allow the boys to choose what sort of people they wanted to be. I stressed how important it was for the boys to feel comfortable talking to their parents if they began feeling troubled by what was happening to them. I said that we could not tell with young boys whether they would turn out to be the sort of people who would prefer the company of other men or of women. What was most important was that they should be comfortable with whatever they chose, and that they could be free to discuss their relationships with their parents. On follow-up, Sebastian seemed to be doing well at school. He was not being teased or bullied for effeminate behavior. His father, however, had had a bout of depression that needed treatment 2 years after the end of the family therapy. Family therapy is often only one therapeutic component in helping families.

ROLE-PLAY, ACTING, AND IDENTITY

Family therapists often use improvisation within role-play as a way of exploring the experience of various relationships. First we discover that we can play parts with which we do not feel identified. Second, virtually everyone can do this in a strikingly realistic way, often much to the surprise of the first-time role-player. For instance, a young man brought up in a family terrified of anger convincingly played a middle-aged woman who battered a child in a fit of rage. This showed that we do not have to have felt identified with the improvised role, or even have directly witnessed anything like it; however, individuals can become temporarily identified with a role that emerges out of the improvised plot.

At the end of a role-play, participants need to be deroled, preferably by stating with whom they became identified in the role-play, and then who they are in their own families and in the professional setting. The danger of failing to derole is that the roles can become scripted in the work context and the individual might be treated by his or her colleagues as being the person portrayed in such a vivid scenario. He or she may also identify him- or herself in that way. This suggests that it is the mutually reinforcing expectations of self and others that script roles which can be maintained across contexts. Given this easily identifiable danger within a professional organization, it is hardly surprising that it can be frightening to improvise in a family context in which you may have to go on living with the consequences of any new family scene.

One additional element I like to add to the deroling exercise, especially with students, is to instruct the participants to try to hold some of their role in their memory. By labeling it as a discrete memory, participants can externalize it; they find that they are no longer organized by the experience. I suggest that they think later about whether what happened did represent something from their own family. This could be either a replication of what happened in childhood or, alternatively, a corrective script in which they found themselves free to play a role they would have loved to have played but never felt able to do so in their own families. I have found that I repeatedly volunteer for delinquent adolescent roles, which I relish and enjoy with great gusto. I had no real rebellion as an adolescent because we were isolated in a dangerous situation during a civil war, and we were all armed with loaded firearms. We had to be prepared to use the firearms at any given moment. No improvisation with rebellion possible there!

Some wrong conclusions can be arrived at, however, if too close a parallel is drawn between nonfamily members role-playing a family and an actual family improvising. The pretend role-play usually starts with a concerted attempt to create a meaningful plot; each individual responds to contextual cues that suggest a particular situation by adding something that confirms the presence of that scenario. Very quickly a plot is developed, reinforced, and elaborated on. The anxiety of not knowing who or where you are leads to a search for something that is more familiar and has meaning.

In contrast a family starts with too much familiar meaning, and improvisation is a search for something outside and beyond the known. Keeney (1991) explores the equivalent process for therapists, in suggesting ways to help them improvise beyond the normal range of therapeutic techniques.

In 1975 I became interested in whether role-play could be used to explore how themes are transferred from generation to generation. A colleague, Jenny Crickmay, and I worked on a project with four actors: two men and two women. The idea was to produce a family in which each actor would play the role of every member of the family over the past three generations of the family. Thus, the actors played all the roles of each sex in each generation. This project enabled us to see whether having the whole family internalized created a family with a recognizable and coherent structure that could be maintained over a period of time. To begin with, I selected a family that I had been working with; I knew the grandparents' generation and what had happened to them. I provided a vignette of the situation of each set of grandparents at the time when the parents in the current family were children. The actors then role-played scenes of family life as the children grew older, and the next generation was born, carrying this through until the present day.

This role-playing evolved over 12 weekly sessions, each of which lasted a morning or an afternoon. All the actors were professional and of a high caliber and there was a professional director who looked after the theatrical aspects. Jenny stayed with the actors throughout this process; unfortunately, I was able to join them for only about half of the time. The power of the role-play was quite extraordinary. The family members were focusing on what was going on within the family and seemed less preoccupied with the audience of three, that is, the director and the two clinicians. Sometimes, however, there was an unofficial audience of the general public who were able to see in through the windows of the Tavistock Clinic and watched in amazement as the various scenarios were acted out in dramatic fashion.

By the end of this process the new family seemed to have gained some coherence and a characteristic way of relating. The "family" then appeared in two conferences: The first was held in London and the second in Cardiff. The Cardiff conference was held in a theater with an audience of about 400 people. The idea was for the audience to suggest situations around which the actors could improvise. The hope was to be able to trace some of the transgenerational patterns as they were played out around current issues. What happened, however, was that the family rapidly lost its previous coherence and started to respond to the audience's input. It became an audience–actor improvisation, and the old script blew away. The result was acutely embarrassing, not least for the professional actors.

This experiment suggested two things. First, the importance of a

deeply ingrained script with which the family could continue to identify itself for maintaining its coherence when responding to the outside world. Playing pretend roles does not provide sufficient identification with the characters. Actors after all learn to escape from roles
after a performance. Second, it demonstrated the power of context.
The actors' home is the theater and this suddenly became the source
of inspiration for the actors, which swept away the temporary script
elaborated back in the Clinic. In short, for a family to cocollaborate
in different and difficult circumstances, they need a family script which
provides a set of roles with which each member of the family can
identify, and which provides a set of guidelines that are broadly based
enough to improvise when facing new situations.

In the early 1980s I experimented with actors once more. I wanted
to see whether actors could portray a family therapy session. This
time I had a transcript of a family session. I found four high-class,
professional actors and a director who had worked for the BBC. The
actors, when confronted with the transcript, were astounded that anybody could say such amazing things. They found it difficult to get
under the family's skin—they could not empathize. I had decided
that I would allow the actors to create their own images of the family
members, rather than asking them to view the videotape (thus protecting the confidentiality of the family). The result was a teaching
tape which was unfortunately rather cardboard as a performance, although effective in making theoretical points. The actors were fully
aware that they had not performed as well as they could have and said
that what they found most difficult was never having witnessed any
family therapy. The context made no sense to them. I discovered that
the words on their own do not necessarily convey what is happening.
A script may have to be learned from witnessing something that can
be given some meaning, or at least from being able to envisage what
it might have been like in the situation described. The plot is the key.

F·O·U·R

Rewriting Family Scripts

For the family scripts to remain helpful to the family there have to be ways of updating them when necessary. This process involves a series of revisions or reedits, in which the family improvises in response to changed circumstances. Any valuable innovations that emerge are then repeated and in time become part of the family expectations, and so the script is rewritten. In this way the family can adapt to developmental changes and new situations. However, the precious asset of stability and continuity that scripts can provide will be sacrificed if revision occurs every time the situation changes. The family would then become too context bound, bowing to every little change. Stability is partly provided by the family script being embedded in belief systems and practices which are shared with the extended family, the community, and the culture. Beliefs are usually deeply entrenched because they are based on underlying models of how relationships function. Models are often even more difficult to reappraise and alter. The key to reediting family scripts lies in the adequate exchange of information between everyday experience of family life and the meanings attributed to the way family members interact.

MEANINGS WITHIN CONTEXT

Finding meaning in what is happening helps to guide decisions about what to do next. Meaning given to interaction is usually based on the constructs that the family already has for the motives behind what is being done. The key issues for change are the conditions in which new information can alter the belief systems. How can exploration lead to the discovery of something new if information is already being processed in a way that is likely to merely re-discover the old meaning?

Any episode of interaction occurring in a family can be given various meanings when viewed from within different contexts or frames. As social scientists Cronen and Pearce (1985) point out, social meanings are hierarchically organized so that one level is the context for construing the meaning of those at lower levels. The hierarchy is usually organized on the basis that meanings emanating from a wider arena—in terms of the number of people involved and/or a longer time span—are likely to be more pervasive than those with a narrower base. When this is taken into account, the following hierarchy can be devised in which family scripts are embedded.

Cultural mythology
Family myths and legends
Family script
Episode or scenario
Act of communication

Beliefs at the top of the hierarchy give meaning to all those below. Implications of changes of lower order meaning do not easily change those higher in the hierarchy. The meanings at all levels may be congruent and so support and maintain each other.

Family Example

We can use an act of communication made by Annabel Morton (see Chapter 1) when she said to her son Jason, "That's it! I'm going to call your father." This episode was given meaning when seen as part of a Morton family scenario in which Annabel cannot manage Jason and calls his father in to help. The episode is given wider meaning when seen as part of the Morton family script in which Jason has the role of getting his father home by behaving in a way that his mother cannot manage. We also have to look at the situation in the light of the family myth that father can manage Jason but mother cannot. Further meaning is assigned by the extended family's myths which, on Annabel's side, dictate that women are expected to be generally inferior to men, and on Frank's side, dictated that depressed mothers needed a man to rescue them. These myths were supported by legends about Annabel's grandmother having nearly been smothered at birth because she was a girl, not a boy, and Frank's widowed and depressed mother having been rescued by his stepfather. All these levels of meaning were further embedded in a culture which, by and large, believes that men have to take the ultimate disciplinary role, while women are expected to care for the children.

Cronen and Pearce (1985) discuss how the hierarchy can be reversed at times—for example, if one particular episode is given sufficient significance, it might give meaning to the family scripts rather than the other way around. Therapists can influence the rules that change the order in the hierarchy. For instance, the attention given by a therapist to what family members do with each other in daily situations has implications for whether the family thinks that what its members actually do is more important than their self-image. A good example of this is provided by Gorell Barnes when she describes work toward changes in everyday management of routine events that can then be generalized. She quotes one father (Barnes, 1983) as saying, "Coming up here has made us aware of one or two 'bits and pieces,' if you like, and we watch points more. That in itself has made a big difference" (p. 51). An episode in a particular family situation, in which something new happens, can create a scenario for future handling of that context. This, if repeated, becomes a regular expectation, which can then generalize to how relationships are expected to be handled within all contexts. The family script is reedited. The implications of the new ways of relating then also challenge the family mythology. The hierarchy thus changes to:

Episode
Family script
Family mythology

Family therapists who focus mainly on belief systems can help to reedit mythology at a high level in the hierarchy. Changes in beliefs systems, if they do indeed influence changes in behavior, are clearly an appropriate way of approaching therapy. Sometimes there are two contradictory hierarchies operating: one based on stated beliefs, the other on what people do. A child will usually take what a person does more seriously than what he or she says. For this reason, I believe it is useful to combine both approaches. The most important change to produce is to believe in the possibility of change. As "seeing is believing," I like to focus on episodes initially. Ideally the episode is one in which the family improvises its own solutions, so that they can feel themselves to be authors of their own script. The focus of the therapist's work is on how to heighten the significance of any successful outcomes so that they finally believe that they can change.

CLINICAL ILLUSTRATION OF THE INTERPLAY
BETWEEN LEVELS OF MEANING

The processes of reediting scripts can be explored as they emerge, starting with an episode in the Morton family (see Chapter 1) in which Annabel took charge of Jason. This was in the fifth session. Jason was disruptive, and Annabel sat him on her knee, holding him facing away from her. Frank in the meantime was playing with William.

JASON: (*crying and complaining*) I want my Dad. (*Frank makes no response to this. Annabel tries a number of strategies to calm him. These are partially successful.*)

THERAPIST: (*encouraging improvisation*) You are very ingenious in finding ways of settling the children.

JASON: (*in a period of squirming to free himself*) You're strangling me.

Up to now both mother and son were replicating almost exactly the scenario in which father controlled Jason in the first session (Chapter 1, p. 8). The holding had been done then with Jason facing away from his father, and Jason had complained about being strangled. Annabel now had to find her own way.

ANNABEL: No, I am not (*strongly*). I am holding you. (*Nevertheless, she allows Jason to slip off her knee and onto the floor. He remains with his head on her lap.*) You're all hot! (*cuddling him and stroking his forehead, thus moving into a nurturing mode*)

JASON: Don't hold so tight Mum. (*Reassured, he turns around and climbs back onto her lap facing her. He reaches up and they hug.*)

ANNABEL: *Not* the strangle one. (*kissing him*) Oh! That's nice! We have nice cuddles, don't we!

THERAPIST: You have been showing us that holding is a caring thing even if it is restraining. It is not hurting like strangling—and holding can be loving.

Here I am narrator to the action, thus heightening the significance of what was going on, but also validating Annabel's actions as valuable. During this time Frank was playing with William while facing away from Annabel in order to let her do it herself. He glanced around occasionally to see how she was coping.

BREAK: [Discussion with observing group.]

THERAPIST: The group thinks that you are a very creative family, finding many ways of doing things. This tells us you will manage.

Jason then tested his mother's determination, and she repeatedly took control, improvising new ways each time, although keeping to the basic strategy of holding him. Each testing, however, was less vigorous. Finally Jason settled. During this, Frank continued to play with William, but now he stopped glancing inquiringly at his wife to see how she was managing. He now expected her to manage.

THERAPIST: *(to Annabel)* You very clearly took charge. *(admiringly)*

ANNABEL: Yes! I can do it! *(pause)* But when I am at home on my own I have William as well.

THERAPIST: We need to work on that.

In fact, there had been another intended message from the group to the effect that Annabel had managed to control Jason, but I delayed that as she continued to take charge of her son with such firmness. When I finally affirmed her success, it was almost unnecessary as she had confirmed it for herself and the rest of the family. This is much more important, and goes some way toward changing the beliefs higher in the hierarchy of meaning. Nevertheless, validation by the therapist with his or her perceived authority, as well as that of a wider professional group, can provide a validating image to an individual struggling at home and doubting herself.

Annabel's demonstrated competence had implications for the family script in which Jason was expected to bring his father in. An attempt to trigger the old script was made by Jason calling for his father when his mother was first holding him. The need for his father's rescue was thus challenged by finding that Annabel coped well. (And I, the therapist, did not move in to occupy the vacant role either.) However, as Annabel pointed out herself, the new emergent script needed to be repeated at home. That task was worked on by reviewing episodes when Annabel was at home on her own.

After an initial improvement, however, things started to slip back, and belief in the new solution started to drain away. In short, the beliefs from higher in the hierarchy were reasserting their influence over the emergent script. These needed to be changed as well.

Annabel had a new 19-year-old Irish au pair to help with the children. In other words, the au pair had been recruited into the role left vacant by Frank who now no longer came home in a crisis. At that time I was seeing the Morton family with two senior female colleagues (Barbara Dale and Charlotte Burck) observing behind the screen, both interested in the gender issues. This team was called the "conversation group," in which each couple that was observing would, during breaks, have a conversation with each other about what they had seen going on. The therapist listens to this discussion and then takes what he or she wants back into the therapy. This, we have found, is a very fruitful way for senior colleagues, who have differing therapeutic approaches, to collaborate. The therapist keeps responsibility for how he or she uses the ideas, while the observers are free of the responsibility for suggesting interventions or sending messages. In the break, on this occasion, the observers had a discussion about how the therapist seemed to be fascinated by scripts, while what they observed was the extraordinary situation of a mother in her 30s conceding greater skill in mothering to a mere teenager. By feeding the gist of this conversation back to the family and saying that the comments came from the women, the therapist was able to help Annabel to start reevaluating her own worth. She needed validation from other women. Since her experience was of men being given precedence and of women being seen as inferior, a man defining her in any way merely confirmed the image of male authority, even if what was said was affirmative. To have the male therapist accept a woman's redefinition of his work also validated the female voice as being at least equal. Annabel could listen to that.

As far as the family is concerned, the observation group can be perceived as speaking for an aspect of cultural values, and hence can be used, if the family wishes to use it that way, as a belief to counteract some of the extended family mythology. Annabel did this despite her mother who still idealized her brother because he was male. I often invite grandparents to some sessions (Byng-Hall, 1982b). This can help to change beliefs about their offspring. It can also release the offspring from feeling that they have to go on fulfilling some role in their parents' family mythology. However, Frank and Annabel redefined themselves as being independent of their families without any prompting by me. They invited their parents to join them in their annual vacation, instead of going to Frank's parents' vacation home in France. This decision resulted in a great deal of pressure from Frank's parents to keep to the annual ritual. The Mortons took a vacation on their own, instead, as they refused to reverse their invitation. Frank felt that at last he was free of his family, and Annabel knew that he put her and the children before his family of origin. They felt married at last.

Meanings that are attributed to actions also involve underlying models of understanding why people behave as they do. The concept of an internal working model is one way of thinking about this.

INTERNAL WORKING MODELS

The idea of an internal working model was first proposed by Craik (1943), a psychologist, who became involved in the construction of intelligent rocket-guiding systems. Craik hypothesized that the organism "carries a small scale model of external reality and of its own possible actions within its head, it is able to try out various alternatives, conclude which is the best of them, react to future situations before they arise, utilize the knowledge of past events in dealing with the present and future, and in every way to react in a much fuller, safer and more competent manner to the emergencies which face it" (p. 61). If this model is used, Craik considered that the individual is much more likely to achieve his or her objectives.

The concept of an internal working model was used by Bowlby (1969) to describe the mental representation of relationships that enable a child to make predictions about his parent's (or attachment figure's) likely behavior so that he or she can feel secure in the knowledge that the parent will be available when needed. For this, the child needs a model of the parent as loving and caring, and of the self as lovable, so that he or she can envisage the parent being pleased to see him or her and willing to help. More specifically, the child needs images of a repertoire of actions that can be taken in order to reach the parent, such as calling or crying and/or running toward the parent. The child also needs another set of images about the parent's predictable responses. The parent also has a reciprocal working model of the child's needs as well as his or her own ways of responding. Together the two reciprocal internal models create a shared working model of the attachment relationship. The part that is shared is the mental representation of the basic elements of the interacting relationship. These two models are, of course, far from identical: The child's model is limited by developmental factors, while the parent's model is based on extensive experience, including that of having been parented.

The individual's working model of a secure family base, in which all members of the family can feel secure, incorporates the various attachments that the individual has within the family. The whole pattern of attachment in the family is taken into account, so that each attachment has potential significance for every other attachment. This raises the issue of whether closeness in one relationship may exclude another, or, to the contrary, may nourish it so that more is available to others. For instance, several children may need to feel that a particular parent is available for each of them. There may be competition for attention, and one child may, for instance, have a model that suggests that the only way of achieving this state of affairs is to capture the parent and attempt to exclude the others, including the parent's partner. A working model of a secure family base, however, is likely to include the knowledge that care can be given by the attachment figure to others, say, to another sibling, without permanent loss of one's own right for care, or being forgotten. In that case you can then afford to wait your turn. Also, children may experience that allowing space for a parent to be with other adults leaves him or her in a better state of mind to respond to demands. The working model also incorporates organizational aspects of the relationships that other members have with each other, the most important of which is the image that any "coparenting" relationship (which might be any effective dyad such as grandmother–mother or elder sibling–father, as well as both parents) will collaborate to provide care. The core shared working model of a secure family base is of a family who will make sure that children will be looked after in all eventualities.

The sense of belonging to one's own family can also be important. This gives a feeling that one has a right to make demands on members of the extended family when in particular need. The family's sense of loyalty and mutual support is likely to support the right to make the request even when there has not previously been much contact, like the aunt who has not seen much of a particular child but cares for him or her when the child's parent is ill. A supportive friendship network can also add greatly to the sense of security within the family, and may be needed to replace an extended family whose availability is limited.

One of the advantages of the concept of a working model is that it takes into account the various active experimental maneuvers that the mind takes in planning some future event based on knowledge of what has happened in the past. It is not just a preset program—like computer software. The idea of a "working" model also implies something that can be built up and experimented with in the mind by imagining the possible effects of trying different ways of relating to people, and then putting some of the more promising ideas into practice; it is a tool for finding a way that works.

A CONCEPTUAL WORKING MODEL
OF FAMILY INFORMATION PROCESSING

A conceptual model is needed to enable us to think about how information is processed within the family so that family scripts appropriate to the context can be enacted. This model is of how information is stored; how stored memories influence the way a situation is perceived; and how information is retrieved and exchanged. Finally, the model must convey how the information is updated. For the model to be useful to a family therapist, it must also address ways in which the processing may go wrong, leading to inappropriate action being taken. The model indicates how information processing occurs within each individual's mind as well as between people.

Some of the general principles of an internal working model might also be suitably applied to a conceptual model. In working models, if something more helpful and consistent comes along, a conceptual model can be adapted or discarded. I find the following conceptual working model both useful and simple enough for the purpose of thinking about scripts. The core idea is that information from the various domains relevant to the context is cross-referenced before action is taken. Although the working model deals with how information is processed within the whole family, it is important to find a model that is congruent with ideas about how it is processed within the mind.

The way in which the brain holds mental representations of the world, however, is still not clear. But we need a model to go along with until it is clarified. Rosenfield (1988), proposing a model that uses Edelman's (1987) theory of the brain, suggests that information in the brain is distributed among many maps and that there must be incessant referencing back and forth between maps. This coupling of different kinds of mapping permits generalization. Nothing, not even memory, remains static but is created anew each time out of the exchange of information between current context and previous patterns (Neisser & Winograd, 1988).

Semantic and Episodic Memory

Bowlby (1980) argued that the internal working model is held in long-term memory, which can be divided into two main categories.

First, there is semantic memory, which holds beliefs, many of which are expressed through language, and includes abstract ideas. These ideas come from either extracting general principles from repeated experiences, or from values and opinions passed on by family members. Second, there is episodic memory, in which memories of events are stored. A particular piece of family interaction then evokes memories of similar events which are then cross-referenced with beliefs held about these kinds of events. Feelings are thus evoked both in response to reliving the memory of the event (e.g., anxiety or fear) and through eliciting attitudes about what should be done (e.g., shame, pride). This mixture of affects then helps to motivate the particular action to be taken next.

Events or Scenarios Held in Episodic Memory

In my imagination I envisage the script for what to do in particular situations like a series of transparent images of what has happened in the past superimposed, one on top of the other, producing a general image that is available for use as a template for what normally happens. Specific episodes can be taken out for recall by cross-referencing with some concurrent event: "Oh, yes. That was Christmas 1982, wasn't it?"

Beliefs Held in Semantic Memory

Semantic memory holds a series of beliefs about different aspects of family life, each of which acts as a frame through which the other beliefs can be viewed. These maps or frames include the following belief systems:

1. Beliefs about *causality*. The model of what makes relationships work is often a mixture of (a) *linear causality* in which one person—or an action—is seen to make something happen in relationships, and (b) *circular causality* in which what happens between people—their interaction—is perceived to be crucial. What people do is perceived as being both influenced by and influencing what goes on. Families vary in which emphasis they place on each mode.
2. Beliefs about *care and concern* within relationships. Do people see themselves as lovable and loving so that they expect care when it is needed? Is loving someone else likely to lead to being loved? Or, in contrast, is lack of concern the model for relationships? So do you give and receive, or do you have to grab what you can?

3. A set of expectations about how *power* will be used. This defines whether those with superior power, say, based on size and strength, or social role, will use that power to care for other people and protect them. Or whether they will use it to impose their will on others, or to hurt other people.

4. The *moral* lens through which right and wrong is judged. This includes the ethics of caring for others, how authority ought to be used, and which behaviors (e.g., sexuality) are permitted or forbidden within a particular relationship.

5. Beliefs about *gender.* These beliefs provide another frame for all these issues. Do men care for or coerce others? Are women compliant or influential, etc?

There are beliefs about how problems are created and solved in relationships. These include:

6. A model of *how problems are caused.* This is usually a function of the model of causality, one aspect of which is whether the cause of the difficulty is seen as arising within the individual, or whether it is seen as a product of what goes on between people. Out of this belief come ideas about responsibility for change, that is, will one person have to sort it out, or is it a collaborative effort?

7. A model of *change* within relationships. One aspect of this that is important to scripts is whether change is seen as a mutual process in which each person relaxes his or her scripted behavior and improvises, coauthoring a new shared script, or is it seen as a battle between each person's script so that one finally dominates? This model is, of course, in turn framed by all the above beliefs. Will loving care and protection lead to growth and flowering of the relationship, or do you have to bully and coerce the other person into fitting into your scheme of things? Are women more likely to use one method and men the other? Etc.

There are also many other belief systems that are involved—for example, cultural, racial, religious beliefs. These beliefs are then applied to who does what to whom and in what way within the family. In this way episodic and semantic memory cross reference with each other. This often happens within the sequence of previewing an event, enacting the scenario, and then reviewing what happened. This information is also processed between family members, and leads to a shared working model. This processing is carried out both within awareness and outside it. Significant issues may be brought into awareness where they can be scrutinized.

THE MONITORING OF THE CONTEXT
FOR RELEVANT INFORMATION

The family is constantly monitoring the situation for whether action needs to be taken, or is to be avoided. Certain family members may become sentinels for particular situations—for example, a mother may monitor for any immediate danger, while a father worries about the long term, but if one is absent, another is likely to take over that role. Another form of monitoring is for anything that might upset a member of the family. Not infrequently, it is the children who monitor their parents for signs of vulnerability. The way in which families defend each other from having to face intolerable home truths by creating an acceptable shared family myth is discussed in Chapter 8.

Cross-referencing between the family script and what is currently happening enables any significant divergence from the norm to be spotted. Family scripts can then operate automatically with a minimum of fuss. However, any new occurrences are rapidly assessed for their significance, especially registering whether or not something has to be done, for instance, seeing whether or not there is a potential threat to security. If the situation is also assessed as urgent, then a script may be invoked quickly with minimal delay for thought or cross-referencing. Here the models from the past become crucial. If past experience suggests that what is happening can be dangerous, then action can be precipitous and may not be appropriate. This is more likely to happen if the model has not been updated, or the family member who springs into action is unaware of the model that is influencing his or her action. This is particularly likely to happen in situations where the past experience was so painful that its recall is blocked. Reviewing the relevance of past models for current situations becomes very important.

REVIEWING MODELS
Developing the Capacity for Metacognitive Monitoring

Metacognition—"thinking about thinking"—is a central mechanism involved in reviewing ideas or models because it recognizes the representational nature of models; for instance, recognizing that "the map is not the territory." The example, par excellence, of metacognition is the capacity to distinguish appearance from reality. Main (1991) discusses the role of metacognition in children's thinking. A child younger than 4 years cannot step back and consider his or her own thoughts and ideas. So scripts cannot be reviewed in early childhood. Children, as they grow older, begin to realize that people can see things differently or get things wrong, and that people can even lie. Children also come to appreciate that the way things are seen can change from day to day—bad on Mondays, super on Saturdays, etc. Many of these capacities are available to them by the age of 6. This allows children to see that one and the same person can also have different characteristics, say, a father can be both angry and loving. Children thus come to monitor critically their own thoughts and those of others for changes and what they really represent. Metacognitive monitoring of ongoing processes allows for "planning activities, monitoring them, and checking outcomes" (Main, 1991, p. 134). This provides a mechanism for accomplishing the sequence of previewing, enacting, and reviewing.

Another important feature of metacognitive monitoring is cross-checking for errors in thinking. This enables children to self-regulate their own knowledge and in particular to see whether the implications of one model are compatible with those of another. This gives them the capacity to reorganize their thinking in order to create only one coherent model of what happens in a particular situation.

Unconscious Processing of Information Held in Scripts

As we know, however, awareness provides only a small window into what is going on. What happens on open stage is a result of a great deal of backstage activity. Information related to many different domains is being processed in parallel, most of it outside awareness. Information held in scripts is also processed by dramatizing the scenarios outside awareness but within unconscious fantasy. One well-known example of this is how life scripts of people who have died continue to unfold in the unconscious of those left behind. This phenomenon is explored further in Chapter 13. Images of children, for instance, who have died often appear at anniversaries of the death or on birthdays. The child may have grown up to the appropriate age in the unconscious imagination.

On a day-to-day level, dreams may pick up a theme from the previous day's events or a task for the coming day, and take the fantasy in a series of associations that connect it with childhood images, previous dramatizations, or unconscious assumptions. The hidden plot is then revealed in a form acceptable to consciousness. These internal dramas can go beyond the constraints of normal experience to climaxes that may be either frightening or encouraging. The unconscious mind can thus make associations with the many potentially contradictory strands—plots and subplots—that always interweave in any interpersonal situation. In this way it is possible to nudge the mind toward or away from alternative solutions or arrive at some unthought-of solution. These may, in turn, enliven or restrict the improvisation within the relationship. Much of the communication between family members about their scripts is also conveyed outside awareness through the symbolism of action, or through the imagery of language. All this processing would totally bombard and confuse the conscious decision-making process. Thank goodness we do not have to think about every little action we take.

McDougall (1986), in her book *Theatres of the Mind,* discusses how unconscious "child dramas" and scripts are reenacted throughout life, and become interwoven with current events. This is one way of processing transgenerational scripts. Freud (1909) saw repetition compulsion—the individual equivalent of redramatizing of attempted solution scenarios—as a way that an individual tries to master some unresolved problem through enacting it again and again. The underlying unresolved drama he suggested has to be understood before it can be played out in the theater of the mind rather than through action.

DIFFICULTIES IN UPDATING SCRIPTS

Problems in Information Processing

There are a number of ways in which the necessary exchange of information for updating scripts is obstructed. This can happen at any point in the cycle of previewing, enacting, and reviewing. Previewing and enacting scenarios involve retrieval of information from past experiences to be used as a guide for what to do. Reviewing means facing the implications of what has happened. The past may be too painful to relive in the imagination; and the implications too disturbing. The blocking or editing of intolerable information happens at both the intrapsychic level (one does not tell oneself) and the interpersonal levels (one does not tell the other person). Usually the two go hand in hand to ensure that only tolerable levels of potentially disturbing information emerge within the family. Difficulties can arise in the following situations.

Contradictions between Semantic and Episodic Memory

It can be very painful to see that what actually happens is not what you would like to believe happens. The family rules may prohibit even looking at the discrepancy between belief and action. Bowlby (1988) wrote a classic paper, "On Knowing What You Are Not Supposed to Know and Feeling What You Are Not Supposed to Feel." In this paper he quotes a study (Cain & Fast, 1972) of children who have witnessed a suicide of a parent, but are then told by the surviving parent that he or she died of some other cause. One example is of a girl who found her father hanging, but was told that he was killed in a car accident. In a similar manner, abused children are often told that the abuse did not happen. Bowlby describes how this process of imposed denial leads to two contradictory models of the same event.

Bowlby argues that the child is likely to identify with the actions held in the episodic memory, even if he or she holds a contrasting set of beliefs held in semantic memory. So that when he or she becomes a parent there is a possibility of reenacting something from a past episode, while believing and saying something quite different.

Defensive Exclusion of Potentially Uncomfortable Information

Bowlby (1980) used the term "defensive exclusion," to describe how painful information is obscured. First, the recall of previous painful episodes may be blocked. Second, any information that might trigger an unfortunate script may be prevented from being processed any further, thus avoiding the potentially painful interaction. The classic example of this is the anxiously avoidant child who on reunion with his parent in the Strange Situation Procedure (Ainsworth et al., 1978; see Chapters 1 and 6) turns away from the parent and turns to a toy instead. This has the effect of switching off attachment behavior, and also switches attention away from anger at having been left by the parent. If the child were to act on the anger, he or she would risk rejection by the parent.

At a transgenerational level there may be an attempt to bury the past by forgetting it, but as George Santayana (1905) pointed out, "Those who cannot remember the past are condemned to repeat it." In script terms a replicative script may be more likely to operate in scenarios in this generation that are similar to those forgotten episodes in the parent's past.

Defensive exclusion may also involve prohibition on discussion of experiences that can be remembered but are too painful to recall. Some parents, for instance, may attempt to bury their past by operating a massive corrective script: trying to live a completely new life, perhaps reinforcing this with emigration or climbing out of the painful circumstances that would remind them of past pain. They may also refuse to talk about their past to their family. This may work well, but some unfortunate aspects of replicative scripts tend to surface.

Splitting into Counterpart Roles

In some families roles are split into complementary counterpart roles: good–bad, weak–strong, violent–gentle, etc. The shared family script encodes the expectation that people are very different from each other. Often this arrangement allows for individuals to disown aspects of themselves which are then projected onto another. The core family script is to blame each other for what goes wrong. Sometimes one person blames him- or herself, but a common form that mutual blame takes is that of scapegoating. This term is deceptive, however, as it seems to imply that the scapegoat is the one being blamed, which obscures the fact that a scapegoat, say, a troublesome adolescent, is usually just as busily scapegoating the family for all his or her troubles. In other words, the family script is to see others as causing any difficulty.

The idealization and denigration involved in this process are maintained by editing information about what is going on in order to maintain the illusion of opposites. This undermines realistic appraisals of what actually happens. As script theory suggests, each member carries the whole scenario—part and counterpart—in his or her head. Each is probably already enacting aspects of the role that he or she repudiates in the other, but cannot, or chooses not to, see it. The shared family script encodes not only the part/counterpart roles but also the splitting process with idealization and denigration, and a block on looking at what really goes on. The split and hence false models that underlie the denigration–idealization split thus remain unchallenged and therefore unaltered.

In summary, all the above ways of disrupting information processing may leave unrevised and increasingly outdated scripts. These unreviewed scripts may then be triggered into action, often by particular interactional cues occurring within certain contexts. This combination of cues may resemble the setting in which the last reenactment of a scenario occurred. This may have been in the recent past or in the previous generation. Smooth changes are more likely to be achieved if the continuity between past and present is acknowledged. In this way there is continual reviewing of old elements that are still present in the updated script. This suggests that reediting or rewriting family scripts is a wiser way of approaching updating rather than trying to write a brand new script. Discontinuous change or transformations have always struck me as an unrealistic and unhelpful aim for family therapy. The same process of discontinuity may precipitate the family right back to where they started.

SOME CLINICAL IMPLICATIONS

It is important to differentiate rewriting or reediting "buried" transgenerational scripts from the psychoanalytic idea of making the unconscious conscious through interpreting how childhood fantasies are being currently manifest in relationships. Obviously there are some similarities in that transgenerational patterns are identified in each approach. However, reediting involves revealing the pattern within a family context so that everyone becomes aware of what this may mean to the parent involved. This shared knowledge makes it easier for family members not to be drawn into reenactments. The particular parent may or may not consciously accept any links. In my experience, however, he or she can more easily let go if the script is given a positive connotation, also in the presence of the family. As described in Chapter 1, replicative scripts can be described as being loyal to one's parents' way of doing things. Corrective scripts can be labeled as struggling to do better than grandparents were able to do. The family's understanding and forgiveness of what previously may have seemed perverse and inexplicable behavior is perhaps even more important than the parents' own understanding. The intense need to repeat or correct something seems to diminish when it is no longer treated as alien behavior. It is then more possible to improvise fresh ways of relating, leaving old ways behind.

It is also important to see that the transgenerational work is only one, fairly small, aspect of work, which involves reviewing what has happened in the past and how it links to the present and future.

Clinical Use of Reviewing and Previewing

The family therapist can harness the creative aspects of reviewing and previewing in rewriting family scripts. One way this can be done is to review a typical episode which occurs between sessions. A therapist can then have a conversation about who did what, when, where, why, and how, and trace the effects of their interaction.

One family I saw reported that the daughter came home late one night the weekend before a session. The late homecoming had followed a disagreement between the parents about the time their daughter should be home. I like to explore the fantasies about the worst catastrophes imaginable in that situation. Father talked about his fear of rape. The mother told me she was frightened that her daughter would never learn to be independent because her father was too restrictive, and that she would be so innocent she might become pregnant. While the daughter, to everyone's surprise, said she was worried that she could be stuck at home forever. Thus, the different motives underlying what happened started to emerge more clearly. I asked them to preview and plan what they would do the next time the daughter wanted to stay out late. The way that evening went was reviewed in the next session. The daughter had rung her mother up half way through the evening as planned, and they found themselves having an unplanned discussion about her mother's fears of going out. It seemed that this had never been openly discussed—the safe distance provided by the phone helped each to feel safe enough to open up in new ways. This then threw light on the daughter's fear of never being allowed to leave home because she had become her mother's companion.

The advantage of using this review–preview process in therapy is that it mirrors a normal process. The therapist can help them to use this process more effectively so that the skill can be taken home.

I asked how each parent had negotiated late evenings when they were their daughter's age. It transpired that mother was given complete freedom by a liberal family. But she had been frightened to go out, much to her parents' dismay. They had pressured her to go to parties, which had only made things worse. She now did not want to do this to her own daughter. Father had been an only son, seen as able to fend for himself. When asked how his parents would have behaved if they had had a daughter, he thought they would have been worried about sex. They warned him about how vulnerable girls were. The family was able to trace the replicative and corrective scripts involved in their attitudes to their daughter's late nights. Drawing a genogram helped with this.

The more distant future can also be previewed. I asked the girl how she might manage her own children when they reach her current age. The uncertainty that this threw her into helped to soften her view that her parents were merely restrictive. She suddenly saw how much more complex the issues were. Here the aim is to create images of multiple alternative models available for the future, thus helping to break up any replicative or corrective scripts that might be forming in a young person's mind. I also sometimes ask what sort of grandparents the parents hope to make. This often has the effect of introducing a playfulness into current relationships, because it sparks off more enjoyable images of parenting. Most parents look forward to being grandparents when they imagine enjoying babies without all the gnawing anxiety of responsibility. I do sometimes worry about encouraging a girl to present her parents with a baby to look after if I ask this question! But it is much more likely that this will happen if this is not talked about. The future grandmother in this family immediately warmed up to the idea, but what she was looking forward to was the limited contact and responsibility. She said that she would like to visit but not too often. This acted as a communication to her daughter that she expected to be able to get over her own fear of going out, but also that she did not want to trap her daughter at home forever.

Changes in Scripts That Can Make a Significant Difference

Clearly reviewing all the family relationships is not a feasible goal of therapy. There is simply not the time. What then are the significant changes to aim for? If there is one key change to be made in a family's script, it is to be found in the problem-solving script. If the family find that they can solve their own problems, it makes all the difference. They can then be authors of their own solutions.

It is worth listing some of the changes that might support the family's problem solving.

1. Reduce those strategies that undermine the family's problem solving. A notable example of this is triangulation in which a third person is brought in to resolve problems in a relationship, but which prevents the dyad from solving its own problem. Conflict avoidance is another self-defeating strategy that the family needs to face up to.

2. Reduce strategies that undermine the family's security. These include distance conflicts (considered further in Chapter 10) and conflicts between authority and attachments (see Chapter 9).

3. Change modes of problem solving toward collaboration, and away from coercion, scapegoating, and blame.

4. Develop the capacity to review their own actions, and update their own models.

5. Reedit scripts to suit the individuals within the family. This includes adapting roles so that they are both appropriate and that each member can fulfill. This may mean less role reversal and fewer replacement scripts.

6. Move closer to an "ideal" script which, according to Nelson (1981), incorporates all the possible and acceptable actions compatible with the script. In other words, one that provides wide scope for improvising within the general guidelines of the script.

7. Develop a hopeful script in which the expectation is of reasonable success and not of failure or tragedy.

8. Promote ownership of the family's own success; not attributing it all to the therapist.

These conditions encourage improvisation. That is what really makes the difference.

A Case Example

Some readers may prefer to approach the ideas in this book by reading this chapter after the Introduction or Chapter 1 since it covers the whole treatment process from beginning to end and touches on most of the important ideas that are elaborated on in the rest of the book.

THE STORY OF THE HERSTONE FAMILY

First Session

A colleague asked me to see the Herstone family urgently because he was not able to do so himself. I had very little information about them. I knew that everything seemed to go disastrously wrong for them, and that the 15-year-old son, Steven, was about to be put into custody, having been caught climbing on a roof with a diamond brooch in his back pocket.

It was not a textbook start. The family arrived 15 minutes late looking flustered and without Steven. The father, Edward, a 40-year-old, overweight grocer, stood by the door and hesitatingly told me that Steven was sitting in the car outside the Tavistock Clinic refusing to come in. The mother, Jo, stood beside him looking flustered, offering apologies. A 38-year-old dental nurse, she was small and fragile looking. Standing behind them was Angela, their 13-year-old daughter who looked like a china doll, dressed in an old-fashioned frilly dress. I suggested to them that they should go down and bring Steven up. They arrived back a quarter of an hour later looking even more upset, reporting that they had been unable to get Steven to come. I realized my mistake in not making this specifically the parents' job. So I asked Angela to go to the waiting room and suggested the parents should go and tell Steven to come up. They arrived 20 minutes later—mother looking distressed and the

76

father browbeaten. Jo explained that as they approached the car Steven had jumped out and attempted to hit her. She then described how Edward had jumped forward and punched Steven, and a brawl ensued. Suddenly Steven gave up and ran off. At this point I remember having a powerful sense of having failed by taking the wrong approach. I had an image of my reputation ruined by the story of this fight just outside the Clinic. However, I asked the parents what was usual about this episode and what was new. At first Jo said that this was just typical. But I pressed her on what was new. She was thoughtful and then said it was the first time that Steven had ever tried to hit her. Also, she said it was the only time that she had stood back and allowed Edward to hit Steven, adding that she normally tried to stop that from happening, because her father had been alcoholic and had attacked her brothers. She could not bear to see that happening in her own family.

I suddenly recognized that a most important change had happened out there on the street. A mother had stopped intervening to prevent a father from disciplining his son. By now I had only 10 minutes of the session left. So what could I do in that time? I said to Jo that I thought that she had been very courageous in allowing her husband to discipline Steven, despite her intense anxieties about what would happen if he did. I said to Edward that he was brave to discipline Steven, despite knowing that his wife was anxious about that. Perhaps he could also have been anxious about what he might have done to Steven. Together they had allowed the father to do some disciplining, which was clearly what Steven needed. I repeated this several times in slightly different language, knowing that when people are flustered they do not always receive the message clearly. I offered them another appointment a week later, which was after the date Steven was due to go into custody.

Comment

When a family reports an episode happening outside the session, my rule is to discover what elements of that behavior belong to an old script and what represents a change that might become part of a new script. By pressing families to think about that difference I encourage them to focus on what could be done in a new way. Even in what appear to be disastrous episodes, like this one, it is always possible to find something new in what happened. This brings hope to the family and a new sense that they can do something differently. If they try a new move again, and it works, then it can eventually become part of a new script. The Herstone family found the concept of scripts very useful as a metaphor. They often discussed whether something was part of an old script, or part of a new one.

The other interesting aspect of this beginning of therapy was just how much I came to mirror the feelings of the family. We both felt as if we had failed. It was important for me to contain these feelings and not to merely accept them as reality. It would have been easy to have conveyed that what I saw happening was a calamity. This would have confirmed this family's script of disastrous failure. By containing my feelings and reflecting on what had just happened, it was possible for me to have an alternative frame for understanding the events. The new frame changed my attitude, so that I could see the father as making a move toward disciplining his son instead of being involved in a futile brawl. I was then able to talk to them about discipline in a way that was convincing. First I had to be convinced myself. I could have said exactly the same things in that first session, but with a sense of failure underlying the words. In a later session, I asked Jo and Edward how they had experienced that first session, since I was very curious. Edward told me that he felt absolutely useless because he had not even been able to get his son into the Clinic. Then he went on to say that he was extremely surprised when I was so positive about him being firm with Steven. I asked him what sort of impact that had on him, and he said he had taken my comments very seriously because he could see that I really meant what I said. This episode illustrates how a therapist needs to contain the feelings generated by a family's scripts and understand what is going on rather than become drawn into the same emotional field as the family, which is likely to lead to the therapist playing a role in their script.

Second Session

Edward told me that the day after the first session he had decided to be firmer with his son, and he gave me an example of a recent incident. Steven had a habit of laying in bed all morning, calling down to his mother to bring up his lunch. On this occasion he told Steven to get up at 9 A.M. Steven refused angrily and stayed in bed. Edward, however, stood in the doorway and quietly insisted that he get up. Edward continued this for 2 hours until, suddenly, Steven gave in. He jumped out of bed and got dressed. I congratulated Edward on finding a way of being firm that did not involve physical intervention, which made both he and his wife so anxious. I also congratulated Jo on allowing Edward to be firm with Steven and not intervening.

I then encountered a problem with what work was to be done next. Steven would be unable to attend the sessions during the 3 months of his sentence. I decided to draw a genogram during the second half of the second session because the mother had indicated the importance of her past. Normally I do not do a genogram until the fourth or fifth session, but Jo had described the image of her alcoholic father and stressed his continuing influence on her.

Jo's family tree was drawn first. I asked for stories about members of the family as I put them in the family tree. When we came to Jo's younger brother, Ted, she told the following story.

Mother's Family Legend (see Figure 5.1)

When she was 11, Jo had been playing with friends in a local park, and Ted, her younger brother who was 9, was with them. When they got hungry at midday, Jo asked Ted to go and buy some ice cream from across the road. He never came back. After a while the girls became anxious and started frantically looking for him. When Jo finally went home, she found the police outside the house who told her that Ted had been knocked down by a van and killed. He had the ice cream in his hands when he died.

Jo was crying copiously while she told the story, as if it had happened yesterday. Angela comforted her, and I suggested that Edward might do so, too. He moved across to her and rested his hand on Jo's shoulder.

She went on to tell how her family blamed her for what happened and how she also blamed herself. Her father made a pact with her that they would not cry. But when it came to midday the following day, Jo burst into tears. For this, she was sent away from home to stay with an aunt and was not even told when the funeral was.

I asked whether Angela knew the story and she nodded. It turned out to be a well-worn story which had been told many times. I call these oft-told tales legends.

Father's Story

Edward told the following story about his older brother.

When he was 5 years old, he had been walking to school one day but was lagging far behind his older brother, Alex, aged 11. He was so far behind that he took a shortcut over a bridge to try to catch up. When his brother looked back and saw him on the other side of the railway line, he scrambled through the fence, ran across the line, and was killed by an oncoming train. The father cried when he described this, sobbing over his guilty anguish. He went on to describe how his parents had arrived on the scene and were told what happened by the other boys. They linked hands, turned and walked away

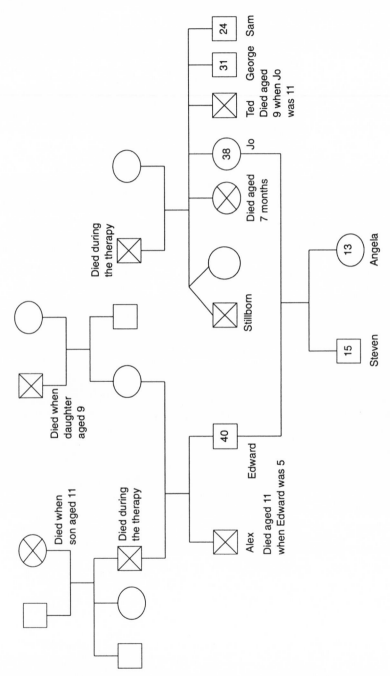

FIGURE 5.1. Herstone family genogram.

from Edward; they seemed to blame him. Edward grew up seeing himself as a disaster.

These two stories of childhood bereavement had led to a distancing of children from parents, rather than eliciting comfort and closeness. The other striking feature of the stories was the similarity between the events: Each brother died because of a sibling. It was now possible to form a hypothesis about why Steven was so completely out of control and why nobody could do anything to really discipline him. He had come to represent the "dead brother" for each, and was being protected in a way that the parents had wished their brothers had been protected. This attempt to correct, or improve upon, what happened in the last generation is an example of a "corrective script."

Third Session

Edward came into this session a different man. He spoke with a clear voice, looked me straight in the eyes, and conveyed a sense of his own authority. He told me that he had never shared the whole story of his brother's death with anybody before, not even with Jo. They had married with the unspoken understanding that they would not talk about each other's brothers whom they knew had died in tragic circumstances. In contrast to Jo, who had told her children her story, Edward had kept his story a virtual secret. After the session Edward went to see his mother, whom he had not seen for a long time. This visit, unprompted by me, was sparked by his desire to find out more about his family's background, which he had either forgotten or not heard about.

While he was there he discovered more information about the family. Edward learned that his maternal grandfather had died when his mother was only 9, following an accident in a mine. His paternal grandmother had died of tuberculosis when his father was aged 11. Since his paternal grandfather had been away in the navy, Edward's father was virtually orphaned and was looked after by a foster family. We were then able to look at what the death of Edward's older brother must have meant to his parents, who had both had extremely impoverished childhoods as well as tragic lives from the age of 9 or 11 onward. They had struggled to provide a better situation for their two sons, Alex and Edward, who were both doing well. Alex had just earned a scholarship to secondary school when he was killed. Until then life had been looking brighter and brighter, as if the new family would supersede the shared family script of tragedy striking when children reach the ages of 9 to 11. However, the script was reenacted. After discussing this, Edward was able to see his parents linking arms and walking away as a sign that they could not face the return of tragedy. It was not an act of turning against their son, which was how he, as a little boy, had seen it.

Why had Edward been able to suddenly take charge of himself and of the situation following the first two sessions? From all accounts he had behaved differently. One explanation is that his role of disciplining his son had been affirmed by both those inside and outside the family: He was able to see himself as effective. The way in which he regained his authority may have had something to do with being able to identify with me. During the first session, I stood in my office, quietly insisting that the parents get their son to come to the Clinic. I did not take no for an answer. Likewise, he quietly stood at his son's door until Steven got out of bed. But why was Edward talking with a much clearer voice? Perhaps it was because he had broken free of the chains of his silence about his brother, which released him to ask his parents about their hidden pasts. What had happened in the second session to help him to make this breakthrough? I had asked who wanted to draw their family tree first. I have found this allows the parent who has the greatest difficulty talking about his or her past to go second. Edward, having chosen second, had seen how Jo had been supported when she cried over her tragic story. When it was his turn, he was ready to let the tears go, which was probably the only way he could tell the story. Once the family taboo of talking about the past was broken, he could explore the implications of what had happened, and reframe the way his parents reacted to his brother's death. He no longer saw himself as being blamed. This illustrates the step-by-step nature of changing a role within a family script by vacating the original role, taking up the new role, incorporating the change into the script, and reviewing the appropriateness of the old model. First Edward released the old script of failure; this was followed by his success in a new role as limit setter, which was affirmed by those around him. Finally, the origins of the personal script, written in childhood, could be revised.

The new role, together with the new self-perception, would however, be maintained only if there was a new family script established which went on reaffirming him in the new image. The 3 months' respite from his son's challenges provided a context in which to work on the transgenerational scripts before Steven's return.

ESTABLISHING A NEW SCRIPT

A Typical Conflict Scenario

A typical enactment of the Herstones' attempted solution scenario, which had happened before Steven left, went as follows:

> Steven stayed out late with his friends, some of whom were established cat burglars specializing in making entries from rooftops. When Steven arrived home in the small hours of the morning, Edward, who had been increasingly furious during the evening, jumped out of bed and stormed downstairs to confront him. A furious row ensued. Jo, hearing this ruckus, quickly ran downstairs and put a stop to it. Edward became angry with Jo for having undermined his authority, and an argument ensued. In the meantime, Angela was standing on the landing watching her parents shouting at each other. She raced downstairs and tried to calm her parents down by standing between them and telling them to stop. The next evening Angela yelled at her brother for what he had done the previous evening. Steven stormed out of the house furiously to join his exciting group of friends. And the scenario was primed for a repeat performance.

The family agreed that this was a typical scenario. It defined each person's role and how the behavior was embedded within it. The core problematic transaction was of triangulation in which conflicts in dyadic relationships were terminated by a peacekeeper, who then became involved in another dyadic conflict with one of the previous protagonists, which then needed another peacekeeper, and so on. None of the conflicts were resolved by such interference. Members of this family often complained of a feeling of "here we go again" because they felt they had to intervene in a situation that always felt potentially catastrophic to them. Each felt compelled to take action despite knowing that it would merely lead to further problems. The family called this their "old script."

Tracing the Origins of Role

Jo as the Protector

Jo was the fourth in her family. Her parents first had twins, a boy and a girl, but the boy twin was stillborn. Devastated, her parents had quickly replaced him by having a baby girl, who died at 7 months of cot death. Jo was then the replacement for both these lost children. Her brother Ted was born 2 years later. Another brother, George, followed 5 years later. This story also indicates how this family grieved.

Rather than shed tears, which was extremely painful because there were so many losses to cry about, they prohibited tears and replaced each lost baby with another baby. Indeed, 11 months after Ted was killed, another boy, Sam, was born. Jo's father had started drinking after Ted's death, and would beat George when he was drunk. Jo remembered feeling so outraged with her mother because she would never try to protect George from his father's violence. She remembered resolving never to let that happen to her own son. Jo's role in the scenario could be seen as a "corrective script" in which she was trying to make right for mother's failure. Her replicative script was that she married a man who also took to drinking, and who, when inebriated, used to hit Steven. In the last few years, however, Edward had stopped drinking. However, the previous phase made Jo forever sensitive to the possibility of violence. Her peacekeeping role could be fully understood. I gave the peace keeping a positive connotation by describing it as her struggle to succeed where her mother had not.

When looking at the replacement scripts in the new generation, Jo was quick to see that Steven replaced Ted, especially in terms of her expectation that something awful would happen to him and that he needed protecting.

Angela, the "Backward" Girl

Angela was at a school for children with learning disabilities. She had been assessed as functioning at below average intelligence. However, behind the china-doll appearance there was a perceptive gleam in her eyes. As I drew her more and more into what went on in the family sessions, it became clear that she was misdiagnosed and that she was, at least, of average intelligence. She was certainly very clever at reading the emotional situation.

We spent some time exploring the issue of intelligence on both sides of the family. Jo had always seen herself as very stupid until she was in her 30s, when she finally decided that she was not as stupid as she thought she had been. She had then begun her training, which led to her qualification as a dental nurse. I suggested that the question now was whether Angela would also have to wait until she was in her 30s before she realized that she was intelligent. Would she stay loyal to her mother's script, or would she see herself differently sooner? Initially Angela could not believe that she could ever change and cried over her fear that she would never get a job. I then approached the problem from a different angle, exploring the origins of the mother's self-image of stupidity. We approached this issue from the perspective of replacement. Jo was very aware that she had been a replacement for the little girl who had died at 7 months. But I pointed out that that girl had, in turn, been a replacement for the dead twin—so perhaps she was the final attempt to replace the dead twin. At this suggestion Jo looked excited because she suddenly began to understand why she used to be expected to share the same bed as her older sister. Often the same things were expected of each of them, as would be of twins. Now her curiosity was really aroused, and she could see that she would inevitably be seen as backward and stupid as compared with her much older sister. Angela and Edward could both see the sense in this, and Angela began to realize that stupidity could be part of people's expectations about someone, rather than due to a lack of brain power. Nevertheless, Angela was slow to accept the new vision of herself, despite being fed increasing evidence of intelligence from within her own family, and from within the sessions.

Edward, Who "Lagged Behind"

I then explored the issue of intelligence on Edward's side of the family. Edward had been doing well until his brother's death. After that, nothing went right and he never did well at school. I explored how that had come about. He had just started school, at the age of 5, when his brother Alex died. Both his parents retreated into their own worlds following their loss. His mother engaged in 40 years of uncompleted mourning. She would spend much of each day at the graveside. Ted's room was never altered from its original appearance. His clothes were still hanging in the closet. Edward's father started working very long hours and became an authoritarian disciplinarian toward his remaining son. As Edward became older he became difficult. He was frequently beaten by his father. Edward's description of how he performed at school was that he was "lagging behind." This phrase, however, was interesting because it was the same phrase he used about himself when his brother Alex was killed. He had been lagging so far behind that it had caused the fateful short-cut that led to Alex's death. Edward could now see that this had then become part of his identity. The phrase became a metaphor in the sessions for Angela's situation because "if you lag behind, then you can also catch up." Edward still saw himself as being stupid compared with Alex who had been clever. I suggested that he might expect his second child to be stupid. He said that it was no surprise to him when Angela was deemed to be subnormal. It is interesting that when children are typecast in their family scripts, it is usually because both parents have a similar role expectation of their child, as did Jo and Edward. Scripting of a child by one parent can often be counteracted by different expectations of the other parent.

Angela steadily changed her perceptions with her family's help. I wrote to the school administrators, who flatly refused to accept my view because they had test results that proved her low level of functioning, and she was still performing at a low level. This is an interesting example of how difficult it is to change a role in one's script because it has to change not only within the family but in the outside world as well. As Angela was not due to stay at this school for much longer, I did not spend a lot of time challenging this version. Instead, I worked with Angela to expect something different in the future. Eventually Angela trained as a market gardener where no one had any doubts that she was of ordinary intelligence.

Steven's Return

After Steven was released from custody he came to two family sessions, but then dropped out of therapy. This was always the risk of continuing family therapy while he was in custody. He felt therapy was something that belonged to the rest of the family and not to him. It was perhaps remarkable that he was able to come at all under the circumstances, but it was important that his parents were able to bring him. There is, however, another way of framing Steven's original refusal to come to the Clinic. His father had had a number of mental hospital admissions during his struggle with alcoholism. It may have been important for Steven to have escaped the mentally ill label which would have been confirmed by seeing a psychiatrist. This was Steven's corrective script: better bad than mad.

I continued to see the parents on their own to help them deal with Steven. I also had the occasional session with Angela when there were issues that affected her. Steven quickly started to create problems. It seemed as if he wanted to get into the old familiar scenarios again. A great deal of work was needed to help Jo from resuming the peacekeeper role in the uproars that ensued. The family situation improved eventually, and Steven managed to stay out of trouble. At one point the two children were having a lot of conflict, so I asked Steven if he would come in for a family session. Steven was angry with his sister. He pointed out several occasions where Angela had set him up to be the bad one, so that she could be seen as the good one. His account sounded convincing. At one point in the session, Angela cried. The parents, especially Jo, seemed to be tempted to intervene to protect their daughter. But they refrained.

EDWARD: I think we have all changed.

THERAPIST: All four of you?

EDWARD: Yes, all four of us have changed. Jo and myself are more sorted out than we have ever been. It just seems as if we had this little bit of conflict between the two of them (*pointing to Angela and Steven*).

JO: I am to blame for a lot of this, I used to stop any arguments between Steven and Angela. All you (*pointing to Angela*) would need to do is to call out "Mum" and I would come running and stop the argument.

STEVEN: No, but you needn't come because if Angela had really gotten too upset, then she would have been able to go off somewhere else

THERAPIST: But Mum is saying that she has changed. At least by not coming in, she is giving you a chance to sort things out. Today I was interested that you (*to Jo*) could have tried to protect Angela, but I noticed you did not do that. If you had, that might have stopped Steven and Angela from doing some work on their relationship.

The discussion moved on to discuss one technique that mother had used in the past: sending the two protagonists to separate rooms. The family acknowledged this to be even less likely to help the two to resolve conflicts.

JO: I used to do that with Steven and Edward as well in the past.

THERAPIST: So these two (*pointing to Steven and Edward*) must now be giving you enough assurance that you don't need to come in.

JO: Yes. I now feel happy enough to just walk out of the room and know that they will sort out their differences. (*to Steven*) I know that you can actually talk to Daddy without going through me.

THERAPIST: So it was a two-way thing. It was you deciding to keep out but also these two (*pointing to Edward and Steven*) doing enough to let you know that you don't need to come in. [I was highlighting the reciprocal systemic nature of the change, thus making them all authors of the new emergent script.]

JO: That was vital. Showing me that you were not going to pulverize each other's brains out.

EDWARD: But why did you used to jump in?

Jo: I know why.

EDWARD: (*interrupting Jo*) It was the drinking again. Whenever I was drinking I used to pick on Steven.

Jo: (*shaking her head*) I meant when my dad used to pick on Ted.

THERAPIST: So you have three scripts. Two from one generation back, and another from the script that you three wrote.

The family was exploring how it had changed its core triangulating script on a number of levels: through beliefs that peacekeeping made the situation worse, by avoiding triangulation in practice, and loosening the links with previous peacekeeping scripts. Both parents readily acknowledged their previous mistakes in this.

The Community Script Needs to Change, Too

Shortly after this session, Steven's probation officer contacted me. He was in despair about Steven, saying that if Steven continued behaving in the same way, he would have no alternative but to recommend his return to custody. I was surprised about this. I asked if he had been reoffending but discovered that there had been no evidence of that. I arranged to meet with the probation officer and Steven's parents together. Steven refused to join us. The probation officer was surprised to hear about the various improvements. It became quite clear that Steven had brought all his anger and despair to the probation officer. He appeared in the probation office unkempt, dirty, smelly, and rude. The probation officer became invaded by the sense of impending catastrophe, just like I had in the first session. We agreed that the probation officer would contact me to discuss how things were going, and that he would also consult me before making any future court reports. It was clear from subsequent telephone conversations that the probation officer still thought Steven had been conning me and his family. One day the police arrested Steven for stealing a motorcycle, and he was held in a police cell overnight. It was not until the next day that he could prove that the bike belonged to him. These two stories show how difficult it is to change the community's script.

Redramatization of the Problem

I anticipate that many families will redramatize their original problem before finishing therapy, to test whether they have really resolved that problem. Sometimes this testing goes to the absolute limit. It is as if at last they feel secure enough with the therapist to bring the problem in its most frightening form. I find that this is an important hypothesis for me because it enables me to handle apparent reverses in fortune as an opportunity to consolidate change, rather than to see it as failure. Six months after Steven's release from custody, trust in Steven had been built up to the point where the family could leave him at home for a week while they went on holiday. On their return it was obvious that Steven had had his friends over for a party. There was some damage, but it was not serious. In the session after this, Edward came in looking very upset. His wife was angry, and Angela looked disapprovingly at her father. He said that he was dreadfully ashamed of himself—"All old script, I'm afraid." The feeling of catastrophe returned to the therapy room. He discussed how he had been furious with Steven about the damage to the house and when Jo tried to protect Steven, the situation escalated. The fight that had broken out between father and son was interrupted by Jo, who had poured cold water over them to make them stop. Edward then grabbed for a bottle of whiskey but Angela took it from him and poured it away. He finally got into the car and drove to the pub. Suddenly the action stopped.

He told me how he sat in the car for an hour, struggling with his impulse to have a drink. He said that if he did, he knew he would go back to the bottle, but eventually he returned home. Edward finished his story with a glum, "So you see, doctor, I ruined everything."

I remembered that they had told me how in the past everyone had tried to remove the whiskey to stop Edward from drinking. I asked them to think of what was not in their old script. Edward thought long and hard and eventually perked up and said, "Well, I did manage to resist the drink myself." I said that an important milestone had been passed. Edward had finally felt secure enough to find that he could resist the drink without any help from anyone else, even in dire circumstances. Until that had happened, the family would have remained haunted by the possibility of Edward returning to drink under stress. I asked him what had helped and he told me that he had had an image of the sessions, and all the work we had done together, and it was then that he decided to drive away.

Laying Ghosts to Rest: The Final Unscripting

A year after coming to therapy, most of the work was done, but I continued the occasional visits for another 6 months. At about the time that I had planned to terminate, both grandfathers died. Edward and Jo asked to continue therapy in order to work on their feelings about the deaths. The situation had brought the return of some old scripted rules against mourning. Jo and Edward quarreled and got angry with each other rather than allowing themselves to cry. At the beginning of the session they sat at opposite ends of the couch, leaning away from each other. Gradually, as the distress appeared, each was able to comfort the other until they were eventually sitting together in the middle of the couch and putting their arms around whoever was most upset at the time. In this context the final grieving for the dead brothers took place.

Jo Completes the Mourning of Her Brother

Jo reported that she had been very distressed when she found some photos of her dead brother, Ted, in her father's belongings. As she was telling me the story, she burst into tears, and Edward moved over to comfort her. She described how Edward had heard her crying and had come upstairs to find out what was happening. This had been a big support for her. We compared this with the old grieving scripts from the previous generation, in which the immediate impact had been for people to move away from each other rather than come closer together. Edward's parents had walked away from him when Alex died. Jo had been sent away from home when she started to cry when Ted died. The new script was to comfort and come close to each other for mutual comfort.

Jo now started talking about the time Ted had been killed. Later she said she had something embarrassing to say.

Jo: I keep planning for when Steven dies. I have been doing so for years. I have taken myself through the mental procedure of the police coming and going into his bedroom, going through his personal effects, and how I would manage.

THERAPIST: So Ted's dying became the future script for Steven's death.

EDWARD: She has had so many men in her life die that she expects Steven to die as well.

THERAPIST: Can you give some of the details of your daydream?

Jo: The truth of it is that what they say is that he has died in a road accident. Then I walk into the bedroom and there are all his personal effects. (*getting agitated*) I just don't know how to cope. (*Edward moves closer to her and puts his arm around her.*) I remember screaming (*pause*). . .

THERAPIST: You remember screaming.

Jo: Yes, crying. . . . I just cannot come to terms with it. It is weird; it has not even happened yet. I seem to find it necessary to put myself through that just in case it does happen (*crying*). I won't be able to cope.

THERAPIST: You talk about it almost as if it has happened.

Jo: It was real. It was very real. That is the stupid part of it. He is alive and kicking.

THERAPIST: When do these memories come most?

Jo: I suppose when he is out late and hasn't come home.

In this part of the session, Jo is behaving as if she is describing a real event, and keeps on having to remind herself that it has not actually happened. I have become interested in whether this previewing of a catastrophe like this was merely the result of Steven's late-night activities.

THERAPIST: Did it happen before that at all?

Jo: It happened over many, many years. To be honest, it must have started before he started coming home late, because he has only been doing that the last couple of years.

THERAPIST: Was this like when Ted died?

Jo: Well, no, actually. I arrived home to find the police there (*weeping*). I feel so embarrassed. He is gone. But he is *not* gone. (*pause*) It is so confusing. It's ridiculous. Why am I crying when he is not dead?

THERAPIST: It does sound as if you have had a similar script for Ted and for Steven, although it did happen with Ted, which makes it very confusing.

Jo: Yes, it is.

THERAPIST: How old was Steven when you started having these day-dreams?

Jo: Well, I can't remember having them when he was a little child. Come to think of it, it may well have been somewhere around the same age when Ted died.

THERAPIST: Steven has been reminding you a bit of Ted.

Jo: I think Steven was really a replacement for Ted. Then he looks very alike. (*long pause . . . while she looks thoughtful*) The thought runs through my mind that if I am not his mother, am I his sister?

THERAPIST: Who are you talking about, Steven or Ted?

Jo: About Steven. If Steven was Ted, then I would wonder who I was. I would be either his mum or his sister (*looking at Edward*). I don't know, it makes me wonder.

EDWARD: I don't know.

Jo: Well, I was Ted's sister.

THERAPIST: Well, maybe that is where the confusion came from. You were given the role by your mother of looking after Ted.

Jo: That is very possible; she certainly gave us all that sort of role. We were very, very close.

THERAPIST: So it must have been confusing as to whether you were mother to your younger brother or his sister. Then you were actually given responsibility for him when he died, weren't you?

Jo: Yes, very much so.

THERAPIST: I guess the problem was that you had these two scripts written on transparent paper, each superimposed upon the other, so you didn't know which was which (*demonstrating with hands how one script could be on top of the other*).

Jo: I certainly was asked to be the mother of Sam who was born to replace Ted.

THERAPIST: So Sam was the first replacement.

Jo: Then I had a son of my own.

THERAPIST: So perhaps what you were doing was keeping the unresolved things about Ted's death on ice, as it were (*pause*). What is surprising is that we are talking about it as if it was something to be ashamed about in this room.

Jo: I have not talked about it before and have never told Edward. I do feel ashamed. It seems so odd to put oneself through that painful procedure (*looking at Edward*).

THERAPIST: It goes through one's imagination—accidents that might have happened to an adolescent who comes home late. It is a universal thing. Millions of parents know that. Why is it so shameful for you? I suppose it was really confusing for you just when you were a little mother many years ago, I mean a substitute mother.

Jo: It just feels wrong that I should do it.

THERAPIST: In some ways that is true, because there is no need to do it. What is puzzling me is that if it is such a normal thing to do, why is it so shameful that you can't even tell Edward and you are embarrassed even talking about it here?

Jo: It is because I can't come to terms with it. I don't know. (*She looks unconvinced.*)

THERAPIST: I guess this all goes back to the time when you were sent away and shamed for grieving over Ted's death.

Jo: I think you might be right. I feel guilty about it.

THERAPIST: And you were told that you should not share it publicly, so that the moment you cried in front of the rest of the family you were sent away. The moment you shared your feelings about it and your distress.

Jo: Yes. They would not even tell me when the funeral was.

THERAPIST: So you were not supposed to mourn. And the shame about crying still haunts you even here.

Edward Faces His Brother's Death

In another session, and following a difficult train journey to get to the session, Edward talked again about his brother's death. This time there were more visual details. For instance, he had heard his brother calling for him and saw him jerking and twisting as he fell dead on the railway line. He was able to do more grieving for his brother, but unlike Jo he was less clear that Steven was a replacement for his brother. Edward had identified instead with his father who punished him for causing Ted's death. In the replicative script Steven had stood in for himself as a little boy. Replicative scripts of this sort often erupt under the influence of drink. He felt that he had repeated his father's behavior when he used to get drunk and physically abuse Steven as a younger boy.

Grieving Scripts Rewritten

The grieving for the two dead brothers was released by the grieving work for the fathers. Each grieving resonated with previous losses. Thus mourning work provides an opportunity to complete unfinished mourning from the past. Grieving scripts can be rewritten. This is discussed further in Chapter 13.

After four sessions with the couple this work was completed. The family rules against mourning had finally been revoked. The rules had previously been "Do not cry," "Keep your distance" (or else you might cry), and "Replace the lost person as quickly as possible." This had been reversed in therapy, which created a new grieving script: "It's good to cry,""Get close together to make each other feel secure enough to face the implications of the death," and "Undo any replacement that is a way of avoiding completing the grieving." One hopes this will help the family to grieve in this and future generations.

THE SEARCH FOR SECURITY

This family had been highly insecure: always feeling on the edge of some crisis. They had two main strategies for dealing with the insecurity: the avoidant/disengaged strategy and the ambivalent/enmeshed strategy. Different members of the family deployed one or the other of these styles. In certain contexts, individuals could deploy both styles. In this family the main exponents of the avoidant style were Edward, Steven, Edward's father, and Jo's father. Those who used the ambivalent/enmeshed style were Jo, Angela, and Jo's mother. So in this family it happened to be gender linked, although this is not necessarily the case.

The *avoidant/disengaged strategy* is used to defend against being hurt as the relationship is felt to be vulnerable to rejection and possible break up. Emotions and memories are inhibited, and getting close to others is avoided. This is an effective strategy for remaining attached to somebody who is equally distant. The pact is that neither person will be emotional, so no one will be hurt or annoyed because that might lead to a rejection. Avoidant individuals are often unaware of their own scripts, so they are also unaware when they recruit other people into roles in that script. Roles are often stereotyped. Children, for instance, are treated as either good or bad, and it is difficult to change attitudes. The individual's transgenerational scripts are often replicative in that what happened in the past generation is often copied. Family legends and stories are few. Edward demonstrated a number of these features, for example, he had forgotten much of his childhood. Although he had remembered the death of his brother, he never discussed it with anybody because that would evoke too much feeling. He also beat his son in the same way as his father had beaten him. Emotionality can change over time, however. In Edward's words, after he became more in touch with his feelings, "My emotions during the early years were so *stunted*. I still have a fair job to get in touch with feelings. I had no idea that people felt so intensely about things, and I feel bad now about how I have hurt everybody."

The *ambivalent/enmeshed strategy* in contrast applies emotional pressure on other people. Individuals feel that this is the only way in which other people will pay any attention to them, or respond to their needs. They tend to be preoccupied with their past and thinking over past issues which are unresolved, and about previous hurts in relationship. To deal with this, they often recruit people around them into their inner drama. This means that there is a lot of confusion about who is who. They tend to replace lost figures with current members of the family. Old feuds which took place in their families of origin are brought into the current family. There is a lot of role reversal and blurred boundaries between people. Their stories are often long and complicated. Jo demonstrated a number of these features. She described herself as being too emotional and expecting too much of people. She also demonstrated how figures from the past could be represented by current members of the family, such as Steven, and how this led to role confusion and boundary blurring. She was often trying to get people to change by applying emotional pressure, whereas Edward was trying to avoid emotions.

MARITAL ATTACHMENT PATTERNS: DISTANCE REGULATION

Classically when an avoidant person has a relationship with an ambivalent, clinging person, it leads to a pursuer–pursued relationship in which the avoidant person moves away to feel less threatened. This then makes the clinging person cling even more strongly, which, of course, drives the pursued even further away in an escalating distance conflict. These marriages are potentially unstable. Often other people are triangulated in to help manage the distance—so-called distance regulators. In the Herstone family, both children acted in concert to regulate their parents' distance. Steven brought them together when his mother came to rescue him from his father. However, bringing his parents together also resulted in him becoming a source of conflict between them. Whereupon Angela would come in to keep the peace and so stop them from breaking up again. Steven, as with many adolescents, had a distance conflict with his parents in that he wanted to be away from them and with them at the same time. This conflict had escalated beyond the boundaries of the family. He triangulated the police in, getting himself taken away from home. I think this became necessary because the intensity of his interactions with his parents made him feel too insecure. Angela managed to maintain her closeness to each parent by acting like a parent to them, causing each of her parents to need her. She gained her security by being close to her parents, but this was partly dependent upon Steven being alienated from them. She thus helped to maintain Steven in the bad role.

CONFLICT BETWEEN AUTHORITY
AND ATTACHMENT

When authority is in dispute the situation often feels unsafe and everyone feels insecure. Authority often breaks down in the context of insecure relationships, and the two problems can then reinforce each other. Steven's protected status gave him enormous power. When Steven flouted his father's authoritarian way of trying to regain control, mother's protective impulses were aroused, as if Steven were still a much younger or vulnerable son. Her attempts to protect Steven reinforced the problems that her husband was having in regaining authority. In the ensuing dispute between the parents over authority, Angela's insecurity was greatly heightened, so she came in as peacekeeper and hence became the parentified child. This role reversal had the effect, however, of further undermining her parent's authority. With these various interweaving factors, the family was no longer able to function as a secure base.

FAMILY THERAPY AS A TEMPORARY
SECURE BASE FOR THE FAMILY

I quickly became established as an attachment figure for this family because I was seen as someone who tackled the dangerous situation of loss of control over Steven. I also related to their positive strengths very quickly, and I came to like them. This enabled them to trust me sufficiently for them to start exploring their own relationships, improvising new ways of relating, but also having the courage to explore the very painful background issues which still influenced their situation.

After the grieving work following the death of the grandfathers, I saw them again with a longer gap—every 3 months for another year. After they were discharged I made it clear that they could, at any time, come and make another appointment to see me. By being available, I was able to provide a relatively long-term secure base for the family.

I think that the most important difference that I made was to

avoid being drawn into the "catastrophe script," which always anticipated the worst. It was this that led everyone—members of the family
and professionals included—to feeling convinced that they had to take
action to prevent a deteriorating situation from becoming a disaster.
The optimistic expectation that the family could manage helped to
create a benign cycle, and interrupted the triangulation sequences.

To do this I had to like and respect them.

CREATING A SECURE FAMILY BASE

S·I·X

Security in the Family

BOWLBY'S PLACE IN FAMILY THERAPY

John Bowlby wrote one of the very first family therapy papers (Bowlby, 1949), which makes fascinating reading. The family therapy that he described consists of some family sessions that overcame impasses in individual psychotherapy. Despite this limited application, and the lack of the inclusion of siblings, it is quite clear, however, from reading his article that he had discovered the power of family therapy. The paper vividly conveys the sense of excitement that we have all experienced when practicing successful family therapy for the first time. Unfortunately the paper was not widely read, and Bowlby decided that it was too difficult in the climate of that time to make family therapy his major approach. He decided to focus on the infant's attachment to a parent as a first step to researching the whole family. He told me that he had no doubt that the exploration of family patterns would be undertaken one day, but that he had to start with units that were researchable at that moment in time.

Bowlby did, however, have some indirect impact on family therapy. When John Bell (1951), one of the pioneers of family therapy, was visiting Edinburgh from the United States in 1951, he was told by Jock Sutherland, who was the chairman of the Tavistock Clinic, about Bowlby's work with families. Bell gained the impression that Bowlby did all the therapy with the whole family and so started doing just that himself. Bell very generously credited Bowlby with the original idea. He did not meet Bowlby until many years later when I staged a meeting between the two men at my house and then at the Tavistock Clinic. It was fascinating to hear how serendipitous the seeding of the idea was. For instance, just as Sutherland finished his description of Bowlby's family sessions tea was served, and Bell never heard about the limited context in which it was practiced.

101

THE SIGNIFICANCE OF ATTACHMENTS
FOR FAMILY THERAPY

Attachment behavior provides one of the fundamental units of family life and has been exposed to increasingly extensive research which has yielded coherent results that are startlingly good for social science. Furthermore, the findings are highly relevant to family therapy. For instance, links have been established between insecure attachment patterns and a wide range of dysfunction (Belsky & Nezworsky, 1988) such as childhood conduct disorders (Greenberg & Speltz, 1988), social withdrawal (Rubin & Lollis, 1988), agoraphobia (Liotti, 1991), suicide (Adams, 1982), adult personality disorder (Patrick et al., 1994). Also, insecure attachment patterns have been associated with at-risk situations such as maternal depression (Radke-Yarrow, 1991) and maltreatment (Crittenden, 1988). Longitudinal studies have shown that attachment in infancy strongly influences many aspects of psychological adaptation such as psychological disturbance (Sroufe, 1989), social behavior (Skolnick, 1986), and cognitive resourcefulness (Matas et al., 1978).

ATTACHMENT THEORY:
ITS LATE IMPACT ON FAMILY THERAPY

Surprisingly, considering its significance, the implications of attachment theory for family systems (Stevenson-Hinde, 1990; Byng-Hall & Stevenson-Hinde, 1991; Marvin & Stewart, 1990; Donley, 1993) and for family therapy (Byng-Hall, 1990, 1991b, Doane et al., 1991; Doane & Diamond, 1994) have only recently been subject to more intensive study. Earlier, however, Lyman Wynne (1984) recognized the importance of attachments when he suggested that attachment behavior was the first step in the epigenetic developmental process within family systems.

There are several reasons for the late start of the exploration of attachment theory within family systems (Byng-Hall, 1991c). Because the early theorizing received so much publicity so long ago, many may think of it as an old theory whose time is past, unaware of recent research findings. Another reason is that until fairly recently much of the research has been directed at the dyad of mother–child. Patricia Minuchin (1985) considers, however, that attachment theory, despite its narrow focus, is one of the more suitable developmental theories to be integrated into systems theory because it explores bidirectional relationships in which each participant provides the context for the other's behavior.

Bowlby's work has also come under attack from feminists (Chodorow, 1978). The first thrust of Bowlby's work was toward the impact of separation of children from their parents, either through evacuation during the war, hospitalization, or death of a parent. This led him to say, "What is believed to be essential for mental health is that an infant and young child should experience a warm, intimate, and *continuous* relationship with his mother (or permanent mother substitute—i.e., one person who steadily 'mothers' him)" (Bowlby, 1953, p. 13; emphasis added). By this he meant that "mothering" could be done by anyone, including a father, so long as the relationship itself was not disrupted. He did not mean that mothers had to be with their children 24 hours a day. This statement about continuous mothering was made in the context of postwar Britain devastated by loss and separations. The idea of the importance of close mother–child bonds fit like a key into a lock. However, the feminists felt that this idea was used by the men who, having returned from the war, wanted to persuade their women that they should leave work and return to the family, thus vacating jobs that the men could then fill. Later on, the misunderstood idea of "continual mothering" ran counter to the trend of mothers working. It also seemed to conflict with the wish to increase the father's role in child care.

Bowlby usually stuck to what was empirical. He would discuss any studies that threw light on the subject. For instance, attachment research has demonstrated that mothers have greater influence on the emotional development of children. He was quite open, however, to the idea that fathers may be shown to be more significant to their children when they have been child caretakers. He also appreciated that the research showed that isolated mothers often became depressed, and that working might well help them, and hence help their children. He did, however, believe that mothers had a highly important and central role in child care and was not afraid to point it out, even when this made him unpopular. Unfortunately the disagreement with the feminists has tended, for some, to tarnish all attachment theory ideas and research findings.

ATTACHMENT THEORY AND THE CONCEPT OF A SECURE BASE

A Secure Base within a Dyad

Mary Ainsworth (1967) first used the concept of a secure base in her fascinating study of Ugandan children and their parents. She observed how toddlers would move away from their mother to play, returning every now and then to touch base with mother. "He is content to move away, as long as he knows that she is there. He can even leave the room on his own initiative, and his aplomb in so doing is sometimes in sharp contrast to the consternation when his secure base gets up and moves away" (p. 345).

Attachment figures are used throughout life (Ainsworth, 1991). Children take more responsibility for managing the attachment relationship as they grow older, eventually taking over the caregiving role in their parents' old age. New attachment relationships are formed with other adults (Weiss, 1982), such as sexual or marital partners or friends, who may then provide each other with a mutual secure base, making care available in times of illness or particular need. In situations of danger or acute stress, even strangers, such as therapists, can also rapidly become temporary attachment figures. The knowledge that there is someone interested and available, if needed, is crucial to the use of a safe base at any age and in any circumstance. The internalized image of the attachment becomes in itself a source of confidence, and supports autonomous behavior even when others are not immediately available.

Family as a Secure Base

A secure family base is defined as "a family that provides a reliable network of attachment relationships which enables all family members of whatever age to feel sufficiently secure to explore relationships with each other and with others outside the family" (Byng-Hall, 1995). The term "network" implies a shared family responsibility that assures everyone that any member who is in need of help will be cared for. For small children it means an expectation of reliable handover to another caretaker and hand-back to the original person either within the family network, or using appropriate outside carertakers. Children need a sense that relationships between the adults are sufficiently collaborative to ensure that care is available at all times. A secure family base involves a shared awareness that attachment relationships need to be protected and not undermined. The shared working model of the secure family base is of family members supporting each other to care for their members. The motto of the secure family base is "collaborate to care."

SITUATIONS THAT AFFECT SECURITY

Two aspects of security need to be differentiated. First, there are observable strategies occurring within particular attachments that are used in an attempt to establish a sense of security. The resulting inter-action patterns occurring between careseeker and caregiver tend to persist over time, and the image of the reliable and interested person can remain as an inner source of comfort for a lifetime. This can be called the security of an attachment relationship. Second, there is "felt security," which is how each member of the family feels at any one moment. This can fluctuate depending on circumstances. For instance, even a secure family base will not prevent members from feeling inse-cure in the middle of a major crisis.

The Effect of Other Relationships on Security

The security of a particular attachment may be affected by the other relationships in the family. Goldberg and Easterbrooks (1984) and Belsky et al. (1989) showed that the quality of the parents' relation-ship influenced the security of the child's attachment. Egeland and Farber (1984) found that in those children whose attachments to their mothers deteriorated from being secure at age 1 to insecure at the age of 18 months, the mothers were more likely to be living without a husband or boyfriend. These studies suggest that a sustained partner-ship, so long as it is well adjusted, helps to maintain the security of a child to his parent. The influence on security of the increasing num-ber of families in which children have many "parents," with birth parents, stepparents, step ex-grandparents, etc., resulting from the increasing trend toward serial partnership breakups remains to be seen. For therapists it is important to focus on the potential for richness in the varied relationships that this produces, as well as to try, where possible, to encourage continuing contact with the important attach-ment figures who have left the home.

Support for parents can, of course, come from a wider group of adults. The art of helping other people's caring relationships lies in concern for, and enjoyment of, what is happening in their care of the child—for instance, the way that a grandparent can support his or her child's parenting. This also involves tolerating being left out while watching what goes on, or—whenever help is given—avoiding being intrusive, competitive, or engaging in a power struggle. At the level of the community Belsky et al. (1989) showed that those parents who perceived their neighbors as being friendly and/or helpful were more likely to have securely attached children. Belsky and Vondra (1990) also demonstrated how the social network influenced parenting.

This suggests that it is important to evaluate the context of the whole family, and its supports, when considering the security that a family provides for its members. As Sroufe (1988, p. 26) puts it, "A relationship system may be far more powerful than a single relationship in shaping development toward health or pathology."

Some Family Situations That Undermine Security

Various family situations can undermine the capacity of the family to provide a secure base, thus exposing the family to feeling insecure (Byng-Hall & Stevenson-Hinde, 1991).

1. *Fear of losing, or actual loss of, an attachment figure.* The effect of loss and separation on children has been studied extensively (Bowlby, 1980). Breakdown of the parental relationship, and how that is managed, is currently the most common source of potential loss, or unavailability, of an attachment figure.

2. *Attachment figure is captured.* Another member of the family may "capture" the attachment figure. This may happen when an anxiously attached child clings onto a parent and excludes all others from gaining access, or when an insecure parent captures his or her partner and blocks the children, the in-laws, etc., from adequate access to that partner.

3. *Turning to an inappropriate attachment figure.* When an appropriate attachment figure is unavailable, an individual may turn to an inappropriate member of the family. For example, this may occur when one parent who, for one reason or another, is not being provided with a secure base from the other, may turn to a child instead. This can undermine the parent's care of the child.

4. *Conflict within relationships.* The most striking example of a conflict that undermines security is that of abuse where the attachment figure becomes the source of danger, as well as being the person the child would naturally turn to for protection. Between adults, as Goldner et al. (1990) point out, many violent partnerships are continued despite the danger because of the value given to attachments. At the level of the whole family, power battles with disputed authority, and family conflict in general, can create a great sense of insecurity.

5. *Expectation of repetition of losses similar to those encountered in previous generations.* When children reach the same age that their parents were when they had suffered major traumas, parents may start to behave as if it is about to happen again in this generation. The family scripts (Byng-Hall, 1990, 1991a, 1991b) that are enacted may be either "replicative," repeating similar traumatic scenarios, or "corrective," trying to avoid the feared situation. Either way, parents may become less likely to respond appropriately to their children's actual attachment needs as they exist in the present.

SECURE AND INSECURE
ATTACHMENT PATTERNS

Although these patterns were introduced in the first chapter it is important to describe them in more detail here as it is often the details that are useful to the therapist. The family therapist may recognize similar patterns, or aspects of patterns, as they are enacted in a family therapy session.

After collaborating with John Bowlby, Mary Ainsworth devised a laboratory procedure which elicits attachment behavior to a figure with whom the child has an attachment (Ainsworth et al., 1978). This was originally done with a Baltimore sample of "normal" 1-year-old infants and their mothers. This is called the Strange Situation (SS) procedure, which consists of seven 3-minute episodes in what can be seen as a little playlet whose plot might be interpreted as the parent preparing to leave the child with a stranger, until in the last scene the parent returns and there is a final reunion. The sequence consists of the following: (1) a stranger introduces parent and child to a strange laboratory room and leaves them there; (2) the stranger comes back, talks to the parent, and finally approaches the child; (3) the parent leaves the child with the stranger; (4) the parent returns while the stranger leaves; (5) the parent leaves the child on his or her own saying bye-bye; (6) the stranger returns; (7) the parent returns and the stranger leaves. The way in which the child behaves on reunion shows how the child has felt about being left and how the parent settles the child. A secure child will trust the parent not to abandon him or her, and anticipates being comforted if distressed. The child, although upset by being left, is soon reassured by the return of the parent. A child who is not secure in the knowledge of the reliability of the parent's care will behave in a different way, depending upon the nature of the insecurity.

The SS procedure has now been modified for 2½- to 4½-year-olds (Cassidy & Marvin, 1992) and 6-year-olds (Main & Cassidy, 1988). In these modifications the time spent away from parents may be lengthened in order to stress the child sufficiently to evoke attachment behavior, and symbolic material becomes part of the assessment as the child now uses talking as well as behavior to manage his or her attachment to the parent. In Mary Ainsworth's study the mothers and children were also observed for many hours at home over the first year of life. This gives validity to the test. Stevenson-Hinde and Shouldice (1995) also validated the 2½- to 4½-year-old pattern through home observations and laboratory tests that explored maternal interaction patterns.

Main et al. (1985) explored the parents' internal working model of attachments. This can be elucidated through the Adult Attachment Interview (AAI; Main & Goldwyn, 1985–1995). Adults are interviewed about their attachment-related experiences in childhood. They are asked to give five adjectives that describe each parent, and then asked to describe an episode that illustrates each of these adjectives. Inquiries are also made about what happened when they were upset as children; whether their parents threatened them, or whether they felt rejected; and whether there were any separations or losses. They are asked why their parents behaved like this and whether these childhood experiences affected their adult personalities. (It is worth noting here that questions about parental cooperation would complete the picture of the security of the family base.) The narrative is then analyzed from the transcript.

What is most interesting is that the coherence of the narrative in the transcript of the AAI can predict with 75%–80% accuracy whether or not the parent has a securely attached child (Main et al., 1985). A coherent account is one that gives the assessor a clear and convincing picture of what childhood was like. It is truthful and succinct, yet is complete, relevant, and presented in a clear and orderly way. Another predictor of security is whether an analysis of the transcript shows that the individual can reflect on the motives of those involved (Fonagy et al., 1991). This suggests that if a parent can make sense of what happened in childhood, and can see the motives behind each person's behavior, then the parent is more likely to be able to respond appropriately to his or her child's signals, and the child is consequently more likely to be securely attached. The research (Main et al., 1985; Fonagy et al., 1991) also shows that the three categories of incoherent narrative predict three matching types of insecure attachment patterns. Although the correspondence between a parent's AAI classification and a child's SS classification to that parent is not always perfect, it is convenient to describe the classifications as a "package."

Secure Attachments

These are the majority (see below for percentages), comprising a *secure* child (Pattern B on the SS) and a parent classified as *autonomous/free* (F on the AAI).

These relationships have adaptable transactional styles. A typical scenario for secure attachments in the SS might go as follows:

> The infant aged 1 year who is exploring the room when the parent leaves the room is initially upset and follows the parent to the door. However this distress is not excessive. When the parent returns 6 min-

utes later, both parent and infant are pleased to see each other and soon get together. Although the infant may also be upset and angry about being left, he or she is quickly settled by the parent and goes off to explore once again.

By the age of 4½ (Stevenson-Hinde & Shouldice, 1995), the child after being separated for 12 minutes greets the parent with full gaze and positive affect. The interactions are calm, while also intimate and indicative of a special relationship.

At home these children and their parents often appear to have fun together. Communications are generally warm and sensitive, and the parent, as we have seen, has a coherent view of attachments and their importance to the child. The infant is not afraid to express anger, the parent understands that anger is a natural component of relationships. There is open communication between infant and parent about both the good and the upsetting aspects of what goes on. There is freedom for parent and child to come together or move apart when each wishes, and when the timing is suitable to both. The parent respects the child's age-appropriate autonomy. Most important of all is the parent's physical and emotional availability at times of distress. Many attachments, however, are not as perfect as this and have elements of insecure patterns as well; however, the overall pattern remains secure.

Insecure/Avoidant Attachments

These are a substantial minority, comprising an *insecure/avoidant* child (A on the SS pattern) and a *dismissive* parent (D on the AAI).

These attachments use a similar transactional style to those of disengaged relationships. To the observer these relationships may appear to be detached, but they are often experienced by the participants as potentially too close unless a distance is kept. A typical scenario is as follows:

The infant does not appear to mind much or even notice when the parent leaves, and continues with exploration. On reunion he or she turns away from the parent and may move toward some object such as a toy. The parent is also cool, looking toward the toys as well.

The 4½-year-old child avoids calling attention to the relationship to the returning parent, either physically or in conversation. The child maintains neutrality toward the parent.

The child's strategy is to attempt to deactivate his feelings of insecurity about the separation by switching attention away from the parent's whereabouts. This, in turn, deactivates his attachment behavior. However, although the infant outwardly seems unconcerned by the separation, he or she is found to be physiologically aroused with an increased heart rate (Sroufe & Waters, 1977). The child then remains aroused for much longer than the secure child, whose heart rate, in contrast, settles rapidly on reunion with the parent. This suggests that the child is indeed anxiously and insecurely attached but does not reveal this to the parent. At home, the child's need for comfort is commonly observed to be ignored by the parent, who may also find the infant's attempts to make physical contact aversive. The parent often withdraws when the child is sad or pushes him or her away when angry. The infants are, however, more openly angry in the safer setting of home than in the laboratory. Main and Weston (1982) suggest that the child's behavior, "avoidance in the service of proximity," represents an adaptive strategy to avoid being emotional—either sad or angry—at the point of reunion, when there is a particular danger that a rejecting parent might refuse to comfort a protesting child, or even refuse to collect him or her.

In the AAI the parent is *dismissive* of the importance of attachments. The parent has often forgotten much of his or her childhood, and tends to idealize his or her own parent, but this idealization does not fit with the account of the care actually given; for instance, one parent described her mother as "wonderful" but then told how, when she had broken her arm, she could not tell her mother because she would be angry. In other words, the narrative is incoherent because it denies the unpleasant implications about the care that was given. The parent also avoids reliving any past painful experiences either by forgetting them or by avoiding being reminded of them when the child is facing similar situations. This blocks any possible empathy with the child's distress.

The shared parent–child attachment strategy is to maintain distance both physically and emotionally in order to reduce the likelihood of emotional outbursts that might lead to rejections or painful reminders. The price is loss of sensitive care for the child when it is needed. The child does not learn to explore feelings and intimacy and, although apparently very independent, is not adaptable. Play tends to be stereotyped, and compulsive exploration is used as a distraction from attachment needs.

Insecure/Ambivalent Attachments

These are a minority, comprising an *insecure/ambivalent* child (Pattern C on the SS) and a *preoccupied/entangled* parent (E on the AAI). This group has recently been well reviewed by Cassidy and Berlin (1994).

These attachments use similar transactional styles to those of enmeshed relationships. To the observer these relationships appear to be too close, but are often experienced as potentially unavailable which provokes clinging. A typical scenario is as follows:

> The infant makes a fuss when left, clinging to the departing parent, and then staying near the door crying for the parent. On reunion he alternately demands to be picked up and then pushes the parent angrily away. The parent fails to settle the child, who does not leave the parent's side and so fails to explore again.

> The 4½-year-old child shows angry, whining resistance directed at the parent, and/or immature, coy behavior, often with ambivalence to physical proximity or contact; emphasis is on dependence.

At home the parent, although committed to mothering is quite often emotionally unavailable. The infant learns that the parent will respond, but only if he works at it. The child's strategy is to keep close and to force the parent to notice him by being demanding and/or overly babyish.

The parent is *preoccupied*; far from forgetting his or her childhood, the parent is frequently ruminating on unresolved issues from the past. Boundaries become blurred with role reversal; the child becomes parentified as he or she gets older. The parent needs the child to comfort him or her. There is a great deal of mutual monitoring and mind reading, all in an attempt to forestall any potential drifting away on the part of both parent and child. One strategy is to ambivalently threaten greater distance. In contrast, however, to the avoidant strategy which does aim to achieve distance, this threat is unconsciously designed to stimulate the other person to actually come closer. The child does this by pushing the parent away, as demonstrated in the reunion. The parent, on the other hand, might threaten to abandon the child, or to send him or her away. These distancing threats activate the other's attachment behavior and so are a highly effective short-term strategy to reinforce closeness. Unfortunately this also threatens the security of the relationship. The price is loss of autonomy for the child.

Ainsworth et al. (1978) in a sample of 105 found 70 securely attached children (B), 22 insecure/avoidant (A), and 13 insecure/ambivalent (C). Van IJzendoorn and Kroonenberg (1988) conducted a meta-analysis of 32 similar studies conducted since then with almost 2,000 infants from various parts of the industrialized world. They found that the variations within a country were as great as the variations between countries. Avoidant classifications were more prevalent in Western Europe, while ambivalent classifications were common in Israel and Japan. This suggests that the community and culture in which the child is brought up has some influence on the attachment pattern. Also at-risk, or maltreatment samples show a high percentage of insecurely attached children, reminding us that family interaction influences attachment. Nevertheless, the percentages in the 2,000 "normal" children (that is, 65% of B, 21% of A, and 14% of C) were very similar to those found by Ainsworth et al. (1978). Despite the variations the similarities in the distributions across cultures were striking, suggesting that a fundamental aspect of human child— parent interaction is involved.

Another minority pattern of attachment has now emerged:

Disorganized/Unresolved Attachments

These comprise a *disorganized/disoriented* child (Pattern D on the SS) and an *unresolved* parent (U on the AAI).

There is also an additional group of insecure children (range 15%– 25% in a normal population, but *80% in the maltreated* group) who are classified as disorganized. This group was discovered by Main and Solomon (1986) when examining the videotapes of SS; they found that some could not be classified adequately under previous categories because the infants did not seem to have an organized strategy for handling the reunion. It is thus not possible to describe one typical scenario for this group. Subsequently it has become clear that this group is an important one, likely to include children who may become part of the clinical population. However, there remains some controversy about the nature of the group. The reunion may include a mixture of avoidant and ambivalent patterns, or an approach/avoidance conflict created by fear of the attachment figure, who may also be maltreating the infant. The infant may manifest this by suddenly freezing while going toward the parent, or veer away from the parent just when getting close (Main & Solomon, 1990). Although the reunion pattern may not make sense in the context of the SS where the parent is on best behavior, the child's pattern might be choreographed to fit the parent's behavior at home. For instance, the child may run off to hide by the wall to avoid an anticipated blow.

On the AAI many parents of insecure/disorganized children are categorized as *unresolved*. That is, they have not adequately mourned a lost attachment figure, or they have had a recent trauma such as a brush with death that they have not got over (Ainsworth & Eichberg, 1991). Main and Hesse (1990) suggest that the attachment figure is frightened by the memory of a past trauma and may dissociate momentarily. This is likely, in turn, to be frightening for the child who is socially monitoring the parent and so assumes that this indicates a real danger, although it is unclear what or where this is located. The child's response to the fear may be a dissociative one as the child has moments of trance-like states that may be observed in the reunion behavior. The general impression I have is that the parent does not have the child in mind, but is scripting him or her into some past drama of which, of course, the child is ignorant and so cannot yet develop an organized strategy. Yet another explanation, then, is that at home there are moments when the parent's behavior flips into a dissociated state and is indeed dangerous or frightening, but because it is triggered by the internal drama cannot readily be anticipated by the child. As the children grow older, however, overall strategies do seem to develop. Children become more controlling of the parent, thus establishing their own structure for the reunion (Main et al., 1985). (See Table 6.1.)

MESHING OF ATTACHMENT SCRIPTS

The way in which the scripts mesh between a parent and a child can be illustrated by how the attachment scripts co-evolve during childhood. This may throw light both on how scripts function in general and on how parents provide a secure base for their children.

For a shared relationship script to function adequately, there must be ways in which the two scripts mesh, so that each person can adjust their scripts so that they are working toward a common end— a "shared goal-corrected system." Each has to come in on cue from the other with an appropriate response. There must also be ways in which each can call the tune at different times. A switch to new shared goals must be negotiated, such as when a child wants to explore autonomously. In caregiving the baby's rhythms are likely to take precedence for much of the time. Mothers of secure infants pace their interactions more appropriately than mothers of insecure infants (Egeland & Farber, 1984). This is clearly an important aspect of meshing, but the infant has to learn to accommodate to the parent's world, especially as he or she grows older.

Stevenson-Hinde and Shouldice (1995) observed mother's interactions with preschool children ($N=78$), both at home when aged 3½ and in the laboratory when aged 4½. Meshing was rated on a 7-point scale, from "intense, unpleasant friction" to "smooth coordinated interactions toward mutual goals." Mothers with securely attached children showed a significantly greater capacity than mothers of insecure children to coordinate toward mutual goals. In a labora-

TABLE 6.1. Features Associated with Parent–Child Attachments during Childhood

	Secure	Insecure/avoidant	Insecure/ambivalent	Disorganized/unresolved
Child's pattern with attachment figure in SS	B Autonomous; explores readily	A Pseudoindependent; avoids closeness; attachment behavior deactivated	C Demanding and/or angry; attachment behavior overactivated	D (or A + C) Disorganized; becomes controlling or caregiving when older
Parent				
AAI Narrative	Autonomous/free (F) Coherent	Dismissive (D) Incoherent; denial of past pain	Preoccupied/entangled (E) Incoherent; preoccupation with past	Unresolved mourning (U) Incoherent; unresolved about losses
Parental style	Sensitively responsive	Rejecting	Intermittently available	Maltreatment (by some)
Attachments				
Distance	Free to go to and fro	Distant	Overclose	Approach–avoidance conflict (some)
Transactional style	Adaptable	Disengaged	Enmeshed	Sometimes disoriented
Shared strategy	Maintain contact with each other	Avoids emotional or physical closeness	Mutual monitoring; blurred boundaries	No common strategy; idiosyncratic reunions; ? dissociation when frightened/frightening

114

tory joint task, mothers of securely attached children showed more monitoring of their own actions for the child, and planning with the child. The mothers also provided a more sensitive framework for their children.

Mothers of securely attached children in the Stevenson-Hinde and Shouldice study also had a more positive mood, enjoyed their child more, were more relaxed, and affirmed their child more frequently. These positive features may also be important in helping the mother to help the child change course toward a fresh task. At the age of 2½ the children in this study and their mothers had been asked to clear up toys in a laboratory setting after only 10 minutes of playing with novel toys (Achermann et al., 1991). The mothers of secure children were more constructively involved in the free play, but then approached the clear-up enthusiastically using a positive tone of voice. They also used a low proportion of control statements. It seems then that a change of goals away from one that is enjoyable to the child to one dictated by adult necessity could be achieved by positively involving the child in the new activity rather than coercing him or her into line.

Parents of insecure/avoidant children monitored their children very little and did not plan much. Surprisingly, however, they also rated themselves higher than any of the other parents on their own parenting performance, despite being rated low by observers. This is congruent with the idealization of parenting that is found in the dismissive AAI. The overall pattern, then, might suggest that the parents had withdrawn from their children, not noticing what was happening to them and also remaining unaware of their own performance. The dyads appeared to have disengaged rather than meshed.

Mothers of insecure/ambivalent children were observed to mesh badly, generating more friction. They were less responsive to their children at home. In other studies (see Cassidy & Berlin, 1994), parents of insecure/ambivalent children show a tendency toward intrusive behavior and toward initiating interactions at times which were inappropriate for the infant, including interfering with exploration. They also drew the attention of the infants onto themselves and away from the outside world. Mothers responded to the children's signals of fear, but did not attune to, or validate, the signs of initiative or exuberance. On self-rating, in contrast to the avoidant group, the mothers rated themselves as more depressed and anxious, and least satisfied with their marriages. The impression is of parents who have their own unsatisfactory inner worlds and induct their children into scenarios in that world as a way of meshing with them. This is at the expense of the child meshing with the outside world.

Despite this picture, when the mothers of ambivalently attached children in Stevenson-Hinde and Shouldice's study (1995) were asked to perform a brief laboratory task they did not differ from the other mothers; indeed, they planned more than the mothers of avoidant children. They also enjoyed the task. This fits with the picture that although mothers are frequently preoccupied with their own inner worlds, they are capable of coming out of this when "prompted by their own moods or desires," which Mary Ainsworth had originally noted.

DEVELOPMENTAL PATHWAYS OF ATTACHMENTS

Children's attachment patterns follow developmental pathways (Bowlby, 1982) depending on the unfolding circumstances in which they are brought up. Bowlby suggested that the original attachment relationship might provide a model for the child's relationships in later life. This issue may be of considerable importance in preventive mental health. In populations that are relatively stable, attachment relationships are likely to remain the same from infancy to age 6½ or longer (Main et al., 1985), while the influence of the security of the relationship has been shown to persist until age 15 (Urban, Carlson, Egeland, & Sroufe, 1991). The pattern can alter, however. In at-risk groups there can be a deterioration toward insecurity (Belsky & Nezworski, 1988). In others there can also be a shift toward greater security.

The investigations of attachment patterns over the first 6 years of a child's life are building up a tentative picture of how insecure attachment relationship may evolve. Parental rejection may influence the way that attachments develop. In "normal" populations, rejection is defined as a combination of interfering with the child's behavior and negative affect. This might reflect the angry rejection of the child's behavior, rather than a rejection of the child as a person, which can occur in an at-risk sample. In avoidant attachments, this rejection has not been shown with infants of less than 1 year old, suggesting that the infant's increasingly active demands—including when distressed— might be provoking rejection, rather than the presence of the baby in itself. The effect of the parent's negative response to a child's distress is very upsetting, indeed often overwhelming, and it can temporarily disrupt the child's internal organization. The infant comes to sense that a risk is associated with engaging with the parent, and develops the strategy of neutrality and avoiding calling attention to the relationship. The parent's rejecting behavior subsequently reduces so that it is no longer evident by age 4½, suggesting that the child's strategy works and that maternal rejection is replaced by mutual avoidance of any meshing that might provoke an emotional response.

Parents of ambivalent infants, on the other hand, show strong rejection of the infant at the age of 1 month. However, this is no longer greater than for other parents by the age of 4 months. This suggests to me that it is the arrival of the child that may be provoking difficulty for the parent, who has to accept a new person with his or her own needs, which at times clash with the parent's needs and pre-occupations. The parent's unpredictable availability provokes the child, as he or she grows older, into constant monitoring of the parent's behavior for evidence of departure—either emotionally or physically. Thus, the tracking function of monitoring, held largely by parents in secure attachments, passes more to the child. In short, it becomes the child's job to mesh his or her own needs to that of the parent rather than the other way around. The child then has to make a considerable fuss to get the parent to mesh with his or her own needs, causing much friction. From the parent's point of view the child is then being infantile. To add to this, the parent may infantilize the child. As Bowlby stated, "Treating the child as younger than he or she is one technique for ensuring that the child remains available as an attachment figure" (Bowlby, personal communication, cited in Stevenson-Hinde, 1990).

The typical picture of a parentified child, often seen in clinical practice, may build up in which the child at first appears to be behaving much younger than he or she is, but at the same time is supporting the parent (e.g., by putting his or her hand around the parent's back in a comforting way, constantly keeping an eye on the parent, and responding whenever the parent shows signs of distress). The babyish behavior tends to obscure or disguise the parentification. The image of a "little old man or woman" can, however, appear—"being his or her own grandparent," that is, looking after his or her own parent.

One way of characterizing the difference between the ambivalent child's dilemma from that of the avoidant child is to say that the avoidant child has a *certainly unavailable* parent, whereas the ambivalent child faces an *uncertainly available* parent. Or, as Marvin and Stewart (1990) point out, the shared strategy that evolves for avoidant attachment is to disengage, whereas that for the ambivalent attachment is to enmesh. Enmeshment has to be differentiated from meshing effectively, which is found in secure attachments. Enmeshment (S. Minuchin, 1974) involves lack of boundaries between individuals, blurring of generation boundaries, and excessive mutual monitoring.

As Hoffman (1975) pointed out, the relationship is "too richly cross-joined," that is, they are tightly interlocked so that every move is immediately known by everyone else, and a response follows. Little independent action is possible; improvisation is restricted, and roles are confused.

The developmental pathway for disorganized/unresolved attachments is less well known. It can be assumed that for some the pathway includes maltreatment because of the 80% incidence in maltreated children. We also know that for those classified as disorganized (Pattern D) at 1 year of age, they are likely to become controlling by the age of 6½. They take over the responsibility for the reunion, and structure what goes on. Some of the controlling is done in a punitive way, while some is done in a caretaking way (Main et al., 1985; Cassidy & Marvin, 1992). I would guess that the parent sows the seed of the style of control, either by behaving punitively him- or herself (or someone else was punitive in the family) or by demanding care from the child.

Stevenson-Hinde and Shouldice (1995) classified a group of *controlling* children at 4.5 years. The mothers of controlling children were significantly lower than all other mothers on those features promoting a sense of security, such as affirming, enjoying the task, and providing a sensitive framework for their children. This suggests to me that the mother's lack of a framework invites the child to take over the organization, especially in stressed situations such as the SS. However, it is not clear that all controlling children have been disorganized in infancy. Some of the mothers in this study seemed to resemble mothers of avoidant children in the way that they interacted with their child.

Research is exploring the developmental pathways of attachments across the life cycle (Parkes et al., 1991): how adolescents (Kobak & Sceery, 1988) and adults (Weiss, 1982; Patrick et al., 1994) evolve their attachments. Attempts have also been made to map the adult attachments formed in love relationships (Hazan & Shaver, 1987), and in closeness–distance struggles in couples (Pistole, 1994). There is not sufficient space in this book to explore these interesting advances. But studies exploring how patterns of attachment are handed onto the next generation are discussed below.

REPLICATIVE SCRIPTS
OF ATTACHMENT PATTERNS

Ricks (1985) reviewed the retrospective evidence about transgenerational transmission of attachment patterns. There are many studies which show that nonoptimal caretaking behavior on the part of the parent is associated with reports of disruption of their own early attachment relationships because of divorce, death, or long-term separations from parents, rather than the experience of short-term separation from parents without disruption. Rutter, Quinton, and Liddle (1983) compared the early childhood experience of parents who had serious family difficulties, defined by having had a child taken into care, with a control group of similar socioeconomic status. They concluded that serious parenting problems in the context of widespread family difficulties rarely arose in the absence of such previous childhood adversities.

Another approach to the problem was to explore the relationship between a mother's sense of herself and of her past, and see how this related to the security of the attachments to her children. Ricks (1985) found that mothers of securely attached children had a higher self-esteem and reported more positive recollections of childhood relationships with mother, father, and peers, than those who had insecurely attached infants. Especially important was a mother's recollection of having been accepted by her own mother during childhood, which was also significantly linked to high self-esteem. This suggests a developmental pathway in which children experience their mother's acceptance and so develop high self-esteem, which helps them to become competent mothers to their own children when they grow up. It was also interesting to note that those mothers with anxiously attached children also reported that the grandmothers were currently unhappy. This raises the question as to how much the mediating factor is the mother's mental representation of her own childhood experiences and how much it is an aspect of their current relationship with their own mothers.

CORRECTIVE ATTACHMENT SCRIPTS:
FROM INSECURE TO SECURE

The study in Berkeley (Main et al., 1985) identified an important group of parents who described disrupted and traumatic childhoods, but nevertheless had securely attached children. This is in contrast to the majority of those parents who had had very difficult childhoods, who had insecurely attached children. The best predictors as to whether or not the parents who have had traumatic backgrounds have secure or insecurely attached children was the coherence of their narrative in the AAI. Thus, a parent who gives a clear and understandable account of his or her painful childhood with all its ups and downs is likely to have a securely attached child. They could reexperience in the interview their feelings of distress, anger, or occasional joy as they describe episodes in the past. They showed a capacity to empathize with the difficulties their parents had in bringing them up. They could also acknowledge their own contribution to the general difficulties.

This is an extremely important finding, as it would suggest that it is not necessarily what happened in the parent's own childhood, but what they made of that experience which influences whether or not they can provide a secure base for their own children. This has implications for therapy. It suggests that to help parents to achieve a coherent picture of their past may enable them to provide a better parenting experience for their own children.

Ricks (1985) also reported a group of mothers who had had traumatic childhoods and yet now had securely attached children. These women had stable marriages and positive self-esteem. They often had exceptionally strong ties to their husband's families. Quinton, Rutter, and Liddle (1984) studied the parenting of women who had been brought up in care. Many had difficulties in parenting; however, those who became successful parents were more likely to have a supportive relationship with someone such as a husband. This suggests that a corrective script is easier to operate with the support and admiration of others. Ricks (1985) considered that the transition from disruption in one generation to security in the next would involve a change in the underlying mental representation of the self and other. This, she thought, was likely to have to include some emotionally corrective experiences, such as (1) change within the same early relationships over time, (2) repeated experience in other relationships that disconfirm the earlier models, and (3) particularly strong experiences within one relationship ("I admire this person; he likes and respects me. Then maybe I am a worthwhile person myself; after all, I respect his judgment.").

Ricks also considered that particular points in the life cycle might allow a reorganization to happen; for instance, when adolescents review their experiences and distance themselves from the way their own parents behaved. This would be a particularly fruitful moment for corrective scripts to be established. Another opportunity would arise when relationships are made that are external to the family and so provide a new perspective to the individual's own past. When partners get together with the idea of creating a new family, there is often an extensive review of each person's past parenting experiences through asking each other about their childhood. Fresh vows for corrective scripts may emerge that are supported by the other. This review is also likely to reappear during the pregnancy of the first child when parents again, often spontaneously, discuss their own childhood.

S·E·V·E·N

Therapy and Supervision as Secure Bases

EXTRAPOLATING ATTACHMENT DATA TO THERAPY: LIMITATIONS AND STRENGTHS

It is possible to both overestimate and underestimate the importance of attachment results. Attachments only represent one aspect of relationships. It is important to recognize that there is a danger of discrediting the theory through inappropriate overextension (Sroufe, 1988, p. 26). On the other hand, attachments, as Wynne (1984) reminds us, provide the core set of relationships around which other family functions develop. Attachments are the ties of family life: Making, breaking, and securing attachments are of enormous importance, and if these go wrong there may be serious consequences (Bowlby, 1979).

Most of the data come from studies of the general population in which the overall pattern of each identified group is distilled out, and any personal content of any one child's reunion behavior is lost in the general pattern. This is both the strength and the limitation of the research. Much of the data relate to attachments found in normal populations—and hence those patterns are likely to be present in some form in any family; but this vision is restricted when taking into account the complexity of an attachment seen in the context of the family and its history. We must also be careful about the way we use the data. Sroufe (1988) reminds us that A and C (or D, for that matter) classifications are not the equivalent of diagnoses, and cannot predict specific problems. Many factors will influence the developmental pathways. Sroufe concludes that insecure attachments represent a developmental context that makes the emergence of problems more likely (p. 30). For clinicians it is important to remember that

121

spotting a pattern of attachment reminiscent of research categories does not confer the same scientific status; its value lies more in pointing to what else to look for.

FAMILY THERAPY AS A SECURE BASE

How can family therapists facilitate a switch from insecure to secure patterns? Murray and Cooper (1994) described a relationship in which the classification moved from insecure to secure following eight sessions of mother–child psychotherapy. The mother was rated dismissive on the AAI (see Table 6.1) prior to therapy and autonomous/free after therapy. The child who was 1½ when therapy started was noted insecure/avoidant but was secure following treatment. An important component of the therapy involved the mother recalling episodes in her childhood evoked by her interaction with her daughters, and by seeing how her daughter and her own parents interacted. Until similar studies are carried out using a variety of family therapy techniques and assessing changes in security, it will not be clear which techniques lead to increased security in the family.

I have been involved in setting up a research project[1] that aims to address some of these questions. It has been necessary to devise six new instruments for this purpose. Videotape of each session is coded for family functioning, for the interventions used, and for problems as they appear in different members of the family, so that it is then possible to link chronologically the changes in the family with what has gone on in therapy. The instruments include data about attachment relationships, authority structures, and family scripts. A Q sort assesses the whole family functioning, while another instrument provides data about each dyadic relationship so that the complexity of the attachment pattern can be recorded. The study is based on a single–multiple case format in which each case is explored in sufficient depth to be a single-case study in its own right, but when sufficient cases have accumulated, collecting the same data each time, acros-case differences will emerge. The data are not yet ready for publication, but the first four cases seem to show promise as a way of demonstrating change.

Bowlby (1988) pointed out that the attachment to the therapist becomes crucial in individual therapy. How can a family therapist

---

[1] The "Attachments and Family Scripts in Family Therapy" project is in collaboration with Professor Issy Kolvin, John Bowlby Professor at the Tavistock Clinic, and includes Andy Cotgrove, Ghazalla Javaid, Angela Roberts, and Bill Young.

provide a temporary secure base for the family during therapy? The overall aim is to use his or her capacity to improve the family's network of attachment relationships so that the family can establish itself as a secure base. This then enables them to explore and solve their own problems during and following therapy.

CONFLICT RESOLUTION
AND EXPLORATION IN THERAPY

An attachment figure creates a secure base because he or she provides safety when needed; it is secure because it is "safety first and exploration later." Clearly the situation is much more complex in a family, but nevertheless the same principle holds true. A major difference is that, in the troubled family, dangers—either from what family members might do to each other or from fears of abandonment and alienation—come from within the family, not from outside. The implication is that attachment behavior is then likely to remain activated, with continuing vigilance for trouble, while autonomous exploration is dampened. This lasts until family members become less weary of each other.

A temporary therapeutic secure base thus includes two main functions:

1. *Protective role.* This includes identifying dangers and conflicts and making sure that any necessary measures are taken. A sense of security comes from knowing that worrisome situations will be tackled; it is not based on being reassured while ignoring the dangers. I try to reach core anxieties and conflicts as soon as possible in the first session. The protective function is reminiscent of structural family therapy techniques (S. Minuchin, 1974) in which anxiety about a situation may be highlighted so that the necessary steps will be taken to resolve the difficulty. An example would be a discussion of how a patient with anorexia nervosa will die if she goes on refusing to eat. Or when children are out of control and the parents are given the task of settling them because nothing can be done until the parents regain their authority. The crisis of breakdown in authority that occurs in some families creates situations that can no longer be ignored. The therapist needs to maintain the intensity and block the family's conflict avoiding moves until the family takes the necessary steps to protect its members. The therapist's role is to provide a setting in which the family can face up to what needs to be done. Calming the

situation by taking charge may remove the impetus to improvise their own way of relating.

2. *Exploratory role.* Exploring how, when, and why these conflicts arise, and trying out alternative ways of relating, comes later when the crisis has settled and everyone is feeling more secure. Techniques for exploring belief systems and alternative futures can be used. Fresh behavior can be improvised and new avenues pursued using the therapy as a secure base where the implications of new ways of relating can be thought through.

AVAILABILITY OF THE THERAPIST

In order to create a safe base the therapist has to make him- or herself available. I make myself available as quickly as possible, to make the most of the crisis at hand, and then maintain contact for an adequate period of time. I telephone the family in order to establish the beginnings of a relationship. I treat this as a preliminary session in order to remind myself of its importance as the first step to an attachment with the family through the member I talk to. I allow enough time, say, up to 20 minutes to talk things through. Often, however, it can be a much shorter phone call. I find that this approach reduces the number of failed attendances in those who are anxious about coming. They need the time to create an image of a warm, accepting therapist who seems to appreciate their difficulties and who is available to greet them at the clinic. During the telephone call I find out how each member of the family is involved with the symptom, which usually makes clear to the person on the phone why all of the family members should come.

I see the family for up to 2 hours (or shorter if there are younger children) in the first session at the clinic, and 1½ hours subsequently. The long first session is a way of adding intensity. I am more likely to see the family in a tense state at some point in the session. Few families can maintain a relaxed facade that long. I also feel that I reach issues of greater significance if I spend more time—patterns become apparent, and the family itself is able to start exploring issues. These conditions enable me to initiate an attachment in the session.

I start, if possible, by seeing families weekly to establish the attachment. Once this is achieved I lessen the frequency to every 2 weeks or once a month and end up by seeing them every 3 to 6 months. After discharge I make it clear that I am always available to them. In this way I see families, on average, about 10 to 12 times but over a period of 1 to 3 years. Thus I offer, in terms of therapy time, what amounts to a brief intervention, but also provide a long-term secure base.

A CASE ILLUSTRATION: THE YOUNG FAMILY

I am going to illustrate some of these issues with the Youngs, a Tasmanian family now living in East Anglia. The referral letter from the family doctor together with the telephone conversation with the mother revealed that the problem focused on Ann, aged 2½, who was not sleeping and was having temper tantrums. Ann was clinging to her father, Bruce, a 33-year-old research chemist, and refusing to go to her mother, Margaret, a 36-year-old librarian. Margaret told me on the phone that this made her feel desperate. However, when Ann was with her mother she would become demanding. Margaret, exasperated, would then push her back to her father. Difficulties had become worse after the birth of Susan 7 months ago. By the end of the phone call, I felt I had made a personal contact with Margaret, and she knew that I appreciated how desperate she was.

ENGAGEMENT:
THERAPIST ESTABLISHES ATTACHMENTS

When I meet a family for the first time, I try to make some physical as well as friendly eye-to-eye contact with each member. This quickly gives the message that I intend to interact with each member. In this case, I shook hands with both parents and touched Ann lightly on the shoulder and said hello as she was introduced. I then touched baby Susan's hand as I looked into her eyes. I then took them to the consulting room. The question now was whether the parents would allow me, a stranger, to make contact with their children. This, of course, is a highly important mechanism in the family attachment system. It is not safe for children to be allowed contact with any stranger who presents him- or herself. Children feel more secure with a stranger once they have observed their parent's response to him or her. As with any potentially threatening situation, the child attachment behavior is aroused until, through social referencing, the child perceives that the parent feels the situation is safe.

The role of doorkeeper—the person who decides whether to let the stranger in—is often held by one parent. It may be either father or mother. The therapist finds out who this is by noticing who the child socially references at the beginning of the session. Ann sat on her father's lap, but kept glancing at her mother. Since I had already won over the mother, it was not long before she gave the go-ahead to the children. If it had been the father, I would have needed to make sure that I engaged him sufficiently to open the door.

Some therapists, aware of the need to get past the doorkeeper, spend increasing time talking to him or her. However, this may not be the best method, especially if children are involved. The way to a parent's heart is through their children in this case. So I spend a brief amount of time talking very directly to the doorkeeper, then switch to socializing with the child, asking about neutral issues (such as their age and time of next birthday). While doing this, the therapist should social reference the doorkeeper. This tells the parent that the therapist is sensitive to the parents' role and that nothing is going to develop between the child and stranger without permission. Talking to the parents at length has the additional disadvantage that it is likely to lead to therapy with the parents in front of the children, who get the message that they are not needed and, in turn, go off to play elsewhere. To maintain communication with the children, even with very young children, it is important to talk to them at some length, and then when they do decide to play or draw, this should be done on a low table set out in the middle of the room so that the children stay central and in everyone's line of vision.

In the course of the first session I try to understand each person's dilemmas sufficiently to make them feel that I might be able to help. In this way I make myself available as an attachment figure to each individual while maintaining my overall focus on family interaction and how they care for each other. During the first session I also try to reach the core conflict and address some of the family's main fears. I was told that Ann had to be comforted to sleep by each parent in turn, waking up as one parent left and then—somewhat surprisingly— calling out for the other one; this process was repeated many times. I also discovered that both sets of grandparents had divorced. Toward the end of the session I said that Ann seemed to need reassurances that her parents were still both there. I commented that when one's own parents have divorced, it is hard not to threaten the same thing in arguments. Margaret laughed and said she threatened to leave about once a week, but that she was not serious. She assumed, it seems, that everyone understood perfectly well that her threats to leave were only designed to get her husband to be more at her side. However, on reflection she could now see how Ann might take her threats literally, and both parents agreed to try to stop arguing. I predicted that they might miss the arguments—a strategic move aimed at provoking them to prove me wrong.

In this session the most striking family attachment pattern was of Ann capturing her father and actively excluding all others, including her mother and sister. Her mother allowed this to happen.

Initiating New Patterns of Attachment

At the beginning of the second session I asked what had been happening, and the family reported that Ann had been sleeping much better. When asked how they had succeeded, Bruce reported that they had stopped arguing. Jokingly, he added, "And we missed it!" Later in the second session Margaret said that she had been thinking about how Ann had been clinging to her husband. She suggested that if her husband were to spend more time with the baby, then she would have some space to look after Ann. I welcomed this initiative designed to change the attachment pattern. Bruce picked up the baby. Instantly Ann started to complain and had a tantrum lying on the floor screaming. I suggested that her mother comfort her. She said, "Ann, give me a cuddle." Father said, "Go on! Give Mum a cuddle." I suggested that Margaret give Ann a cuddle. She went toward Ann reluctantly, saying she had tried it before but it had not worked. I persisted and eventually Margaret came over and crouched down beside Ann. Bruce stood up, moving away carrying Susan. At first Ann continued crying; then she settled for a few seconds but started up again, at which point Margaret started to rub Ann's back overvigorously. I encouraged Margaret to leave her hand gently on Ann's back. To everyone's surprise Ann stopped crying; I pointed out that she had succeeded. Bruce pointed out that Ann in fact always wanted her mother when she was really upset. A first step had been achieved and affirmed.[2]

Correcting Role Reversal

I had noticed that both parents were treating Ann as a little adult: Ann was asked to cuddle mother, not the other way around. Every angry gesture that Ann made was taken as a major reprimand, not seen as merely a fractious toddler having a tantrum. I said that I thought we needed to do some work on why Margaret felt so rejected. One image that the parents appeared to have of Ann was of a powerful, controlling, tyrannical person who could reject them. Both parents, for

[2]This part of the session has been analyzed in greater detail elsewhere (Byng-Hall & Stevenson-Hinde, 1991). Ann's behavior was considered to be typical of insecure/ambivalent attachment.

instance, regularly asked Ann if she loved them. In this way parent–child roles were reversed—at least sometimes. But where did this shared image come from? Often the parentified child is scripted to represent individuals from previous generations. For the child to become type-cast, the roles scripted from each side of the family often have some similar characteristics.

In the third session I commented that Margaret talked about her own mother in exactly the same language as she described Ann—"shouting, throwing things, saying ridiculous things." She reflected on the fact that she did indeed see Ann as being like her mother, whom she described as also being a dominant personality. This created a focus for work, which was to relabel Ann as a frightened, vulnerable, little girl who tries to be big and to control relationships in order to make herself feel more secure. I started by illustrating how they unwittingly supported Ann's controlling role. In one session Bruce picked Ann up and put her on top of a high cupboard so that she was sitting way up above the adults. She then proceeded to shout out orders to her father below. I pointed out that playing at being in charge of parents was fine, so long as it was only pretend. What made children anxious was, I suggested, if they felt they actually had to look after their parents. In this way I managed to avoid criticizing the father, but was able to point out one of the real dangers of parent-ification.

Transgenerational Patterns (see Figure 7.1)

When things were less tense, I explored the history further. Margaret was an only child. She had been 2 years old when her parents split up. Margaret's mother, Isabel, had gone back to her parents, taking Margaret with her. Isabel had been so depressed and angry that she had to be looked after by her parents. Margaret then, as a child, had been brought up to see her own mother as being in need of help: inclined to go into fits of rage if she did not get what she wanted. Margaret had tried, fearfully, to take care of her own mother. It was clearer now where the image of Ann as a demanding tyrant came from. It also helped to explain why, when Ann was 2, Margaret was so anxious about the stability of her own marriage.

Bruce's parents had separated when he was 10. His mother had suddenly left one day with another man. So the trigger for Bruce's uncomfortable memories now were his wife's threats to leave. After the separation Bruce had stayed with his father, and had been moth-ered instead by a sister who was 10 years older than he was. Bruce holding on to Ann in a rather competitive way in the face of his wife's

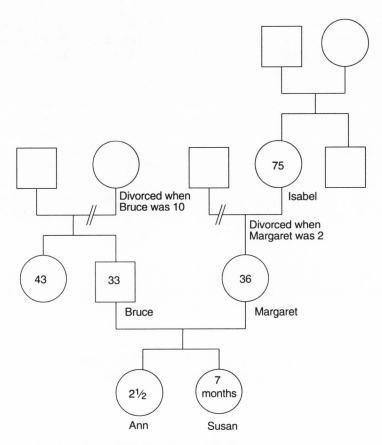

FIGURE 7.1. Young family genogram.

threat to leave now made sense. In his family tradition, fathers and children stay together following separations. From another angle it also became clear why Bruce now asked for care from his eldest daughter. Here then was an overlap between each parent's experience that helped to explain why Ann was scripted into the role of the parentified child, to represent both her maternal grandmother and her paternal aunt.

I invited Margaret's mother, Isabel, on two occasions to join the family sessions. She was still somewhat formidable at the age of 75. We talked about how Ann reminded Margaret of Isabel when she got angry, and how Margaret could, at times, be frightened of Ann as a result. Putting the reality of Margaret's aging mother and her tiny toddler who was sitting on her mother's knee alongside these old memories enabled Margaret to feel less frightened of her mother. It also helped her to see her daughter as only a little girl. Exploring the past also enabled Margaret to perceive her mother's overbearing behavior as stemming from vulnerability and her tragic background. Perhaps even more importantly, Margaret reported afterward that she felt more able to stand up to her mother's behavior. She began to feel less coerced by shouting or demanding out-of-control behavior, whether it came from her mother or her daughter. Margaret's own tendencies to shout and scream did not disappear, but they were less frantic and frightening for Ann. During this work, Bruce's help was enlisted to support his wife's changing relationships and it was also balanced by work on his own transgenerational issues. Bruce was much more wary, however, about exploring issues. He watched, like many wary partners, how things went for his engaged partner. When he saw that there could be something to be gained he became fully involved himself.

Other Caretakers for the Children

For a family to function as a secure base the management of nonfamily child caretakers becomes very important. Transgenerational patterns should also be explored. In Isabel's family, nannies were always asked to take the children the moment there was any upset, or when the parents wanted space for themselves. Margaret said that she refused to have a nanny as she had felt so rejected by this. But when I explored what care arrangements were currently being made for Ann, it transpired that they had a series of unsatisfactory au pair girls, instead, who they used in exactly the same way; that is, whenever mother was upset she handed the children over. She also asked the au pair to look after the children when she was at work. It is an interesting example of a conscious corrective script—"I won't have a nanny"—while unknowingly operating a replicative script by using an au pair as if she were a nanny. After reviewing this, Margaret and Bruce decided to employ a properly trained middle-aged nanny. This worked much better and Ann settled down. However, when the nanny left, mother decided that she would prefer to look after the children herself. This had followed a series of occasions when Margaret suddenly—and distressingly—realized that her own rejecting behavior was very similar to that of her mother's.

Resolving Distance Conflicts

Much of the latter part of therapy, which spread over 18 months, was spent on the marriage–distance conflict (Byng-Hall, 1985a) and how to remove Ann from her role as a distance regulator (Byng-Hall, 1980).

The marriage was characterized by a too close/too far conflict in which both partners felt at times that it was too close and intrusive, and so Ann's capturing of her father, with which both parents colluded, created some space between the couple. At other times their relationship felt too precarious and distant; then Ann's problematic behavior brought them together in nonintimate coparenting roles. In this way Ann had been stabilizing a potentially unstable relationship. As a therapist I took on some of the distance regulator role by bringing them together in a safe way, which released Ann somewhat from having to do that. Work on mobilizing each partner's concern for the other's distress and vulnerability, as well as building respect for each other's autonomy, helped to establish a more secure mutual attachment relationship.

Play as a Sign of Security

Toward the end of therapy, Ann started to play imaginatively on her own; in other words, she was sufficiently secure to explore. This is one of the surest signs that the parents' conflicts were being contained and were not involving the children. On one occasion Ann passed a tray, on which some dolls were arranged in a circle, to her father. Bruce moved the tray so that Margaret could also see it. They then both enjoyed watching the play unfold. This interaction greatly contrasted with any interactions that took place at the start of therapy, in which all play had been between father and Ann, actively excluding mother. The content of the doll's play included a little girl sitting on her father's knee who then moved to her mother's knee, and then went off to school. This led to an exploration within the therapy of how relationships were changing and developing. By now Ann was much better except for occasional intermittent bouts of stubborn, angry behavior. These episodes, however, were perceived by her parents as Ann behaving as a difficult little girl—not as a tyrant.

Termination: Looking to the Future

At the point of termination I am usually preoccupied with helping families to establish contexts in which their problem solving can continue. I discuss this openly with them and ask them to think about how they will allow time for discussions in the future. I ask them to practice this, giving them an opportunity to establish a workable negotiating format in the session, where they are in a better position to iron out any difficulties.

I also ask a lot of questions about the future, especially about how they are going to deal with anticipated difficulties. For instance, I asked Bruce if he might get caught up in anxiety about his marriage when Ann reaches the age of 10, which was the age when his parents separated. I also discuss how families will deal with the predictable bad patches in the future when they feel that everything has gone back to square one. I asked the Youngs how they could keep in mind the knowledge that the improvements had happened and will return again. I also discussed how they might use me. I state that I am like a family doctor—I am available when there are problems. I see it as a strength if a family comes to me as soon as a problem arises. Clearly this metaphor is suitable for a doctor working in the British National Health Service. It might not be so appropriate for others. Attachment theory is relevant after therapy has terminated because it suggests that the knowledge of my availability would make the family feel more secure and hence less likely to need to come to see me or to use me unnecessarily. This is indeed my experience. I do have a number of rereferrals, but never when it is unnecessary, and the rereferrals are usually highly productive within a few sessions.

SUPERVISION GROUP AS A SECURE BASE

The supervision group can provide a secure base in a way similar to the family. Many of the same principles apply. The aim of the supervision is for each of the supervisees to explore family therapy techniques and to improvise his or her own variations. The group has to be experienced as secure enough to enable each member to explore their own issues with the knowledge that any difficulties will be heard and responded to. Likewise, the supervisor, also under pressure, has to feel secure enough to improvise some new ways of supervising. This innovative ethos is important if the students are to adopt a learning mode. The supervisor needs the group to be sensitive to his or her stresses; I may share some of these with the students, but not in a way that demands care from them, or prevents them from putting pressure on me. Sharing the human experience makes the whole group much warmer, but sharing the dilemmas of supervising with the group enables the students to learn about supervision, as well. The supervisor needs support from other senior colleagues. The supervisor group, the training in which the group is embedded, and the agency from which the student comes must collaborate sufficiently to ensure that the students' needs are cared for. Any unresolved conflict between those in authority can jeopardize the sense of security felt by the trainee.

I will illustrate some of these principles from the Advanced Family Therapy MSc course at the Tavistock Clinic, which has evolved since its inception in 1974. The group runs for 2 years; supervision is "live" with the supervisor behind the a one-way mirror observing the therapy done by one trainee, while the other members of the group are also observing. Each group session lasts for 4 hours, and two families are seen during that time. Since I improvise variations in the way I supervise each year, I will refer to those practices that I found most useful.

Engagement with the Group

Live supervision can, especially in anticipation, be highly anxiety provoking. I start with two sessions in which the students introduce themselves, first by presenting their professional backgrounds, and second by drawing a genogram in which the aim is to explore the supervisee's caring script—that is, the script that brought them into the caring profession, and in particular into family therapy. We also explore the cases that each supervisee finds most difficult to handle. McGoldrick (1982) refers to these situations, which overlap with difficult aspects of the trainee's own family script, as the trainee's "trigger" family. An attempt is made to select such a family for the trainee to see, recognizing that the trainee will have inside knowledge of the situation but will also be prone to be recruited into the family's script. But as McGoldrick pointed out, this is to the advantage of the family as well as the student. The family gains from the student's inside knowledge, which is complemented by the supervisor's skill; at the same time the supervisee learns ways of dealing with those situations that are most likely to trigger him or her into unfruitful and painful interactions.

Communication between Supervisor and Supervisee

Live supervision closes the gap between the supervisor and the trainee, both in time and space (Byng-Hall et al., 1982). This maximizes the potential availability of the supervisor during the time of most stress. The trainee can come back behind the screen to be with his or her "secure base" for a consultation. The student can choose his or her own time to come out, or the supervisor can suggest a consultation, often saying, "Come out when you are ready." This flexibility is reminiscent of a secure attachment in which there is freedom to go back and forth when either feels it is appropriate. Occasionally I go into the room to be with the trainee, but I have doing this less frequently because I have found it to undermine the trainee's authority with the family. Also, I have discovered that the use of a radio earphone to

make suggestions from behind the one-way mirror to the trainee conducting the therapy is a better way of taking him or her through very
difficult patches of therapy (Byng-Hall, 1982c).

The idea of the earphone is often frightening for the trainees who
feel it will become intrusive and controlling. They are often surprised to
find that, although it has its problems, it often makes them feel more
secure (see Loewenstein, Reder, & Clark, 1982, for a discussion of the
difficulties and advantages by three of my past supervisees). I find the
earphone preferable to using the telephone. It brings the supervisor's
skill"into the room" but in a way that does not come in between therapist
and family. The earphone does not interrupt the process, and the interventions are experienced as belonging to the supervisee. The trainee
discovers that saying things that he or she may not have said otherwise, or
thought of saying, has surprisingly helpful effects on the family. The
attachment of the family to the therapist is thus strengthened.The therapist
can also say that he or she is receiving a message so that the family has to
pause in what they are doing. Thus, one of the advantages of the telephone—that of breaking up a flow of destructive interaction—can also
be gained from the earphone.

The style of supervision should be congruent with what the
trainee is being asked to do. Structural therapy needs to be supervised
in a clear and authoritative way—for example, when adult authority
is being tested by a child, the supervisor might say, "Ask the parents
to get him to sit down." The trainee is then more likely to use a
similar authoritative style, which will enhance the supervisee's authority, and the parents can use it as a model when they start to take
charge. An exploratory phase, on the other hand, can be fostered
better by the supervisor inquiring over the earphone, "Do you think
father could be . . . ?"

I often do not use the phone much during the first half of the first
session with experienced trainees so that I can observe their normal style.
I explain this to the student beforehand. I try to involve trainees in the
decision about how much to use the earphone. Often they ask for a
greater input when employing a technique with which they are not familiar. At times of minimal use, however, it can still be useful to feed
back positive affirming comments such as "That's great!" or "Good, stay
with that." A supportive presence is maintained. The amount of use of
the earphone diminishes over the life of the 2-year group, until it is
hardly in use—or is removed entirely—by the end of the group.

The main risk of the use of the earphone is the supervisor talking too much. This can lead to "echo therapy" in which the trainee
merely reiterates what is coming through the earphone. Although
this can occasionally be helpful in a crisis, it reduces autonomy and is

reminiscent of enmeshment. It may leave the trainee unable to identify with what he or she has just been echoing. This makes it difficult
for the trainee to integrate it into his or her own therapy "story."

Learning New Skills

The learning process uses patterns similar to those in family therapy,
that is, preview/enactment/review. Preview involves a presession discussion of hypotheses and possible strategies. Ideally the trainee will
have reviewed the videotape of the previous session, and located a
place on the tape that is of particular importance. In this way preview
is based on review. Incidentally, if the equipment is available (a VCR
with two-track sound input: one track coming from the therapy, while
the other comes from a microphone that the supervisor uses), it is
useful to put the supervisor's running comments on videotape. Often
the most telling points made while teaching those behind the screen
are lost to the supervisee unless this is done.

At each consultation, the reunion of the therapist with the group
is important. I usually affirm what he or she has just done and then
ask the therapist how he or she feels. This acknowledges the importance of these feelings and what information they can provide about
family processes, rather than seeing such emotions as anxiety or hope-
lessness as the therapist's problem. It also helps to debrief the therapist,
who can then think more clearly. Although there is a group discussion, I usually decide at the end of the break what to suggest next.
This keeps the authority for decision making clear and reduces the
confusion that follows if the whole group proffers advice. However,
by the end of the break, the decision of what to do in light of the
discussion is made by the therapist. I see supervision as helping the
therapist to learn to work on his or her own, not only as part of a
team. Autonomy is steadily increased and trainees improvise their own
ways of working. As the course is part-time, the students continue to
practice on their own throughout the course. I tell the trainees that
the place that I expect their best therapy will be carried out is in their
own agencies, where they are free to use their own imagination in a
familiar setting with their own client population. I like to hear how
their therapy is progressing; this is reminiscent of a secure child telling a parent about what he or she has just been exploring.

Distance between Supervision Group and the Family

The families are given the choice of meeting the team behind the
screen. The family hopefully comes to perceive the team as a friendly

helpful extension to their own network. The therapist's use of the team can model for the family the value of using other people—a good example of a secure base. Messages from the team after consultations, or given via the earphone, are respectful, and occasionally playful, in order for the message to be less persecutory or authoritarian. The use of the reflecting team, in which the family watches the team discuss the session, makes the team even more familiar and hence less threatening.

Collaboration within the Supervision Group and within the Training

The group reviews what is happening within the group once during the term; any rivalry, or sense of being deskilled, is particularly focused upon. Feedback to the supervisor about his or her input is also sought and given. The supervisees meet every 2 weeks, without the supervisor, to prepare for the supervision later that afternoon. This mutual support has a strong bonding effect. The supervision group becomes experienced as the place to turn to for help at times of any crises in the course, or even those occurring in a member's life outside the training. In short, the group becomes a secure base.

Like the family, however, the "outside" world is also involved, and can help or hinder the sense of security. One very useful involvement is a once-a-term, three-way meeting in which the trainee, the supervisor, and the tutor meet together. This provides a setting in which the supervisor and trainee have the use of someone outside the group to make comments on what might be going on. These meetings are often pivotal in clarifying what is happening in the learning curve, what has been achieved, and what goals to set for the next term's work.

The supervisor also needs support; live supervision is one of the most demanding of all skills. Once a term all the supervisors meet, and at another meeting the whole staff group meet so that notes can be compared as to how a trainee has been performing across the various parts of the course. The trainee group also feeds back to the supervisors how they are experiencing each aspect of the course. To complete the circle, the managers of the trainees' agencies are invited to visit the clinic. Communication is thus kept open between all parts of the course and the extended network. This is essential for maintaining a secure base.

E·I·G·H·T

Myths and Legends about Security

Family mythology (Ferreira, 1963; Byng-Hall, 1973, 1979; Bagarozzi & Anderson, 1989) consists of shared family images of itself, and legends that portray those images, which help give the family its sense of identity. To the family their myths represent the truth. To the observer, however, these beliefs may be perceived as highly colored: like the father who was perceived to be very strong despite his heart failure, or the decorated "war hero" grandfather, who on closer examination never, in fact, saw any action.

Ferreira (1963) considered that all families need some mythology, but too much deadens. To return to the analogy of color: Any one particular color is created by filtering out the remainder of the light spectrum; if this filtering is too extensive, mythology no longer acts as colorful heraldry but as a restrictive set of blinkers. Ferreira suggested that myths provide a blueprint for action, which in my terminology is a family script.

Myths about the present family may consist of attributions of particular roles to certain members of the family—for example, the "crazy one," with all the accompanying expectations. Family stories often back up these ideas. The images then become established because they are not challenged. Sometimes the whole family may be seen in monochrome—for example, rose-tinted for a "happy family." In other families each character is seen in sharp contrast—for example, "the helpful one" and "the irresponsible one."

In summary, a myth is an interesting set of contrasting constructs. Outsiders may consider it to be a distortion and hence might call it a myth; family members see it as their reality. Constructionism has taught us that there are many realities and no absolute truths, so it is unwise to state whose construct is the most valid. However, therapists have

137

some ideas about what is helpful to the family and what is unhelpful. In my experience the most unhelpful aspect is the self-deception involved in some myths, in which the expressed belief is quite different than what appears to happen. An example is the parent rated dismissive (D) on the AAI (see Table 6.1) who may describe his or her parent in one way, say "wonderful," but when asked to illustrate this with an example tells a story of neglect. In other words, there is a discrepancy between semantic and episodic memory. The same set of idealizing blinkers may also be obscuring uncomfortable events in the present. As we have seen, parents who display this self-deception are more likely to have insecure children. Some family myths and legends, on the other hand, are a source of family solidarity, helping to strengthen resolve and providing a motto for family life.

ROLE IMAGES IN FAMILY MYTHS

Three sets of role images can be described in families (Byng-Hall, 1973).

1. *Ideal images.* The behaviors toward which each strives, or pressures other family members to adopt.
2. *Disowned or repudiated images.* Those behaviors and attitudes that are prohibited and disapproved of in others or denied in oneself, even if they can be observed by others.
3. *Consensus role images.* Those role images about which there is unchallenged agreement that each fulfills. Individuals away from the family group may admit to secret reservation about these images; thus, the consensus role images represent a group phenomenon. Attempts at questioning these images are collectively rebutted. The end result is that each individual is reliably supported in his or her own self-image by the family as a whole. This gives the set of role images a stability that may be valuable to both the individual and the group, and is necessary for staying together. The family myth represents the final compromise between each individual's need to have him- or herself seen in a particular light and evidence that that is not the whole story. The bargain is often, "I won't point out your bad points so long as you leave me in peace."

Families differ in the degree to which they tolerate the contradictions between observed behavior and consensus role images. Family shame comes if there is either too great a discrepancy between the consensus role images and the ideal images—the family knows it has fallen short of its ideals—or, even worse, if the consensus is that the image is now near to being what is usually disowned. Few familes can stand that. Someone will have to be blamed—even extruded.

Family myths can be defined as follows:

> The set of "consensus role images" that are accepted by the whole family as representing each member. This gives each member an allotted role in a particular pattern of interaction. The images of interaction can, however, be seen to be either distortions, or only a segment, of observable behaviour. The integrity of the role images is not irrevocably challenged from within the family. (Byng-Hall, 1973, p. 244)

Or, put another way, the family myth is the family's consensus about which home truths cannot be told.

One danger is that a family myth may become a closed belief system, unable to integrate new information. This is particularly likely to happen if the family feels that a challenge to its beliefs threatens its very survival. If the myth becomes closed, family interaction loses some of the advantages of the beneficial stability gained from the myth and can become rigidly unadaptable to changing contexts.

If a family member does challenge the myth in a persistent and effective manner, and the family can no longer just dismiss these home truths as trivial, the challenger is likely to be scapegoated. This is especially likely to happen if the challenge comes from an adolescent. After all, adolescents are often challenging the authenticity of old beliefs.

FAMILY MYTHS AND INFORMATION PROCESSING

Family myths, although endowed with some permanency, are also, potentially at least, open to review. This review may be done in several ways, depending on the family's style of processing information. These styles (described below) can be usefully divided into those characterized by the narrative styles of the various attachment relationships. It is important to remember, however, that there probably is no consistent attachment pattern throughout any one family. There is likely to be a complex mixture of attachment styles, but often with one predominating.

Coherent/Secure Style: Beliefs of Mutual Acceptance

In these families there is a realistic and coherent view of relationships in which both good and bad behavior are expected and accepted. The consensus role images thus cover a wide band of behavior into which ordinary people can fit. The ideals are not set at unobtainable levels, and pressures to reach them are not too intense. Similarly, the shaming and disowning of unacceptable behavior, thoughts, and wishes are not too stringent. As the family scenarios are reviewed, the images that the family has of the roles people play become modified to fit realistic views of what happens. In short, the family myth is demystfied when reviewed and replaced by a mutual acceptance of what members can do, and can be seen to do. The family's legends and stories provide a coherent picture. They are rich and varied, telling of the mixed experiences of life without being judgmental.

Incoherent/Avoidant Style: Shared Denial

In these families there is a high degree of defensive denial of past and present happenings. Role images are split between good and bad, with individuals either being idealized or denigrated. There is a large discrepancy between what an outsider observes and what the family perceives. Review of events is restricted because facing the implications of what family members do to each other is too painful. Typecasting of individuals is common, although it is possible to be knocked off an idealized pedestal and rapidly become denigrated. Parents who are categorized as dismissive (D) on the AAI often give sparse, rather concrete accounts of their past. Family legends are similarly restricted but stark. Family stories and legends are often parables about good and bad, success and disaster. They are simplified, and may sound unreal. Attempts to review the myths are resisted. Challenges, perhaps made by an adolescent who is incensed by the hypocrisy, are likely to lead to disowning the challenger and scapegoating him or her, thus preserving the consensus in the rest of the family. These families are particularly likely to extrude members, and throwing members out may be a feature of their legends.

Incoherent/Ambivalent Style: "Ghosts from the Past"

In these families there is continual reviewing of the "rights" and "wrongs" of the past, both recent and distant. But they are never resolved. Family members are caught up in strong feelings about injustices and imagining how things could and should have been handled. They often feel that they are owed something. But, true to an ambivalent style, there are also feelings of both obligation and gratitude to past figures. Because of this consensus, role images are muddled and deeply colored by past experiences. Roles are often reversed, say, with children taking parental roles vis-à-vis their parents. Children may be perceived as childlike as well as responsible; parents, likewise, may be seen as responsible but demanding and childish at times. These varied images may also reflect glimpses of figures from the past. Consensus role images are also often in flux; thus, they do not provide individuals with a steady view of themselves. Family mythology is often full of rather convoluted stories about the past. Parents categorized as preoccupied/entangled on the AAI give a similar, lengthy, rambling account of their past, with stories rarely coming to a firm conclusion. This does not create clear-cut myths, but presents fleeting images and ghosts from the past flitting across the stage.

A Case Illustration: The Johansen Family

In work with the Johansen family, I challenged three interconnected myths. Family mythology is often like the many layers of an onion.

Sven Johansen was an apparently compliant 54-year-old horticulturist of Norwegian origins. His Scottish wife, Donagh, was 38. She could be formidably forceful when crossed in any way. They had three children—Jean, 12; Edward, 11; and Prue, 6. Edward had been referred for stealing money and then, strangely enough, giving it to medical charities. Donagh became so violently angry with Edward about this that it frightened her.

Sven, who was a keen sportsman, had a coronary thrombosis 3 years before, following a game of squash. The family, in particular the parents, went to great lengths to point out how he was now "fully recovered." This was their first myth.

During the first five sessions, the hostility between mother and son declined. In the sixth session Donagh announced that the doctor had given the go-ahead for Sven to take part in sports. He told me he would be playing squash after leaving the session. I became worried as there had been no fundamental change in this family. The intense underlying anger between the parents had, up to now, been rerouted through Edward. Sven was depressed and I felt that he was potentially suicidal. Edward's stealing had diminished, but problems seemed likely to reappear elsewhere. Would it be a further, perhaps fatal, coronary? This would dramatize Donagh's murderous anger and Sven's suicidal depression; and if it happened after a session I would be to blame.

Between the sessions I rang the family's doctor. It appeared that Sven's coronary had been serious, and he was currently experiencing incipient heart failure. The cardiologist was gloomy, but the doctor felt that it was much better not to turn Sven into a cardiac invalid, and hence he had suggested some exercise which he understood, in current medical practice, was advocated anyway. He had, however, had something like golf in mind, not squash.

In the next session I told the family why I was worried and about my conversation with the doctor. Donagh became increasingly angry with me, saying that her husband had his medical "go-ahead": "A man needs to be able to enjoy himself." Edward, however, pleaded with his father not to play squash. I pointed out that while the parents were apparently not concerned, Edward had to do all the worrying, and that he had repeatedly done so in earlier sessions as well. Donagh denied any worrying by the children. Edward said, "You must be kidding!" which is an interesting confirmation that denial of danger by parents does not increase security in their children. I was incensed by Donagh's blatant denial that the children were worried. I explored the children's ideas about why their father had a heart attack. Both Jean and Edward attributed it to the squash. Jean produced a sensible physiological reason, but Edward's first idea had been that the squash ball had hit him on the heart. No wonder Edward felt he had to channel all violence toward his mother and not physically toward his father. I suggested that Edward had been wanting to look after his father by getting money for medical charities including one for heart transplants. Now, although in full battle with the me, Donagh conceded that Edward was now worried—"But it was only because you put these fantasies into their heads." I was now not only anxious but angry as well.

This episode illustrates beautifully the point that anyone, including the therapist, who challenges a current family myth is liable to become scapegoated. Skynner (1979) discusses the role of family therapist as the scapegoat. Here it will be noted that I had completely taken over Edward's role, doing the challenging, worrying about father, acting as lightning conductor to mother's fury, and expressing Sven's anger as well. Father was once again protected from the fury and anxiety which it was feared might kill him. The doctor had also been drawn into colluding with the myth of recovery and admitted to feeling that he had colluded with the family's wish to believe it.

Once the therapist is recruited into the family script, he or she has to emerge again to be of help to the family. Immediately after the session, I role-played the mother, using the group that was observing the session to simulate the family. I found that I ("she") became furious with the "therapist" for failing to realize how much "she" had protected the children and her husband from worrying about the coronary by saying it was better. The "therapist" appeared to me, in the mirror of the role-play, to be intent on tearing this vital work to pieces. After the role-play, I no longer felt angry with Donagh.

In the next session I started by reporting to the family that the group had helped me to see that I had not properly recognized the good work that Donagh had done in protecting her children from worry, although I pointed out, "As we all know, you cannot stop them from worrying." She softened quite remarkably and said it was her maternal instinct. I said that I would like to know where this maternal instinct came from.

The family tree (Figure 8.1) on mother's side of the family revealed some remarkable similarities between the generations. Donagh's father had cardiovascular trouble which had recently led to some heart failure and a mild stroke. Donagh's mother had not even noticed his swollen ankles before the family doctor discovered them. After leaving the hospital, she had refused to tell her husband that he had a

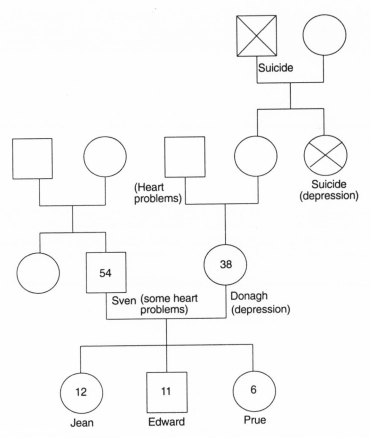

FIGURE 8.1. Johansen family genogram.

stroke and then forced him out to walk the dog. The therapist asked Sven what he thought his father-in-law felt about that. He laughed and said, "Depressed, I should think." This started the challenge of the second myth which was that "if you accept illness you will sink into despair." Sven had acknowledged that the pressure to deny illness could equally lead to depression. The family began to draw parallels with the present. The children thought that their grandfather would "give up" if he admitted that he was ill. I asked about Sven's response to illness and found that he had given up sports for a year following his coronary: Playing squash again was seen as a way of keeping him on his feet. Donagh, like her mother, denied evidence of illness and kept her husband active.

Tracing the genogram back several generations, I found two suicides on maternal grandmother's side. I pursued the theme of depression and suicide down the generations again and discovered that Donagh's mother had severe depressions and that she would tend to be very "down" if her husband was "down." Bringing this theme into the present, I asked Donagh if she ever became depressed. She glanced at her husband and agreed that she did. I asked the children if they knew about the depression. They nodded and said that their father usually warned them. Donagh was very surprised about this. The myth of a mother "always fighting on" could finally be dropped after the myth of her own mother as "the forceful fighter," had been transformed into "someone who is forceful but vulnerable."

Following this session there was a radical change. Each parent took much more responsibility for his or her own difficulties: mother for her moods and father for discussing sensible exercise arrangements with his cardiologist. The depression was accepted by Donagh, and her "fighting" came to be seen as her way of trying to avoid suicidal depression. Each spouse recognized that accepting an "illnesses" had been thought likely to precipitate a catastrophic depression.

The school reported a remarkable improvement in both of the older children's work. They no longer had to look after their parents' health in the face of parental denial. Therapy stopped after 12 sessions.

FAMILY STORIES AND LEGENDS

To support the family's consensus images, stories are told to illustrate how the forebears, and the family members themselves, behaved in a way which led to the present state of affairs. Thus, past and present mythology is interwoven. The family's current view of itself may change, and the past will also have to be seen in a new light. The family stories will then be given a new twist.

Stories can take many forms. Some, although perhaps based on an actual event, are openly acknowledged to be richly enhanced. Others might be presented as true. Family stories (Byng-Hall, 1979) include:

1. *Family yarns or tales.* These are told for fun, often by a particular family member, say, the grandfather. Everyone can chuckle at each new elaboration or exploit. These yarns give permission to fantasize, to play with a variety of potential images. Heroes are often preposterously larger than life and, as a result, are always just about to step on a banana peel—which may indeed provide the punch line to the stories. They effectively provide a balance between the stereotyped hero and his inevitable scapegoat counterpart.

2. *Fables or cover stories.* Occasionally whole episodes are fabricated and presented as truth. This may be done quite consciously, say, to explain away a father's absence in prison. A psychotic or demented member of the family may, however, also start up a story which joins the mythology.

3. *Family secrets.* One way of ensuring that a story is told and retold is to make it a secret. It is then told in private. Everyone passes it on to another family member while swearing him or her to secrecy. What cannot be acknowledged is the break of trust in passing it on. The secret then becomes the fact that it is no longer a secret. The function of these forms of secret is often to bind the teller and the listener into a hidden coalition. Pincus and Dare (1978) describe how secrets can be based on either pure fantasy or reality. However, even "real" secrets, because they cannot be openly explored, frequently become bathed in fantasy, or become redramatized unwittingly.

4. *Recalled events.* Some events are recounted, often in response to an inquiry, in a way that shows there is a real struggle for accuracy. Supporting evidence is sought: Other people are asked for recollections; photos and old letters are produced. This represents the family's attempt to discover what historians call historical actuality. Although the final account will inevitably still be colored, the aim is to inform, not to indoctrinate. These accounts should not be included in family mythology. They provide the building blocks of a healthy family history. Fables, lies, tales, yarns, legends, and secrets provide the story components of mythology.

5. *Family legends.* Legends are colored and often colorful stories that are told and retold down through the generations (Byng-Hall, 1982a, 1988). All families allow many fascinating episodes to fade

into the past unless someone takes the trouble to go and ask the aging members of the family before they die. Why, in contrast, is great care taken to make sure that certain stories are told to the next generation? My hypothesis is that these stories are often moral tales that convey the rules and obligations of family life. Legends are molded by the narrator and are "here and now," not "past," phenomena. Each telling produces a version that is edited to fit current distortions in family myths and family rules. Thus, while the family structure remains unchanged, the family stories and legends remain unchanged, as well. They can help to prevent changes because they can have a homeostatic function. Being shared, there is some constraint on alterations and revisions. Neither teller nor listener is usually aware, however, when reediting does takes place, in line with a shift in family beliefs. Each person imagines that the past, as now depicted, led up to the present family predicaments—a far cry from the idea that the past has just been altered by the present. Thus, legends can also consolidate and maintain change, reinforcing the new "reality."

A Case Illustration: The Brown Family

In the Brown family, as will become clear, violence was considered to be the problem. The mother, a physiotherapist, referred her family over the telephone because her two teenage sons were fighting, but added that she was worried about telling her epileptic husband about making the appointment. He would, she said, be absolutely furious. She was worried about his violence. The father, an architect, told this story in one of the sessions, following a discussion about his fury with his sons for misbehaving: "My father threw his father out when he was only 10. My alcoholic grandfather was drunk one day when he came home and started beating up my grandmother who was blind. My father got hold of a piece of wood, hit him, and threw him out of the house."

The therapist asked whether the rest of the family knew this story. They all contributed additional snippets of information showing that this was a well-worn legend. "He never came back, leaving his blind wife to look after grandfather and his five blind brothers and sisters!" (There was a form of congenital blindness in the family.) "The only one who could see properly was grandpa who was the youngest." The imagery of legend is often vivid. In this case it was epic in quality. There was a hero, a heroine, a villain, and victims. The villain not only assaulted a blind wife but also deserted his pathetic, almost totally blind, family.

Legends as Condensed History

Legends are often condensed history. What takes a minute or two to tell often depicts something that unfolded over several years. The legend encapsulates a scenario, which then stands as a graphic analogy for the whole process. In the Brown family, it was, of course, not one but many episodes which would have led to the breakup of the grandparents' marriage. The blame implied in the legend was isomorphic with the current view that the father in this generation was also responsible for the problems. It also pointed to who should be the rescuer, with implications for the boys in the current generation. They would be expected to rescue their mother if their father became violent.

REEDITING FAMILY MYTHOLOGY

The Illusion of Alternatives

It seems that one of the reasons that certain legends are told and retold is that there is an unresolved theme in the family involving an illusion of alternatives (Watzlawick, 1978). This implies that one of two particular choices has to be taken—for example, either you fight your father and get rid of him, or you let your father beat up your mother. Either way the son is wrong. The theme also remains unresolved because the way the problem is framed implies that it is only the son(s) who can provide the answer. The chooser has to select one of the alternatives. This is the illusion. A third alternative would be for the son not to get involved in parental battles at all, leaving them to resolve their own difficulties. The real alternative is either to get involved or not to get involved. By posing the question as, "In what way are you going to be involved?" the real choice is obscured. Watzlawick (1978) illustrates the illusion of alternatives with the Nazi slogan, "National Socialism or Bolshevik Chaos?" The real choice was, of course, between dictatorship and democracy.

The Brown family's legend illustrating the illusion of alternatives was then told to maintain the family structure—for example, keeping sons triangled in, reminiscent of the binding dimension of double bind. The function is to avoid even more feared situations: The parents might be left on their own together, or they might separate. When this pseudodilemma is resolved by discovering other options (e.g., marital rows can be survived and sons can leave home), the stories pertaining to the dilemma may die out, unless that is, they are so entertaining that they survive for "after dinner" purposes.

Editing the Past to Fit the Present

Editing the past to fit the present is, of course, a well-known phenomenon. Linnemann (1966) describes the editing of Christ's sayings by the gospel writers so that the parables carried significance for the young church at that time. He describes a parable as a "language event." At each telling the context is different. Christ preaching in his lifetime to his uninitiated followers was done in a very different context from that of the gospel writers who believed him to be the Messiah. Preaching is, in Linnemann's words, "updating or providing new exposition to each generation." The moral to be drawn in each context, as with family legends, is somewhat different. In a secular context, history has also often changed to fit the present, or rather to support change in attitudes in the present. Mrs. Thatcher called on British Schools to teach a more patriotic version of British history, to reflect her role as "patriotic" leader. One is also mindful of how Hitler and Stalin rewrote the past histories of their countries, in addition to actively changing the course of history.

Legends in Family Therapy

Family stories told in therapy are often linked symbolically with the current dilemmas in therapy. These stories provide quick access to how the family sees the current situation, and often reveal unconscious aspects of perceptions.

In the Brown family with the epileptic father, following an exploration of their profound fears about epilepsy, I asked for the first stories that came into their heads. Father's story was as follows: "It is curious but this keeps popping into my mind. . . . My father telling me about how he used to stand on the bank of a river and dive right under the barges, and then coming up again on the other side."

The family then produced a rich network of interlocking stories about danger at sea, near drownings, and saving others who were drowning. It was then possible to link these with the many aspects of the epilepsy experience; the father going under while everyone else is anxious about whether he will "come up" again. Like all fantasy material, it is so rich that it is necessary to focus on, and to select the relevant stories. Like metaphor, the story that resonates best with the therapist's own imagination provides the most potent communication. The imagery that evolved out of the above stories included dying, but also violence, madness, and loss of control—images often associated with epilepsy. The Browns were able to share with me how frightening the father's grand mal seizures were now that the imagery was available to describe them.

In long-term therapy, the genogram (McGoldrick & Gerson, 1985) provides a useful format for exploring legends.The main modification of the technique to elicit legends is not to ask what an ancestor was like, but to ask for a story about him, or better still a story to show how the "ancestors" (e.g., grandparents) got along together. The story is then written down on the genogram (the paper needs to be large enough) and any subsequent editing can be noted.The other advantage of constructing a genogram this way is that the stories are interactional, which is congruent with working with the family's interaction. Direct comparison can then be drawn between what happened then and what is happening in the session, or in current family life.

In the Brown family, as the family system stabilized, the legend of the drunken great-grandfather thrown out by his 10-year-old son was revisited several times.The family decided that he could, after all, have chosen to come home some time later, or perhaps his wife did not want him. It emerged that the blindness was of late onset and so only the great-grandmother would have been affected, not her children.

Mr. Brown came to one session complaining bitterly about his son's rudeness to him. I asked the family to recall the legend. I suggested that perhaps it was becoming all too familiar for them now, which could be frightening. I asked them to use their imaginations and put themselves inside that legend, as if it were happening now. They could hardly bear to think about it, but by keeping them to the task, they eventually brought themselves to imagine the scenario.

Not only did the scenario seem unreal but it was in such contrast to the family as they sat in the therapy room that it did not seem to haunt them any longer.The father then discussed with Brian whether he felt he had to intervene in order to prevent him from beating up his mother. The reality of the present family interaction was compared and contrasted with that of the legend. I pointed out how in the current family they had corrected the legend so that now the father was seen as the strong one who could control his sons if necessary and could not be thrown out.The fighting was largely restricted to between the brothers, a much more appropriate place than between father and son. I also suggested that they felt that they had to dramatize the conflict between the boys, perhaps unnecessarily, because they were haunted by the father–son violence in the legend. Father's epilepsy also made potential violence feel more threatening than it might have been otherwise. Fact and fantasy, past and present, were disentangled in this way.

A THERAPIST'S LEGENDS

Family legends provide a useful source of data about a therapist's own family. I have described one of my family legends (Byng-Hall, 1982a, 1988) which revealed the complex attitudes of my family toward bravery and cowardice. For this book I decided to select some stories about insecurity and security, or about going out to explore and what happens if you do. I made this an experiment to see if it was feasible to build a picture of the security or insecurity of the family base one generation back. To see whether it was possible to make transgenerational connections, I set myself the task of asking what is replicated, what is corrected, and what compromises are made? What lessons can I learn about telling stories to the next generation? I leave it to the reader to judge whether or not it would be a useful exercise for themselves, or for students.

I was brought up in Kenya on a large ranch full of wildlife. Not surprisingly many of the family stories were about animals; leopards were featured in many of the stories that involved danger.

Legends about Insecure Situations

The Leopard Legends

My father told a story about when he was a young man living alone in a forest in Kenya. One night he woke to see a leopard, silhouetted against the night sky, crouching on the windowsill. It then jumped down into the room and, quick as a flash, scooped the dog from under the bed and departed with the howling dog between its teeth. Not surprisingly, I grew up terrified of wild animals coming through the window at night. Leopards were an ever-present potential danger. Because of their camouflage, one could pass within a few feet of a leopard in the bush near the house and never see it. The fact that leopards do not usually attack humans but are killed relentlessly by man made no difference to my childhood fear of them.

One of my mother's favorite stories about me was also about leopards. When I was about 5 years old and my sister 7 years old, a leopard had killed some calves in a thicket a short distance from the house. The next day the family was driving near this thicket when my parents, whose hobby was ornithology, spotted an unusual bird and both got out with binoculars to look for it. They disappeared into the thicket. My mother told the following story: "After we had been gone a while, John got out of the car, found a stick and a stone, and came looking for us to rescue us from the leopard. Caroline, in the meantime, sensibly wound up the windows, curled up on the backseat, and read a book." This story was told to celebrate my bravery.

Originally I thought that it was only another cowardice–bravery story, which indeed it was. I then realized it was about gender, also. The male role is to go out and defend; the female role is to stay indoors. This is certainly another aspect; however, it struck me that it was, above all, an attachment story. Here was a little boy frightened by the situation, desperately searching for his parents, and arming himself with sticks and stones to protect himself on the way. The reframing of these signs of fear to imply courage was convenient for my parents because they had chosen to live in a very isolated and dangerous place by English standards. Many years later they were very surprised when I told them that I spent most of my childhood frightened and lying awake at night watching the open window.

The next story comes from a year or two later. My father had shot a leopard which had been killing sheep. We had an English woman, a friend of my mother's, staying with us. She was rather frightened of Africa. She was sleeping in the "guest house," located 20 yards away from the main house. My sister and I arranged this dead leopard so that it looked as if it was crouching and facing the woman's bedroom door; she would be terrified when she came out in the morning. Her actual response was not included in the story, although the woman may well not have been fooled at all. This story, I think, was trying to convey how our family was not frightened; only those silly people from England who would be scared.

My mother, who had been brought up in London, admitted after my father died that she had always been frightened while living on the farm. What better way did we have of perceiving her as the fearless local, in contrast to this frightened English woman? Incidentally, my mother's fear was probably pervasive, because, in contrast, the African children appeared to be entirely natural and relaxed with the wild animals, as were their parents. To feel secure both she and we, as children, needed a myth that she was not frightened. Presumably this image was also important for my father, as he often left my mother on her own while he went around the farm.

Reediting the Leopard Legend

My widowed mother, as she became very old, started to tell the story of the "rescue from the leopard" more frequently, often in front of my sister who felt aggrieved because she saw it as an insult to her. I told my sister that I had always taken the story to mean that she had been the sensible one who stayed in the car, but, not surprisingly, this did not alleviate her sense of being insulted by my mother. I then decided to reedit the legend on a trip back to the farm almost 45 years after the event. To my surprise and delight the setting had hardly changed. I took a video of the thicket standing near our old house, and talked about my version of the legend as being about a frightened little boy, knowing that this commentary on the video would be heard by both my mother and my sister when I showed it to them later.

I then surprised myself by realizing that I had swung around and filmed the place where the dead leopard had been placed to scare our visitor, and I told that story as well. It was the first time I had connected the two stories in my mind.

When my mother saw the tape she made no comment, but when she and my sister talked about it later my mother apologized for making my sister feel that she was being criticized, and she was very surprised that my sister had taken it that way. This led to a discussion about how worrying it had actually been for my parents bringing up two young children on the farm, and how they tried to save us from being frightened by playing the danger down and being straightforward, when, in reality, they were frightened themselves. This helped to correct our image of our parents being insensitive to our fear. It is interesting that one of the effects of my parents pretending not to be anxious, and modeling "bravery" instead, was that I felt that they were never aware of real dangers. As a result, I steadily took on the role of sentinel—the one who kept watch for the family. This became an increasing preoccupation for me when I was an adolescent, and the situation became genuinely dangerous politically. This is a good example of being recruited into a role in the family script by perceiving an apparently vacant but necessary role. One explanation for the discrepancy between my sister's sense of being criticized and my mother's lack of awareness of this was that it was entirely acceptable in Kenya in the 1940s that a female should stay inside, not venturing out, while the males were defending. This was no longer so one generation later in England.

Perhaps my widowed mother told the "John to the rescue" story more often, not only because she was reaching the age of repeating stories, but also because she was now frightened and living on her own in the English countryside. The attachment relationship was now reversed. She now actually wanted me to rescue her.

Epilogue

When I showed this piece to my sister, she said she could not, as hard as she tried, feel anything other than criticism of her in the leopard story. My mother never told it to her as "Caroline in the meantime *sensibly* wound up the windows." She left out the term "sensibly." Eventually she recalled my parents being angry with her for not looking after me and not stopping me from getting out of the car.

Either my mother told the story with a different "message" to each of us or I edited in the word "sensibly" to screen out the criticism. Either way the whole scenario now makes much more sense. It had to do with attachment and protection of a child, and my parents knew it. But why create the illusion that I was the protector? Was the idea of being a sentinel also an illusion? Now, my story about the legend is that I was being scripted to be the strong, brave, unanxious male who would take over the protective role when an adult. I was expected to run the farm eventually. The sentinel role was a partial fulfillment.

Legends about Security

To create an effect, I will sometimes say to friends that I was brought up by a collie sheepdog. I will then say that this was not a comment on my parents but rather a fond memory of a collie, Meg, who used to protect us when my sister and I were toddlers. The house had no fences around it and Meg used to round us up like sheep if we wandered off too far; she was always just a few feet away, watching us intently. Meg was a kind of attachment figure for us and helped us to feel safe. My sister and I would play happily for hours out in the garden without any need to go in to make contact with our mother. Meg provided one aspect of the secure family base. A secure family base can also include siblings and pets!

The Message Is in the Telling: Leaving-Home Stories

I find myself telling leaving-home stories. Here is an example.

When my father was 15, his father sent a telegram to his school in England from Northern Nigeria. The telegram said "HAVE BEEN SHOT IN ARM BY POISONED ARROW STOP WILL DIE STOP GO TO UNCLE THEO IN NEW ZEALAND STOP." My father was delighted to leave school rather than be bored while waiting to go to Oxford. His uncle had bought a small island off the coast of New Zealand in order to sell plots of land to would-be ex-Army settlers. These buyers never materialized and his uncle, getting bored, returned to the mainland, leaving my father living alone on the island with some cattle and a herd of wild horses. He was now 16 and his father had recovered, but he stayed on the island rather than return to England. Every month at the neap tides, he could ride his horse over to the mainland at low tide and replenish his supplies. After about a year there were such severe storms that he could not ride across. He and people from the neighboring island were beginning to become hungry. Eventually my father was able to get across to their island and from there to the mainland. My father went to give notice to his uncle and swore he would never go on an island again. However, when he eventually got back to England and was met by his father in strike-bound, rain-swept Southampton, he said he wanted to leave England. When asked where he wanted to go, he said Kenya because he had a friend there. He did not want to go to Oxford.

This story conveys admiration for being an explorer and pioneer, as opposed to being a stay-at-home academic, but it also warns against dangerous loneliness in which one's life is at risk (father and son) and, interestingly, about sons being given too much responsibility, which turned out to be dangerous. It also conveys complex messages about distance. First, "use the globe to get away from home." (My father's relatives were scattered all over the world.) But "stay in contact." My father's choice of Kenya was interesting as he went to live on the same continent as his father, but 2,000 miles away.

My mother lived at home with her family in London until, in her late 20s, she visited Kenya and met my father. One of her leaving-home stories was about going to stay with some friends when she got there. "We arrived at Ulu Station where I was met with a horse. We rode through the most beautiful rolling country, full of game, and arrived at the house where we were given such a warm welcome." This was then followed by stories to illustrate the hospitality and kindness of this family. My mother had an overclose relationship with her parents from whom she tried to escape. The message was how wonderful it was to be free and far away from home—so long as it was going to the bosom of a welcoming family.

The compromise solution my parents made with their overlapping distance conflicts was to live abroad in an isolated farmstead, but, as a result, in a very close-knit family group.

My Own Story

This has to be told here and now as I write it, as I am not repeating stories told to me.

When I left home in 1956, aged 18, I set off to Cambridge to read agriculture, with the avowed aim of returning to the farm to take it over when my father retired. Secretly, however, I wanted to research animal feeding. On the boat going to England, I contracted polio with paralysis of the trunk and legs, and was taken off the ship at Brindisi in southern Italy. Luckily I was with a friend, but in the hospital I waited for my parents to come. They never did. After a month my friend arranged for me to be flown to London. It was not until many years later that I plucked up the courage to ask my parents why they never came to Brindisi. They told me that they had immediately booked a flight when they heard I was ill, but then my father developed a very high temperature He was assumed to have polio as well, but luckily developed no paralysis. Then they had the message from Italy that I had polyneuritis (wrong diagnosis), which has a more benign prognosis, so my mother stayed to look after my father, concentrating her efforts on getting my flight arranged to London. They had not told me before because they said it would only have added to my worries. At last I could feel sorry for my mother's acute and horrifying dilemma over which member of her family to be with. However, I certainly learned that not telling people about painful situations, far from protecting them, exposes them to terrible misunderstanding and resentments.

During the 9 months in hospital in England, I became fascinated by the dynamics of a long-stay ward, and especially by the way people responded to their own illnesses. This was the era marked by terrible cases of people with total paralysis being kept alive on life-support machines.

When it became clear that agriculture was not a feasible career, I decided to be a doctor instead. To my surprise, my father told me, for the first time, that if he had taken up his scholarship to Oxford he had wanted to study medicine.

When I eventually went to Cambridge to study medicine and then on to London (to live with 10 million other people, as opposed to being on an isolated farm), I remember feeling a great sense of relief. This was partly due to the ending of a continuous sense of insecurity and pervading fear in the dangerous situation that prevailed in Kenya in the 1950s. There was another component, however: a feeling of excitement about doing the right thing.

It seemed I was enacting a corrective script by going "home" (which is what my parents called it) to England, as opposed to exploring abroad; living in cities instead of isolated farms; and going into academia, instead of farming. However, it was replicating what my parents did by going abroad to leave home. Both my parents, I think, secretly yearned to have done what I did, especially my mother who yearned for the culture of the city life and plenty of company. In this, I felt supported by them as they expressed enthusiasm for these moves, except for my father who could never understand how I could live in rows of houses. If he could see another house from where he lived he felt crowded.

I realized that if either of my parents had felt too many unfulfilled roles, or envy, their vicarious wishes might have interfered with what I was doing. That might have spoiled my path and left me feeling as if I were not the true owner of my own identity. Finally my identity as a doctor was supported by finding that this was my father's hidden ambition. However, he could not bring himself—a true-blue British farmer—to approve of psychiatry! That was quite upsetting to me. But it certainly left me knowing that I had carved out my own niche. My identification with a caregiving role raises the possibility that I had been a parentified child. This suggests that the legend about rescuing my parents from the leopard probably may have had yet another layer of "truth," and that I indeed had been expected to take care of my mother even at this age, not on the physical protection level but more on the emotional level—when my mother felt anxious or frightened, for instance. That would fit with a career as a psychiatrist and family therapist. This legend could now be seen to relate to many levels: protection and attachments, cowardice–bravery, gender roles and role reversal. Such is the richness of storytelling.

Review of the Exercise

I find that on completion of this exercise I am pleased to have done it. Although I had already thought about the significance of some of the stories—in particular the "rescuing from the leopard"—many I had not. The whole exercise of writing down the stories took a few hours, and felt relatively uncensored. It then led to further thinking and reediting.

I am aware that I have edited the stories to fit this telling, at this time, and in this book. But then my theory tells me that must be so. For instance, if I tell my family these stories they are full of embellishments that might interest them (or bore them to tears through repetition), but they would not interest the reader. I am aware that I selected stories that supported my thesis. On the other hand, I was surprised how well they did so, and the original selection came off the top of my head in response to my prompts: "Now I must think of a leaving-home story," or "Are there any stories about security?"

In all my writing in which I theorize about human nature, I am aware that I am uncomfortable about what I have said until I can see where I personally might fit in. It cannot be valid as a general theory if it is not at least potentially true for me. For instance, when I search my family for attachment patterns I glimpse at some scenarios that suggest secure attachments and others suggest insecure/avoidant and insecure/ambivalent attachments. I am thus inclined to see families as having the capacity for all three, but one might predominate in particular contexts and relationships. Of course, it also means that I have to acknowledge the theoretical story as representing my own construct, even though I have tried to validate it through work with families, my research, and research data. Nevertheless, it is important that the reader knows where my constructs originated. Perhaps all family theorists should research their own constructs?

Finally, what about some stories about my family of creation? It is easier to talk publicly about my parents now that they are dead. Although the exercise helped me to think about my role as storyteller in my own family, it is not appropriate to share these thoughts publicly.

Readers interested in doing this exercise for themselves might be put off by the nature of my stories. Some families have unusual stories to tell, or are storytellers; others are not, but communicate in other ways. Although this is true, the students I have worked with have usually found, sometimes to their surprise, plenty of stories to use. Others have claimed that their families are not interesting. I have, however, never met a set of family stories that are not fascinating, especially when the interconnecting patterns emerge.

N·I·N·E

Resolving
Care–Control Conflicts

CARE AND CONTROL ISSUES
IN AN ADOLESCENT UNIT

I first became aware of the interplay between authority problems and insecurity in the family when I worked at Hill End Adolescent Psychiatric Inpatient Unit in St. Albans, England, in 1969–1972, as a senior registrar under the leadership of Peter Bruggen (Bruggen et al., 1973). Many of the adolescents who came were out of control and in the process of being extruded from the home: both care and control had broken down. The unit had just opened and rationalization for the work was being sought. Of the utmost importance was that the adolescents should have an understandable reason for being admitted. To be treated in a mental hospital is potentially damaging because it might establish an identity of being mad, both in the adolescent's mind and in the eyes of his or her family. The rationale that came to mind was that for an adolescent to require inpatient rather than outpatient treatment, those caring for the adolescent must no longer be able to cope with the individual at home. Establishing this as the reason for admission allowed admission and discharges to be made by the adults who had parental responsibility—usually, but not always, parents. It was no longer purely in the medical domain, and the authority that was restored to parents proved to be a very powerful therapeutic tool (Byng-Hall & Bruggen, 1974). Most of the family work would focus on the parental decisions in family meetings before admission, during the stay, and at discharge. Once it was possible for parents to make the agonizing decision to admit the adolescent, sometimes against immense pressure from the young person,

158

parental authority and control could be restored. Parents also decided to discharge when they felt they could cope once more.

Some significant things happened using this approach. One was that young people stayed for periods much shorter than those admitted to adolescent units where the medical staff made decisions about admission and discharge. In the first years the average length of stay was 3 months; over the last 10 years it has been 4 to 6 weeks. Family attachments seemed to improve: The family at the point of discharge wanted to be together much more than at the point of admission, and it was possible for families to be much more open with each other. For some, a preliminary meeting prevented the necessity for admission: Knowledge that the unit was there and available for when they might want it enabled parents to cope on their own with their adolescent at home. The support that the institution gave to families could be likened to that of a secure family base in the sense of a group of people known to be available and interested in helping, when need arises.

Since this was the only adolescent unit serving a population of 4 million, the children eventually admitted were very disruptive and difficult. They represented an extreme end of the spectrum. Much of the skill of the staff was in helping the parents—some of whom were separated or divorced but still shared authority—to work as a team and stop fighting each other in order to make a sensible decision about their offspring. Within the unit, the staff worked with the adolescents on what it was that they did to make it difficult for adults— their parents in the first place and, sometimes, later for the staff themselves. This provided a focus of work in helping the adolescents to take charge of their own behavior.

What impressed me was that a benign cycle could be started in some families, about whom everyone had felt hopeless. This could sometimes happen with startling speed. It was as if, once the authority in the family was no longer disputed, the anxiety went down and family members could start thinking, collaborating with each other, and even feeling some affection.

FROM A SENSE OF BLAME TO A SENSE OF PAIN: CHILDREN IN CARE

After leaving the Adolescent Unit, I worked part-time in the Social Services Assessment Centre which had the role of making decisions about whether children should, or should not, come into care. Once again, I worked with the family; on these occasions I met with them in their own homes. It was possible to involve the parents in thinking about what would be the best alternative to recommend to the Court. This recommendation had to be one that the Court would accept. For instance, it was no use recommending that a Probation Order should be assigned to the youngster who had committed a serious crime. Parents understood this. They were able to feel much more allied with the final Court decision—and the plans that evolved— because they had been involved in what to recommend to the Court.

These families were often initially extremely hostile to myself as the psychiatrist and to the social workers who came with me. I found that I needed to spend enough time at the family home in order to break through the barrier of hostility. This usually meant spending a whole morning or a whole afternoon with the family, allowing for any distractions: mother making tea, letting the dog out, neighbors calling, etc. I would probably have two of these meetings with each family. I found that it was extremely powerful to explore the family history in the first session. Almost all of these families who were at the point of losing or extruding an adolescent had a history of terrible loss. Often it was possible to move from *a sense of blame to a sense of pain* in these meetings. Blame created rifts between the adolescent and the family, the family and the professional workers, or between all these groups. Pain and sadness about the past could, on the other hand, bring everybody together. Crying over a lost relative could evoke a caring response in others, which was, of course, just as important for the professionals as for the family. We felt quite differently about these apparently impossibly difficult families when we knew what awful times they had been through.

I vividly remember visiting one family to be greeted at the door by an angry, barking dog. It was obviously being egged on by an equally angry heavily built man. He was frightening. I noticed, however, that the dog was wagging its tail. I knew that it was not always a hostile home. He was the father of the 14-year-old girl who had come into care. The court had asked for a report about whether or not she should go home. In the sitting room there was a picture of a middle-aged woman framed in black. It was the only picture on the wall, and it hung over the fireplace. When it came to drawing the family tree, I learned that this woman was the father's mother— the matriarch of the family. She had been killed by a hit-and-run driver 16 years before. The father had become convinced that the hit-and-run had been a deliberate killing. Terrible battles ensued between the father and the rest of the family because he became increasingly controlling. Eventually the daughter had started to run away. Her father then became so agitated by her refusal to stay at home that he eventually disowned her and locked her out. She was picked up by the police in the early hours of one morning.

We discovered that the family had not changed their residence since the grandmother was killed, even though it was now incredibly cramped with four children. The situation was magnified by the fact that the grandmother's room had become a mausoleum—unused, with nothing touched since she had died. On hearing about this, we went up to the room and stood around the bed while father talked about his mother and how he was so sad that she was not there to know his children. The dog did not bark the next time we came. The girl went home after the second meeting. I heard that the family moved a year later. This family is an example of what appeared to be a dispute over authority, and it might have been handled that way, but it turned out to be a problem of unresolved loss instead.

INTERPLAY BETWEEN THE AUTHORITY AND ATTACHMENT SYSTEMS

A sense of insecurity can arise when one is unsure whether those looking after oneself actually care, or when they are so preoccupied with other issues that they cannot be relied upon for help. One of those situations occurs when there are power battles in the family and authority is in dispute. The influence between the two systems of authority and attachment goes in both directions. If the family has a sufficiently secure base, then the normal conflicts and challenges to authority which occur in families can be explored and resolved. At the same time, functional authority within a family can be used to support the caring arrangements provided by the secure family base and to protect individuals within the family from attack. One example would be to ensure that sibling rivalry and conflict does not get out of hand, putting a child at an unfair disadvantage in the family. Another example is that the authority of the caregiver is supported. At times, caring may involve unwelcome procedures (e.g., dressing, washing, or medical care) that a child often tries to avoid or delay. In short, the two systems of care and authority mutually reinforce the capacity to provide security within the family. (See Figure 9.1.)

The corollary, however, is that insecure families undermine the capacity to resolve disputes in authority, while dysfunctional authority leaves the family even more insecure. The dysfunctions within the two systems thus may become mutually reinforcing.

The way that attachment and authority have developed is impor-

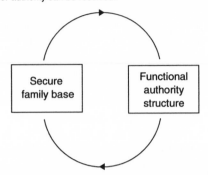

The secure base provides the context in which disputes over authority can be resolved.

Functional authority supports caregiving: For instance
• Supports caregiver's authority in unwelcome aspects of looking after children, for example, bed time.
• Prevents sibling conflict from putting a child at an unfair disadvantage, or at risk.

FIGURE 9.1. Mutual reinforcement between a secure family base and functional authority.

tant. Transgenerational scripts will influence the way in which these two systems function. Then the pathways along which attachments and discipline evolve side by side influence the final shape of authority and attachment.

Conflict Developing between Parental Authority and Insecure Children

Greenberg and Speltz (1988) explored how attachment insecurity created conduct problems in preschool children. They reviewed the research on attachment patterns carried out on children up to school age and found that security is related to optimal parent–child interaction, whereas insecure attachments were more likely to show behaviors with their parents that are associated with later clinic referrals. These behaviors include whining, noncompliance, and negative attention-seeking. They concluded that insecure children may be more at risk than secure children for behavior disorders in the preschool years. They hypothesized that this was due to problems in the planning of whose needs are to be met. In script terminology this is competition between individuals' scripts. Greenberg and Speltz described four different patterns: (1) when the child tries to coerce the parent into caring for him by being very demanding and difficult, and the parent is also overcontrolling—a contest develops between competing plans, in which the worse the child's behavior the more likely it is that the child will at least gain some attention; (2) when a child of such parents always gives way to the parents' overcontrolling behavior and becomes a "compulsive complier," thus becoming a meek and "good" child; (3) when the child coerces and controls the parents who would not otherwise respond, but who also have laissez-faire discipline and thus allow the child's plans to always predominate (the child then never learns to accommodate to other people's plans or perspectives and remains unsocialized); (4) similar to the above, but when parents reach the end of their tether they suddenly become punitively controlling, often in a way that is unpredictable to the child. This pattern of inconsistent discipline is more common than pure lax discipline, as the children usually eventually force their parents to react. In contrast to these patterns, the securely attached child accommodates to the parents' plans knowing that when the need arises the parents will drop their plans in order to care for him or her.

Patterson and Dishion (1988) studied the effects of parental discipline on their children. They found that parental irritable discipline was associated with antisocial children. The parents had irritable explosions during discipline confrontations with their children, and they also nagged their children. They threatened or hit them, and were inconsistent. Patterson and Dishion also found that these parents remembered punitive discipline in their own childhood and distant negative home environments. The parents also showed more antisocial traits themselves.

The above findings would suggest that transgenerational scripts and current generation discipline both contribute to poor authority structures and antisocial behavior. (See Figure 9.2.)

Strategies That Mutually Reinforce Dysfunction

The strategies for dealing with insecurity that can undermine authority include the following:

1. *Capturing.* An insecure individual may attempt to capture another member of the family, excluding others from access to that member in a desperate attempt to guarantee care for themselves. This process may include one parent capturing the other parent and excluding the children, but more usually it is a child who captures one parent excluding the other parent and any siblings. One effect is a reduction of the authority of the excluded parent, who often feels very hurt and put down. He or she, quite correctly, perceives that their partner has colluded with this process.

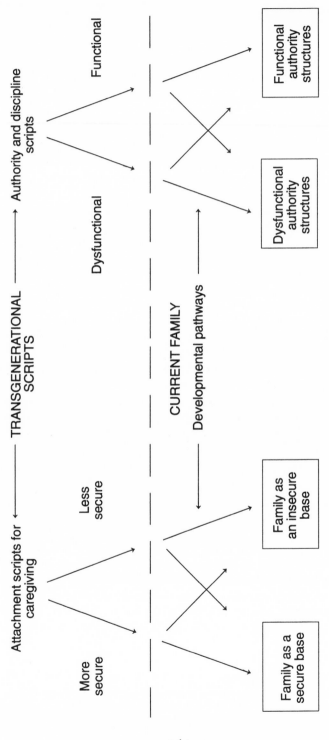

FIGURE 9.2. Past history of authority and attachment systems.

164

2. *Role reversal.* The role reversal that is associated with insecure/ambivalent relationships or disorganized attachments can further undermine the authority of both parents. Role reversal includes controlling behavior that may be punitive, or parentified behavior in which the child looks after the parent.

Some Strategies to Gain Control
That Undermine Attachment Security

In addition to the general sense of insecurity and uncertainty that dysfunctional authority generates, there are specific strategies that make the situation worse. These include the following:

1. *Conflictual competition between scripts.* This is described above. Conflict over who is to get what care is available is damaging to the secure family base, whose purpose is to provide care for all its members.

2. *Cross-generational coalitions.* The parent or adult who feels most vulnerable may recruit other members of the family, such as children or their own parents, in a coalition in order to counteract the perceived power of a partner. This has two effects: First, it undermines the caregiving role of that parent to the child; second, it also distances the child from the caregiving of the other parent. Although it is a strategy that may give the vulnerable parent a sense of support in the short term, this further undermines the authority structure of the family. The outflanked parent may either become more and more authoritarian in an attempt to compensate for loss of actual authority, or give up and provide no authority whatsoever. These responses are probably influenced by their own family scripts for authority. The authoritarian response is, of course, likely to further cement the parent–child coalition as this often leads to the child in question being protected by the allied parent from the "cruelty" of the authoritarian parent.

3. *Dysfunctional discipline.* Parents' discipline may be authoritarian, lax/permissive, or inconsistent/explosive. Each of these can create a sense of insecurity. Authoritarian parents are frightening; lax/permissive parents allow their children to run wild, which is anxiety provoking in a different way; and inconsistent/explosive discipline (or "irritable discipline," as described by Patterson & Dishion, 1988) combines the worst of both worlds. The children are out of control and then, suddenly, a frightening explosion of rage erupts from the parents without warning. (See Figure 9.3.)

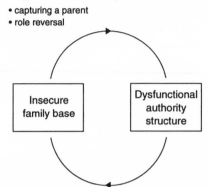

FIGURE 9.3. Mutual reinforcement between insecure family base and dysfunctional authority.

THERAPEUTIC IMPLICATIONS

The overall aim is to use the temporary secure base of the therapy to shift from a mutually reinforcing dysfunctional system to the mutually reinforcing functional one. Focusing on any one of the following therapeutic strategies may help, although I find it most useful to work on as many of these domains as possible. The focus can be on:

1. Resolving authority conflicts within the family using structural family therapy techniques.
2. Resolving distance conflicts within the family and increasing the security in the attachments.
3. Working with the families of origin if they are actively involved within the family dysfunction. This may involve bringing them into the sessions, or helping the family to go and do something different on their visits to the grandparents' homes.
4. Working with transgenerational scripts by exploring the family history of attachment and loss, as well as authority and discipline (see Figure 9.4).

Figure 9.4 illustrates how the various interventions can help to shift the dysfunctional systems into more functional pathways. The priorities for which system to focus on first vary from family to family. Families may make it clear which is the most pressing issue. For instance, the Young family (discussed in Chapter 7) came with intense anxieties about attachments, with Ann capturing her father and her parents' relationship being threatened. However, the Herstone family (discussed in Chapter 5) came with an authority problem, with Steven being out of control. I usually anticipate that having helped with one system the problems with the other will emerge quickly. Research into a number of families that I have treated[1] shows that I, in fact, tend to raise both issues early but initially focus more on one than the other. The overall rule is, however, that if the authority structure is dysfunctional and the children are out of control, or if there are unresolved power battles between the parents, these must be dealt with first. It is not possible to think creatively until control is reestablished, and the chaos created by out-of-control children is reduced sufficiently to start exploring.

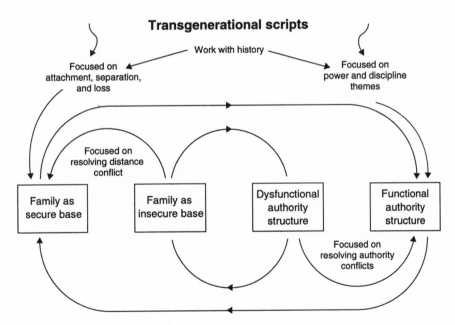

FIGURE 9.4. Family therapy interventions: toward mutually reinforcing functional pathways.

[1]Research project in collaboration with Professor Israel Kolvin, John Bowlby Professor, Tavistock Clinic, exploring process and change in family therapy.

Disputed Authority: When Is It Dysfunctional?

What family therapists have to be sensitive to is that there are many different ways of structuring authority within a family that can function perfectly well. Some families appear to be able to manage well on almost egalitarian lines, others on what seem to be rigid, patriarchal lines. Whether or not these styles function well is influenced by the culture in which the family lives, but also by past family traditions. As a clinician I take the view that it is only when the authority structure is clearly dysfunctional for a particular family that work needs to focus on establishing viable authority structures. My rule of thumb is to accept that the authority structures are dysfunctional only when the power dispute can be linked clearly to the problem. This helps to differentiate dysfunction from normal renegotiation of power—for example, a mother redefining her position in the family, or an adolescent growing up. Usually there is no difficulty in identifying the dysfunctional situations when the parents are complaining that the child is out of control, or the parents cannot agree on how to discipline the children. Sometimes, however, parents do not see authority as being a problem while everyone else has no doubts at all after meeting the children. Those parents may come to see the lack of discipline as a problem only after tracing some of the consequences of not setting any limits. Even more convincing to them, however, is the effectiveness of parental teamwork in settling their children.

Modified Structural Family Therapy

Most of this work is along the lines of structural family therapy. The way I do this, however, differs from structural family therapy in a number of ways. The family work in the Hill End Adolescent Unit, 1969–1972, that I described was established without any knowledge of structural family therapy, but when Salvador Minuchin came for a sabbatical at the Tavistock Clinic in 1972, it was clear that his basic approach was surprisingly similar to ours (Byng-Hall & Bruggen, 1974). The Adolescent Unit staff would quietly insist on the parents making the decisions that they had to make. All attempts to divert from that process were blocked. The resolution of the conflict over authority was achieved through the parents making their decisions about admission and discharge. This was similar to Minuchin asking parents to take charge of the feeding of their hospitalized anorexic daughter. The style, however, was very different. We were British, laid-back, and "correct," while Minuchin was vivid, charismatic, and engaging. Both approaches were absolutely insistent, however, that the potentially dangerous situation could be resolved by the parents using their own authority.

After leaving Hill End, I was exposed to a lot of structural family therapy theory and practice through Salvador Minuchin's two sabbaticals in Britain and also a number of other contacts with the Philadelphia Child Guidance Clinic. I discovered that I needed to adapt the technique to fit both my personal style and the overall aims of helping families to find their own solutions. My style is more of quiet insistence than of dramatic intervention, which is the hallmark of some structural family therapy in which the therapists actively confront the family and make them do something different. I like to let things happen more slowly. The first session is usually taken up with exploring what happens within the family: trying to discover what it is that the parents are attempting to do and how they are trying to do it.

There is one type of family in which the children become out of control because the parents treat their children with great respect, discussing everything with them, rather than telling them what to do. This permissive style is often associated with corrective scripts in which the parents are trying to avoid what their parents did, which was to be very authoritarian and harsh with them. I found that if, at the moment that their children misbehave in the session, I demand that these parents should discipline them, they react against the suggestion. I was, after all, then behaving as their parents had behaved, and against which they had reacted.

In the first session I often try to find out how the discipline patterns are similar, or dissimilar, to the parent's own childhood experiences. By appreciating why they are now trying to discipline their children in this particular way, the parents will feel supported rather than undermined. What is most important is that they feel respected instead of criticized. It is then possible to explore the consequences of the way that they discipline the children, and it is much easier for them to see that they have overdone the respect for their children's rights. In the process of this discussion we explore some strategies that might work better, especially those that involve the parents working as a team. By the second or third session, it is usually possible to ask the parents to take charge of their children within the session. The way that they do this is likely to reveal some further reasons why discipline has not worked previously. But the fact that the parents eventually do take charge is what is important, and this has to be done in a way that is their own and not imposed by the therapist. This requires a lot of restraint. Therapists often want to jump in and stop parents from doing certain things because it looks like the wrong way to treat a child. In the context of a family therapy session, parents, in my experience anyway, do not actively abuse their children, even if that has happened at home. So that particular danger is not one that need constrain the therapist from helping the parent to discipline the child. Even if what happens is uncomfortable for the therapist, it is likely to be only a watered-down version of what happens the whole time at home.

The great problem for the therapist is not to feel that he or she is condoning bad parenting practices during an enactment. The illusion is that disapproving of something done in the session will stop it from happening day in and day out. Instead, it is more likely that the family will discontinue therapy.

Once the parents have settled the child in their own particular way, the family needs to be affirmed and congratulated for their achievement. Working out even better ways of gaining control can come later. While the parents are taking charge of their children in the session, two inputs are provided by the therapist: first, quietly insisting on the parents achieving what they hope to do and not to give up; second, helping the adults to act as a team during the restructuring. The team may consist of parents, or cohabitees, or an adult and a grandparent, etc. In single-parent families it may involve helping the parent not to use one of the children as a member of an adult discipline team.

Sometimes success requires prolonging the work past the formal end of a session, as trouble can brew toward the end of a family meeting. This is the only situation in which I will break the rule of finishing on time because for parents to take charge for themselves is such a powerful intervention that it helps to transform the therapy. Structural family therapy is, in my experience, by far the most potent and valuable technique in family therapy with out-of-control children. In my view, therapists who do not learn how to use this technique in this situation deprive the families with whom they work.

The solutions that parents improvise in order to control and settle their children vary greatly. In one conflict-avoiding family, the father picked up his 7-year-old son, put him in a seat, and stood over him, angrily insisting that he stay seated. There was enormous anxiety about this, especially from the mother who wanted her husband to be more lenient toward him. To the parents' amazement, the child stayed put for 20 minutes. The maximum time of sitting in one place had, up to now, been 1 minute. While father stood up to his son I talked to the mother about how she could support her husband. Afterward she revealed that she was terrified that her husband could not manage it and would be devastated by failure. The father's competence was established and the parents were devising their own techniques for settling him at home.

Other episodes in which parents gained control of their children are described in Chapters 1, 10, and 11, and in the following case.

A CASE EXAMPLE: THE THOMAS FAMILY

The Thomas family was referred because their 8-year-old son, Geoffrey, had been behaving in a dangerous way. He had been playing with matches and dangerous implements such as knives, and he had been found trying to operate a chain saw. He was also rude and generally out of control. Geoffrey's mother, Cilla, was 35 and worked in a flower shop. His father, Bert, was 32 and worked in electronics. Both parents were very worried because Geoffrey would also make his younger siblings, 6-year-old Astra and 2-year-old Tim cry. They were afraid that Astra and Tim were at risk.

First Session: Taking Some Control

Surprisingly, in the first session the two younger siblings were much more unruly than Geoffrey himself. Tim made himself center stage by climbing up onto the table in the middle of the room, jumping up and down, and shouting at the top of his voice. Astra insisted on talking loudly to everybody and would listen in on other people's conversations in order to give her views on everything. Geoffrey was much more subdued and spent a lot of time watching his mother's reaction to what was going on. He and his mother would frequently exchange secret glances. The father seemed out of it. While the children ran wild and were extremely rude to the therapist and their parents, Cilla would smile—sometimes apologetically. Bert would ask them in a soft and polite way to come and sit down. It was noticeable that neither parent looked at the other, but both faced the therapist and took turns becoming active, either by interacting with the children, or by talking to the therapist. This configuration is commonly found in parents who avoid conflict with each other by never putting their scripts into competition. Needless to say, it destroys teamwork. For this configuration I often use the "weather couple" metaphor. I described a barometer, in which the man comes out in one type of weather, while the woman retreats back into the house. When she comes out he goes back inside again, so they are never together to sort things out. The parents understood the meaning of this metaphor, and this led to a discussion about the need to support each other and to act as a team.

Although Geoffrey was losing out, in terms of attention to his younger brother and sister, I noticed that he had quietly taken a knife out of his pocket and was playing with this, opening up the blade. As his parents did not seem to notice this, I pointed it out, and we discussed the various dangerous activities that Geoffrey got involved with. Both parents described these activities in rather a deadpan way. There was a noticeable lack of sense of anxiety within the family, as if this discussion was indeed about the weather. Geoffrey put the knife away in his pocket, and the conversation went on to other things. I was interested to explore where the ultrapolite approach to the children came from, so I inquired. Cilla's parents had been very rude to her which she hated, and she was determined not to act in the same way with her children. However, when the children finally pushed her to becoming very angry, she would lose her temper and shout abuse at the children. Bert, on the other hand, had a more distant and unemotional relationship with his parents. I noted to myself that the father seemed to be replicating a more avoidant/disengaged style, whereas Cilla seemed to be more ambivalent/enmeshed with the children. I told them I was impressed by their struggle to be so protective of their children, by trying not to be cross with them despite all the provocation.

Right at the end of the session, as the family was preparing to leave, Geoffrey took out his knife and made a sort of playful lunge toward his mother. Taking control of a dangerous weapon could not be delayed until the next session.

CILLA: I think you had better put that away now.

THERAPIST: Can you two (*pointing to both parents*) decide together now what you are going to do about it?

CILLA: (*Inaudible; quietly says to husband what she thinks should be done.*)

BERT: (*nodding in agreement with his wife*) Right. Geoffrey, you have finished playing with the penknife now. (*leaning down to talk quietly to Geoffrey*) You can have it back later on when the others have gone to bed.

GEOFFREY: (*whining*) I don't want to.

BERT: (*raising his voice slightly*) Well, give it to me now, it is *my* penknife.

GEOFFREY: Why should I?

BERT: Because if there is an accident, or somebody gets their hands on it. These things do happen.

GEOFFREY: I just want to hold it.

BERT: Okay. Well, you held it all the way here, so I'll hold it all the way back.

GEOFFREY: I just want to look after it (*whining and looking irritated*).

BERT: I would like it *now*, to take it home, please (*a bit more authority in his voice*). You can look after it later on when we get back.

CILLA: Perhaps he could put it in his bag (*countering her husband's work*).

BERT: (*with more assertiveness*) As we have asked him to do something, I think he should do it.

CILLA: Okay (*but she turns slightly away in disagreement*).

GEOFFREY: (*Reluctantly hands the knife to father and runs out of the room.*)

BERT: Thank you very much. (*Puts knife in his pocket.*)

THERAPIST: That's great. You really stuck with that one. And it worked.

Although it was a demonstration of many of the things that were undermining the authority of the parents in their attempts to work as a team, nevertheless it was important to affirm their success. After the session, I decided that it would be useful to do a video review in the next session so that they could see exactly what happened. The use of video is a particularly useful technique for parents who readily feel criticized. They are more likely to be able to see for themselves some of the difficulties that they were creating, but also to see what it was that made them succeed.

Second Session: Video Replay

The parents came on their own because the children had chicken pox. I decided to view the tape with them. I always select a piece of videotape in which the interaction is not too conflictual to show first. I use this to enable families to watch themselves. Later I show them a more fraught sequence, which they might find harder to take in. The effect of doing this with the Thomas couple was to move them into an audience position in which they could be observers to some of their own processes. They discussed their different emotional responses to what was going on. Even the quietest piece of tape that I could find was chaotic. Cilla described how she felt her rage rising in her chest when things were going wrong. Bert, on the other hand, just felt rather sad and distanced from everything. I stopped the tape and asked each parent to describe how they deal with their distress. Cilla said that she counted up to 3 out loud. The children would then know that she was about to explode. Bert, however, just moved away.

I then became aware that the two were taking turns talking to me. There was no dialogue or eye contact between them. So I said, "I have been joining your dance, like talking to each of the weather people in turn. Can you turn your chairs more toward each other so that you can talk together?" Bert turned his chair toward his wife and said that he could not connect with Cilla's feelings. Cilla complained that he did not let her know what he was feeling. For instance, when he had pain of a physical nature he would never let her know. Bert said, "I feel you criticize me if I tell you about my pains." I extended the metaphor of the weather barometer by talking about it giving messages to each of them when the atmospheric tension reached flash point. I then asked them to point to where in their bodies they felt the tension. Cilla pointed to her stomach and described how it seemed to rise up toward her throat when she was getting angry. Bert pointed toward his chest and said that he would get a feeling of tightness when he was feeling upset and that he had some asthma recently. Cilla said that she had difficulty admitting to herself that she could get very angry until the children came along. She said she felt that Geoffrey needed help because he was so frightened of his uncontrollable anger and rages. Bert disagreed. Geoffrey seemed to him to be, on the exterior anyway, more callous and calm. I said that both parents appeared to be sensitive to aspects of themselves in Geoffrey— Cilla, her rage; Bert, his detached quality.

At this point I felt they were ready to look at some of the more disturbing videotape. Before showing it to them, I asked that they concentrate on their thoughts and feelings during the clip. I showed the section in which Geoffrey was fiddling with the knife and had exposed the blade. The parents first reacted to the fact that neither of them had noticed what was happening until I had pointed it out. I said that I thought that Geoffrey may feel sometimes that he had to raise the stakes in order to get attention. Cilla said that she had thought Geoffrey was playing with dangerous things merely because he wanted to. She had not realized that it was his way of trying to tell them something. Cilla and Bert then discussed how they were giving mixed messages to Geoffrey—they allowed him to have dangerous things, but they were constantly reminding him that these things were dangerous. I explored what damage had actually been done in the past. Geoffrey had cut his fingers on a couple of occasions, but what the parents were really worried about was that he might hurt the other children. They admitted that playing with matches could be very dangerous if he burned the house down. On the other hand, he seemed frightened of matches, and so to help him overcome his fear they had given him some to play with. I was trying to focus the parent's attention on some real dangers. There was lightning in Geoffrey's storm if they did not notice the clouds gathering.

At the end of the session I gave them a task of meeting two or three times a week for 20 minutes in order to discuss issues relating to the barometer: how to listen to their own barometers, but also notice Geoffrey's, so that they could do something to help prevent a storm. I asked them to keep track of when they did something different and note its effect. I also suggested that they spend one evening a week sharing an activity that they both wanted to do together. During that time they should not discuss the children. This is a typical example of how I give tasks to parents: One half focuses the task on the problem; the other half finds a way of switching attention away from the problem onto their own shared enjoyment.

Third Session: Marital Problems Emerge

The children were still ill with chicken pox and so the parents again came on their own. When I asked what had been happening, Cilla reported that Geoffrey had got out of hand and that he had been hurting his younger siblings. She finally lost her temper, shook him, and then "attacked" him. She quickly added that she had not intended to hurt him. Geoffrey had then tidied up and was subsequently very affectionate to his mother. She said, "I don't know whether what I did was right or wrong, but it's *bullying*." I asked how she could use her husband to feel okay about what happened. Bert was hesitant and said that he didn't feel it was wrong, but "it would be nice if there was another way." Cilla was scornful of Bert's suggestion of distraction. I asked Cilla what it would take for her to value her husband. Cilla said (turning away from her husband), "Oh, my values are too high. I shall have to get on with it on my own. Our partnership is only occasional anyway." Bert said to her, "I feel you are not interested." The threat of marital breakdown was now out in the open. I asked them about how their families of origin responded to their marriage—grandparents loomed large in their discussions. This is often a key question in an apparently uncommitted marriage. They told me that the announcement of their engagement led to endless disputes between their families about what should happen and who should do what. They then described how Bert had a terrible accident a few months before the marriage. He had fallen off a ladder in the garden and landed on a garden fork which penetrated his chest. He had been near death's door initially. They had sorted out his medical problems only 2 years ago. Cilla commented, "We managed to get married, okay, but we couldn't have a honeymoon." The injury resulted in the family moving in with Cilla's parents. Bert was looked after by his mother-in-law and became very close to her.

I tried to get back to the original romantic story of their meeting by asking what attracted them to one another. Cilla said, "It all got lost. My parents just liked him. It is hard to dislike him." I said that it seemed that mother-in-law and wife were competing to care for Bert. I asked Bert if he found it difficult to marry a family rather than a wife. He laughed. I said that I thought the accident had been tragic because it had prevented Bert from carrying out the role of enabling his wife to move into the next family.

They still lived close to Cilla's parents. I asked to whose family Bert felt he belonged, Cilla's parents or the new one? He said he felt he was somewhere in the middle of the two. Cilla said she felt that he was in the new family with the children. This was a hopeful sign. They told me that they had plans to move to Norfolk sometime. This planned move provided a major focus for the work. It helped to differentiate Cilla from her family and to establish Bert as being centrally involved in the new family.

Work with Mother and Son: Transgenerational Scripts

In the next two sessions, Cilla and Geoffrey came in on their own because Bert had now come down with chicken pox. In the first of these two sessions, mother started off by being very polite to Geoffrey—for instance, asking him diffidently to go and fetch something for her. I inquired about from whom she got her tremendous politeness. Did her parents ask her to do things? Apparently they just used to tell her. Cilla said, "I think it is very rude to order people around." I positively labeled her attempt to correct that form of rudeness in her own family. It did turn out, however, that her parents were nevertheless very concerned about the formal terms of politeness like "please" and "thank you." I commented on her loyalty to her family in keeping to this tradition of politeness. This is a fairly typical example of how replicative and corrective scripts interweave. Part of the behavior is corrective (Cilla not being bossy), while part of it is replicative (teaching a formal politeness that must be followed).

I asked Cilla whether she thought that she had been successful in teaching Geoffrey how to be polite. Cilla said that she thought that he knew how to be polite. But I reminded her that I had seen him being very rude. Cilla did not want to accept this, trying to label it as "challenging" instead. I traced her reluctance to call a spade a spade, and it turned out that she had not wanted to put him down. She said, "I guess I tried to boost his ego a bit because he is so shy. I tried to give him confidence." I was amazed at this, because he seemed to me to be a very rude, assertive little boy. So I asked Geoffrey, "Did you know that your Mum's afraid that you are too shy?" He answered with a firm "No." I then asked him whether he thought that his mother should worry about that, and he said, "No," shaking his head vigorously. So I asked Geoffrey to find out whether his mother had been shy when she was small. She told him she had been very shy when she was a little girl, and added that she still was shy. I said it did not look to me as if the problem was Geoffrey being too shy. Cilla said, "Well, if we go anywhere and people talk to him, he tunes out and does not respond. He won't answer." I commented that this was not necessarily being shy, it was being rude, and added, "I don't see someone who is shy being like Geoffrey. (*to Geoffrey*) I am thinking that if Mum was shy when she was a little girl she wants to help you not to be shy. (*turning to mother*) You have done a good enough job!" Cilla was thoughtful and said, "He has come into his own a lot more recently."

Resolving Authority Conflicts in the Sessions

During one session Geoffrey did not respond to his mother's attempts to control him, which led her to look at me questioningly throughout the episode. I realized that there was a confusion of authority within the session itself as to who was in charge. That was just like at home. I clarified my authority by saying that if I was in charge of the therapy, could she be in charge of the discipline in the room? Cilla agreed with this. Geoffrey then settled down again. I pointed out that the moment there was an uncertainty about who was in charge Geoffrey took advantage of the situation by being impossible. I went on to emphasize that the lesson we had learned was that both parents should act as a team: Make it clear who was deciding what and agree with each other about that.

On another occasion Geoffrey became more and more intrusive while I was discussing with his mother how it would feel for her when she went to Norfolk and was no longer seeing her mother every day. Geoffrey finally managed to break right across this conversation and switch his mother's attention onto himself. He did this by standing between us and talking to her so that she could hardly see me. He eventually started signaling to her in some secret code, which effectively left me out all together. However, although distracted, Cilla managed to avoid being drawn into this. I pointed out that her refusal to be drawn in was a change from the usual secret alliance that she and Geoffrey had which excluded other people. Cilla was then much firmer with Geoffrey and told him to sit down which he did. I com-

mented on how she had been successful when she had been firm with
him.

Toward the end of the session, I became scripted into a family
scenario. When I returned from a break in the session there was a
different atmosphere in the room. Mother and son were exchanging
glances and giggling. Geoffrey presented a drawing that he had done
which looked to me like the place they were planning to move to in
Norfolk. I use children's drawings as stories about situations, and they
had come to expect this. So I embarked on getting Geoffrey to tell
me the story in his picture. Mother and son continued to giggle even
more. Eventually the truth emerged that Cilla had drawn the picture
and not Geoffrey. In my attempts to make a story out of the picture I
had, of course, made a fool of myself, and that was what they were
enjoying. After this, Geoffrey's behavior deteriorated rapidly. He tore
up the picture, tried to eat it, and was totally disruptive. At one time
he kicked his mother who kicked him back again. I was puzzled as to
why this had got out of hand suddenly and why mother's authority
had gone again completely. She was trying hard to tell him to stop,
but he took no notice. It was only after the end of the session that I
realized that it was the coalition between mother and son against me
that had undermined the adult authority within the session—just as it
did at home. I decided to take this up in the next session when the
father was due to be back.

Father Reintegrated: Triangles and Distance Regulation

In the next session I could hear some scuffling in the corridor just
before the family came into the room. Bert had to run down the
corridor to grab Geoffrey. This opened a discussion about how
Geoffrey was trying to test whether the adults were together and would
support each other. His father had not been able to be an active supporter when he had been very ill in the past. His mother had to
struggle against a lot of odds while her husband was ill and had to do
all the looking after and running after Geoffrey herself.

Cilla told me that her friends were noticing that Geoffrey was
behaving much better at home, he was much calmer. I reintroduced
father into the therapy by filling him in on what happened during
his absence. In particular, I reported how his wife had been able to
settle Geoffrey down when it had been made clear who was in
charge of what, and there was no longer any confusion about authority. I also told him about how I had been teased by Cilla and
Geoffrey, but that this had led to Geoffrey being out of control because suddenly he and his mother were in collusion against me. I

asked Bert whether he ever found himself in a similar position. He told me that he had been made to feel like the "third person" on occasion, when the two of them sided with each other. I speculated that such situations had probably occurred in both of their families in the past. So we reviewed this through a genogram. On the mother's side, it was very clear that the regular pattern was for two people to get together in order to tease a third. For instance, she and her father would form an alliance while leaving her mother out. During this discussion, Geoffrey came over and started whispering to his mother, excluding the others, which was reenacting the script in the room. As we discussed this Geoffrey started creating a distraction so that it was difficult to carry on the discussion. I said that it was up to the two parents to determine what they felt was the proper behavior in the room. Together they made him sit down and keep quiet. This was done in a quiet and reasonable way but with clear authority, each checking with the other to make sure they were in agreement. I commented on their success. Geoffrey now settled down and became involved in the session.

I took the chance of asking about Bert's parents. On Bert's side of the family, his own father distanced himself so much that most interaction in the family went on between Bert and his mother, or between his mother and his sister. We saw that although Bert now appeared to leave himself out, when compared with his own father he was discovering ways of coming more and more into center stage. He was pioneering a new script in which the three could be together.

Session with Grandparents

All three children came with their parents and maternal grandparents. I asked about discipline. Grandfather was very forthright: He said, "Our way is to discipline, but it is not Cilla's way. I feel the children need a lot more discipline." I said that his style of discipline seemed to differ from his daughter's. Both grandparents said that they considered discipline and good manners to be very important. Cilla's mother thought that Bert had also been a bit soft with the children. Cilla said that she felt her parents' input was unhelpful and went on to explain that they were asking her to behave in a way that was "not us." Cilla now pointed out to her parents that she had found that being more direct, avoiding double messages, and avoiding hitting and screaming was much more effective. I said that the complicated thing about three generations is that each generation has to find their own way. Grandmother nodded, but persisted in saying that it nevertheless makes it easier if the parents are a bit strict with the children. Grandmother said, "They just have to be told sometimes." Then I asked, "If you say that, will your daughter have to do the opposite?" Grandmother said, "Possibly," then laughed.

I asked whether once the family had moved it would be easier for them to get along. Grandmother explained that she did not think it would make any difference because she felt she did not have any influence anyway. Genuinely surprised, I exclaimed, "You think not!" Grandmother, on second thought, said, "Oh, perhaps we do." I said that each generation has to mark out its own ground by doing things their own way. At this point the children started making more demands and more noise. The grandparents stopped and listened while the parents sorted out the disagreement over some toys. I sat quietly, letting the parents get on with it, and then went over and sat by the grandparents. I told them that I was impressed by the fact that they had been able to sit quietly and had not tried to take over the disciplining. They said that it was no problem. But I teased them a bit by pointing out that I had noticed their faces wincing, and they all laughed. In the meantime, the children had been settled by Bert and Cilla. I pointed out that they had done a good job and both grandparents agreed. I then spent some time talking to the grandparents about how they might miss the family when they moved. Grandmother, in particular, said that she was going to miss them. I then said that, as they probably knew from their own experience, when you are bringing up your own family you still have in the back of your head the image of your own parents disapproving or approving. At first they did not understand, but then I explained it in a more concrete way. "Cilla will have a picture of both of you in the back of her head (*pointing to the back of my head*) when she goes up to Norfolk, and Bert will also have his two parents talking to him in the back of his head, saying, 'I like this, I disapprove of that.'" I then turned to Cilla and said, "What would make you feel you can do this your way and that you don't have to do either exactly the opposite or exactly the same as your parents?" Cilla said, "Well, if they stood back from it for a while and did not get caught up in the chaos."

Grandfather had obviously become intrigued by the image of wanting to react against the criticism of parents. He said, "My sister and I also had this with our parents. We had a tyrannical mother. I always objected when they criticized our children, and wanted to do the opposite." He suddenly seemed much more thoughtful. He could at last empathize with his daughter.

Preparing to Make a Separate Home

The parents came on their own to the next session. We focused on how Bert could tell his in-laws to stop interfering with the family. I asked him to role-play. Bert looked awkward and said quietly, and very politely, "I'd be extremely grateful if you'd let us bring up our children ourselves." I exclaimed, "Surely not *that* rude!" There was laughter and merriment over this, but Cilla was warm and supportive, not ridiculing. Bert was amused by his own politeness. He had in practice become much more assertive. He was clearly on Cilla's side now. I asked him how he was going to make an honest, monogamous woman out of Cilla. At the moment she was married to her parents, to him, and to Geoffrey. The discussion moved to Bert's family, and I saw how they had also had to struggle to extricate their marriage from the previous generation. Bert was now fully identified with the process of differentiating and establishing their new family.

In this family, although the loss of control of the children was the urgent presenting problem, the attachments—overly strong bonds with the previous generation, and an unconsolidated marriage—had been creating a great sense of insecurity. Dysfunctional authority and insecure attachments were mutually reinforcing.

Follow-Up

The family came to see me after the move to Norfolk. Although there were still some worries about Geoffrey, they centered mostly on difficulties in settling in his new school; a far cry from worries about burning the house down.

Bert described how he had carried Cilla over the threshold of their new home. They were "married" at last.

Resolving Distance Conflicts

People who have secure attachments do not often have ongoing conflicts over how close or distant they should be from the attachment figure. They are able to alternate between being together or apart. In a secure relationship each person may want a different distance at any one time, but this is negotiable because there is confidence that care will be given when needed. In insecure relationships the situation is different. There may be anxieties—about either being too far away, getting too close, or both—which interfere with the free flow of coming and going in the family. This may create distance conflicts within family relationships. This chapter will consider how some of these conflicts might arise and how they may be resolved.

We all need ways of defending ourselves against unpleasant experiences or situations. We can usually find ways to prevent them from becoming overwhelming or interfering with everyday life. Unfortunately, some of the strategies used, although perhaps helpful in the short term, may interfere with long-term functioning. The two main methods of handling unpleasant experiences within attachments, avoidant and ambivalent, take different routes, as we have seen in previous chapters. It is worth summarizing and comparing these two contrasting methods of processing information about unpleasant experiences before considering how they contribute to distance conflicts.

AVOIDANT/DISENGAGED AND AMBIVALENT/ENMESHED STRATEGIES CONTRASTED

The insecurely attached individual, either during childhood or as an adult, is vigilant for signs of danger within the attachment relationship; this vigilance is, of course, focused through the lens of past experiences of being hurt. The ambivalent/enmeshed person is afraid of being abandoned; the avoidant/disengaged person is afraid of feeling affection, in case the anticipated rejection will be too painful. Each is fearful about the survival of the relationship but has different strategies for dealing with it. The ambivalent/enmeshed individual is on the lookout for the first sign of loss of interest or departure in order to stop the other leaving; the avoidant/disengaged person is highly sensitive to any signs of impending closeness or intimacy and tries to stop it in order to preempt the pain of rejection. The ambivalent person is preoccupied with past experiences, either from previous generations or from what has happened in the present relationship. This represents an attempt to resolve those uncomfortable issues, but the issues usually remain unresolved as there are so many ambivalent mixed feelings about what happened. The avoidant person defends him- or herself from feelings about what has happened, or is happening, that might be painful. To do this, he or she uses defensive exclusion (Bowlby, 1980) which prevents painful memories being recalled, but also blocks access to uncomfortable feelings.

Each also has a different way of viewing the implications of what has happened in the past or is happening now. The ambivalent person is sensitive to and preoccupied with old memories as well as recent happenings. He or she is constantly looking for implications of what happened and feeling either aggrieved or guilty. The avoidant person denies any implications of what is happening. Indeed, he or she dismisses the importance of attachments, so what occurs within relationships is of little consequence. In short, ambivalent/enmeshed individuals review the implications, while avoidant/disengaged individuals stop themselves from seeing the implications or feeling strongly about them.

The two groups tend to handle self–other boundaries differently. The avoidant/disengaged person may see the other as being very different and separate—nothing to do with him or her—whereas the ambivalent/enmeshed individual may blur the boundary, creating an inner theater of the mind in which the characters can be interchangeable, including the recasting of the current generation in the roles of the previous one, as old dramas are constantly brought to life.

To summarize the difference: Avoidant/disengaged individuals feel that relationships may become too close, and so they keep at a distance; ambivalent/enmeshed individuals feel that relationships may become too distant and so they cling on. It is important, however, to be cautious about this. My impression is that everyone knows and has the capacity to use all three strategies—secure, avoidant, and clinging—given particular situations. Trying to categorize an individual within a family session will often lead to the sudden realization that even though he or she seems to be one way, a different aspect can be revealed unexpectedly. For instance, a distant father shows a flash of intimate sensitivity, or one person who seems close, even enmeshed, with one member of the family is distant with another. Individuals usually have predominant strategies within particular relationships and will revert to those modes when under stress and when attachment behavior is aroused. The Strange Situation (SS) procedure allows for subcategories that include features of another strategy as well as the predominant style. The Adult Attachment Interview (AAI) also allows for similar subcategories. The combination, however, of avoiding/ clinging does seem to pose a particular problem. Crittenden (1988) identified both features in disorganized/disoriented children who are at risk.

    If everyone in a family were to adopt a similar strategy, these strategies might be relatively successful. Distant families can feel comfortable with their remoteness; close families are proud of their connectedness. Family therapists often encounter families in which both contrasting strategies are present to some degree. This can be called the too close/too far family system (Byng-Hall, 1980), which creates particular forms of distance conflict.

CONCEPTUAL FRAMEWORK FOR DISTANCE CONFLICT

The Instability of a Too Close/Too Far System

Sometimes the degree of closeness in a relationship needed to allay fears of separation is itself too intimate for comfort, generating a sense of insecurity. This is a quite common situation in many relationships at some point in their history. Many couples go through patches when intimacy feels threatening to one or the other partner, while at other times the degree of freedom enjoyed by one threatens the security of the other. This distance conflict can also affect other relationships, especially parent–adolescent relationships in which it is a common experience for both parent and child to be greatly relieved to have some distance from each other, while the parent feels considerable anxiety about the adolescent being out of contact, especially at night. These distance conflicts, through which we are all likely to pass at some time or other, may, however, become scripted as an ongoing state of affairs. This is especially likely when each of those in the relationship has contrasting strategies for handling insecurity; for instance, one partner may have a predominantly avoidant strategy, the other an ambivalent one.

The too close/too far system created by this contrast can become unstable. A greater effort by one partner to reach a safe distance provokes greater effort in the other to cling more tightly, which produces even greater efforts to get away, and so on, with escalating intensity. Each person's move produces the opposite of what was wanted, which then provokes even greater efforts. In terms of cybernetic control systems, there is a mutual positive feedback system which leads to escalations of pursuer–pursuing behavior. In attachment behavior terms, avoidant strategies are likely to provoke clinging in insecure/ambivalent individuals; in turn, the clinging leads to greater distancing in insecure/avoidant individuals. Thus, when individuals who use predominantly avoidant strategies in attachment behavior get together with someone who uses a predominantly entangling/clinging strategy, an escalation of pursuing–pursued can occur. Hoffman (1971) called these cases "runaways," which, if unhalted, lead to the breakup of the relationship. Hoffman pointed out, however, that "runaways" often come to a sudden end—they are aborted. How does this happen? One mechanism is to triangulate other people in to stabilize the dyad.

An Individual's Ambivalence or Symptom Used to Regulate Parental Distance

A couple in a too close/too far distance conflict is particularly likely to resolve this potential runaway by triangulating in another person, often a child, to regulate the distance between them (Byng-Hall, 1985a). Each becomes linked to the other through the child. The child becomes a distance regulator, holding the parents at a safe distance, neither too close nor too far from each other. The child monitors the parents' relationship, ready to pull them together when they get too distant or to come between them when they are too close. Family therapists know only too well the myriad ways in which children can be involved in these maneuvers. For the couple it provides an effective solution because they can avoid the frightening escalations that happened when they were only responding to cues within their relationship.

The main hypothesis in this chapter is that the distance regulator is also prone to become the designated patient (Byng-Hall, 1980). He or she is often felt by the family to be responsible for the remaining marital discomfort. The parents are held at an unsatisfactory, if safe, distance. They have neither satisfactory intimacy nor freedom. The child is perceived as "coming between us" or a "constant drag." A child who is ambivalent about the marriage makes a good recruit for this job. Most children have appropriately mixed feelings about their parents' relationship: They want them to stay together but also like to get in between them to get something special from one parent. A classic example is the "oedipal" triangle. Once triangulated, the child's ambivalence provides all the negative feedback necessary to prevent excessive marital distance or closeness. The child's intrapersonal conflict created by ambivalent feelings about the parents' relationship thus becomes important for the survival of the family unit. This ambivalence has to be maintained by everyone in the family. It is a small wonder that symptoms then arise.

The child's symptom itself can then become the distance regulator. When the fear is of the parents breaking up, the child creates a problem that brings the parents together again as coparents. This is a nonintimate role, and hence safe. This represents a perfect compromise to the too close/too far dilemma for the parents. It is the symptom that now has to be maintained for the sake of family survival. The solution of the distance conflict includes the child's problem behavior. This particular solution is likely to become scripted because to give it up exposes the family to the parents' unstable relationship.

The child who makes the best recruit, however, is often insecure/ambivalent and might regulate closeness by capturing one parent, clinging to that parent and excluding the other. It is usually the ambivalent/enmeshed parent who allows him- or herself to be captured, as this provides a substitute closeness with the child. The avoidant/disengaged parent is also happy about the arrangement because it reduces the intrusive closeness of the partner. The demanding, attention-seeking, controlling behavior of the insecure/ambivalent child can then come to represent a problem with which the parents have to cope. The clinging child who will not sleep or comes into the parental bed is also typical.

Distance regulation might also be provided by a group of siblings; perhaps one is close to the mother but excluding the father, while the other creates problems and brings them together. Excessive sibling fighting can also bring parents in to stop the battles and is often effective in interrupting parental intimacy. A symptom in one of the parents may also become a distance regulator. For instance, a chronic illness or a symptom such as agoraphobia can act as a distance regulator. The agoraphobia means that the partner has to be present much of the time, but in the role of supporter, not lover. This provides protection from fears about intimacy as well as desertion. The in-laws also traditionally come between husband and wife, especially those who disapprove of the marriage in the first place. Therapists can also become distance regulators. They bring the couple together for therapy but in a safe context in which intimacy is limited.

The enemy of these ways of regulating too close/too far distance conflicts is improvisation: "Where will it lead? Could we become more intimate? Then all my secrets will be exposed. That would be the end. Or could we wander even further apart? It is unlikely he or she will want to come back to me then. Better to stick to what we know—stick to our script—and focus on the problem."

The fears about loss and abandonment have been dealt with previously. But why can intimacy be so frightening?

Perceived Dangers of Intimacy

Ryder and Bartle (1991) discuss the distance-regulating role of the boundaries in intimacy. The issue they point out is not so straightforward. To have a perceived limit to closeness can foster intimacy, as it curbs fears of getting too close. You might have expected that having a boundary to closeness would hinder intimacy instead. Adequate limits then on closeness and distance help. It is only when the relationship is simultaneously too close *and* too far that conflict arises. Kelvin (1977) describes the individual's need for an area of totally private fantasy. If no one knows about it, no one can change that part of him or her. This area of constancy helps to maintain the sense of self as being unique. In the unfolding intimacy of courtship, however, more and more of this privacy is given up, running the risk of loss of identity. Kelvin also holds that physical sexual contact involves primitive responses that may further threaten the sense of control over this unrevealed area. For some, the image of mutual orgasm is clouded by the fear of cataclysmic loss of identity and of self, far from the ecstatic abandon hoped for. Ryder and Bartle (1991), however, discuss how transcending boundaries can happen within passionate sexual love in a way that can avoid catastrophic loss of sense of self. This requires a very clear sense of self with constant awareness of the indissoluble separateness of individuals. Then, through the sense of transcendence, there is a sense of becoming "one with the loved person." If there is felt to be pure fusion of the intimate fantasy world within that union, then the partners may feel that private space remains sacrosanct, now because it is safely within the boundaries of the sexual dyad. In some couples the illusion of knowing each other's fantasies and responses can be maintained for a while, and the partners can feel validated by this.

The blurring or loss of boundaries is, however, a feature of ambivalent/enmeshed couples. Within the conceptual framework of attachment behavior, the illusion of reading other people's minds relates to the individual's need to try to assess whether or not the other is likely to respond to his or her needs. True intimacy comes when one or both partners have to acknowledge that their image of the other's thoughts and feelings belongs less to the partner and more to their own imagination. The potential loss of security inherent in this acknowledgment can feel catastrophic and may be avoided either by separating—disengaging from shared intimacy—or by increasingly intrusive attempts to control or "read" the other's mind. In the latter case, as Kelvin's ideas suggest, the partner is likely to respond by becoming more secretive, in turn provoking further intrusion from the other partner. Another runaway is created. Once again an outside, shared preoccupation can come to the rescue and can halt these processes. The child may provide this focus either by switching the parents from a "sexual" into a "parenting" (nonsexual) dyad, by becoming someone they can disagree over—hence maintaining each parent's separate, because differing, self-identity, or by becoming a substitute partner.

THERAPEUTIC IMPLICATIONS

In those families that use triangles in order to regulate their distance, the therapist, whether he or she likes it or not, will also be used in the same way. The therapeutic use of this phenomenon involves first entering the arena as a go-between, then taking precedence over other go-betweens, and finally changing this role from an unhelpful one into a healthy one. The work will entail helping the family with their anxieties about both loss and intimacy, and then handing back the responsibility for distance regulation to the couple.

Case Example: The Jones Family

The Jones family originally came from Wales. Cindy, aged 13, was referred to the clinic because of school refusal.

In the first session, the family distance regulation mechanisms are often evident. If they are posing a problem for the family, it is valuable to build a simple picture of how they evolved. Some of the past go-betweens are often still involved.

Cindy was a typical truculent adolescent. She plonked herself down close to her mother whom she used as a shield between herself and her father. Brian, aged 10, sat beyond her watching intently. Cindy peered around her mother and accused her father of being embarrassing and generally disgusting. The father, Dai, a lean balding man of 42, defended himself against this attack. The mother, Evelyn, aged 40, glanced sideways at her husband in a way that showed she was on Cindy's side.

Mother was apparently helping to keep father and daughter apart for some reason. But Cindy demonstrated through her reaction of disgust that she had already taken responsibility for keeping herself distant from her father. Disgust is a particularly useful way of creating a barrier when the relationship might otherwise be too close. But, by siding with Cindy, her mother also avoided closeness to her husband on the pretext of caring for her daughter.

Questions about onset of symptoms, and about family moves, often reveal how the bonding pattern has evolved. Symptoms had begun after the Jones family had moved to Bristol from Wales 4 years before, leaving behind Dai's mother, who was a depressed and difficult old lady. Evelyn said that her husband was "married" to his mother. The children laughed. Dai shook his head but did not refute the charge. Evelyn told the following legend about their wedding reception. A waiter had approached her to ask if he should start serving the next round of champagne. Prudently she suggested waiting 20 minutes. One minute later, however, she observed to her fury that the same waiter was serving drinks. When asked why, he explained that the senior Mrs. Jones had told him to do so.

This legend was told to show that Dai's mother was the cause of all the marital problems. But the story also revealed that she wanted more champagne—more fizz—more quickly in her son's marriage. Thus, she had a role in encouraging both distance and closeness.

After the family's arrival in Bristol, Evelyn had been agoraphobic, and a psychologist, Mr. J., had helped her with this. As Evelyn improved, Cindy developed phobias and became Mr. J.'s patient as well. After coming to London a year previously, Cindy had started to refuse to go to school.

The distance regulator had changed over the years. Dai's mother had been the distance regulator in Wales, and Evelyn had taken over after the move to Bristol. Evelyn had also complained of being frigid as well as being agoraphobic, thus limiting both separation and intimacy. Owing to her refusal to go school, Cindy had finally taken over the role upon arrival in London. Cindy not only stayed at home with her mother, but she also very actively captured her mother. They told me that she used to go to her parents' bedroom and "force" her mother to come to her bed, "because I am afraid of the dark." However, on another occasion she had locked her parents in their bedroom for 6 hours before releasing them. Therapists, past and present, were also, of course, involved.

Therapist Takes Over as Distance Regulator

This family attempted to recruit therapists into the role of distance regulator but on their terms, thus rendering the therapists useless as an agent of change. For the first three sessions the Jones family applied relentless pressure on me to become like Mr. J. who had befriended Dai and had invited him to join his psychotherapy seminars. Dai, in turn, became my "cotherapist" to both his wife and daughter, and in this way distanced himself from them but at the same time made himself indispensable to them. After the start of therapy with me, the Jones family recruited Mr. J. back into the role of Cindy's therapist helping her to go to school. There were a number of telephone calls to him from Cindy. During Dai's continuing visits to Mr. J.'s seminars, Dai told the seminar how badly I was treating the family. Upon discovering this, I became angry. On the one hand, I felt like saying to the family, "If you don't want my help—go," but, on the other hand, I wanted to tell Mr. J., "Leave the family to me." It can now be seen that the ambivalence—"wishing out, but wanting in"—was to be found in the whole system: family members, and now the therapist as well. The distance regulator, as we have seen, is likely to be designated the cause of the problem and, as the tug of war intensifies, is also likely to feel the discomfort. For a while I became the family scapegoat. This process is described by Skynner (1979). I experienced something of their discomfort about the too close/too far conflict.

I became the ambivalence container; that is, I held their mixed feelings. It was important to understand this in terms of the system. I discussed it with colleagues and found another way out. It was clear that the therapists were being invited to form a rivalrous dyad who would cancel each other out—thus not threatening the distance pattern in the family by asking them to face what was happening. Instead of courting the family away from Mr. J.—a step in the rivalry dance—I contacted Mr. J. and asked for his help. I then agreed with Cindy and her father that Mr. J. was extremely helpful, and told her that she should ring him not once a week, but every day instead. I never heard about Mr. J. again.

Displacing Other Distance Regulators

The fourth session was held without Brian, who was in his school play. I put stress on the distance pattern in the family by seeing Cindy on her own for half an hour while the parents sat in the next room. This separation was what was being avoided by the school refusal. When she went to fetch her parents from next door, Cindy became very childish; she sat on her mother's lap, clinging desperately to her. I waited for the parents to manage the situation. Initially they tolerated it, but I asked whether they were satisfied with this. Dai asked his daughter to go and sit down on the couch. He tried to move her physically but failed. He said she was too strong for him. Her mother then tried to move her but with an equal lack of success. Each tried again while I sat and observed. I said that I was surprised that Dai had not been able to manage his daughter. Cindy explained that her father had a bad heart. He denied this, although later it emerged that there had been a scare about a possible heart attack. I remarked that father only had to put out a hand to help his wife and they might be able to manage as a team. Cindy tested them to the end, and only when both parents were totally determined to move her and to act together did she get up and go to sit on the couch. I then asked whether Cindy had ever slept in her parents' bed. Somewhat shame-faced, the parents admitted that Cindy had been in their bed the previous night. I discussed with the parents how they might work together as a team to get her out that evening.

In the next session the parents came on their own. Cindy had gone back to school without any trouble the following day (and then remained at school). She had not even tried to get into their bed that evening. Dai, smiling, added that at 4 o'clock in the morning they had both awakened and had intercourse for the first time in a long while.

To summarize, I had acted as a distance regulator between Cindy and her parents, first by seeing Cindy separately, and then by insisting that her parents get her off mother's knee. I handed the performance of the task, however, back to the parents and exploded the myth that father was not strong enough to help separate his wife from his daughter. Having completed this structural move in the session, I helped the parents to dispense with Cindy as a distance regulator in their sex life.

WORK WITH THE COUPLES

Coparenting or Couple Therapy?

The switch from working with a couple on coparenting issues to work on the couple's relationship or on sexual dysfunction has to be handled carefully. The family has located the problem in the child for good systemic reasons. My policy is to be very cautious about making the shift. The question may arise, however, when the therapist has managed to help the family to see that the child has been a distance regulator for the couple. Partners not infrequently start to acknowledge the conflict in their relationship and may then be eager to work on resolving the conflict. However, what must be remembered is that the moment that the difficulties surface, past strategies are likely to be brought back into action. A formal switch to couple work following some family therapy quite frequently leads to a resurgence of the child's problems. Even if the child is no longer there, discussion about the child will often be used to defuse the anxiety generated by the couple therapy. My initial response when a couple asks to work on their relationship is to be cautious and say that the issues for them as coparents have not been sufficiently dealt with yet. I agree neverthe- less to see them on their own to do that work. The couple is then often able to do some useful work on their relationship from within the relative safety of being able to switch to the nonintimate topic of their children. I usually ask about the children at each session even if they have not mentioned them. This may lead to pressure from the couple to focus exclusively on their relationship rather than spend time on the children. If this pressure is sustained, then I do change the contract to that of couple work. Sometimes, however, it is clear that a child is no longer triangulated, as in the Jones family, and so the switch to couple therapy can follow.

The reverse situation exists when parents refer themselves for couples therapy. I am similarly slow to shift the focus to the children, even after the partners begin to see more clearly how they are involv- ing the children in their relationship. I will nevertheless discuss the children in light of the couple's relationship. If the children have real problems, I will bring them into the sessions for specific pieces of work. An earlier case study (Byng-Hall, 1985a) illustrated how I work with the distance conflicts in couples.

Couple Work with the Jones Family: Further Detriangulation

After Cindy had returned to school, I asked the couple what further work they might want to do. They both agreed that their own rela- tionship left much to be desired and asked for help with that. I en- couraged them to discuss the difficulties together. Soon the topic of conversation became Dai's mother. He was always wanting her to stay, but Evelyn always refused because she caused all the "trouble." I pointed out that they were avoiding talking about themselves by bring- ing in a third party, this time the mother-in-law. This family, how- ever, used words to avoid action, and so I used a nonverbal technique. I announced that I was now going to role-play the mother-in-law. I asked them to go on discussing their relationship, and at the first mention of the mother-in-law I got up and stood between husband and wife, blocking their view of each other. They were somewhat startled, but I insisted that they continue with their discussion. As each of them tried to peer around me, I moved to obscure their view. After a while they became irritated by this, and Evelyn asked me to sit down. At this I turned around and looked at Dai inquiringly. They continued with the discussion, until eventually Dai also asked me to sit down. Instead, I turned around to look at Evelyn, who now quickly asked me to sit down. Once more I merely turned around to look at Dai. After a surprising length of time and with steadily rising tension, husband and wife finally asked each other whether they wanted me to sit down. At the moment they agreed I sat down. They both laughed and were able to see the parallel between the previous session in which they had to act together before Cindy would move.

I commented on how difficult it must be to get close to one another with the mother-in-law always between them. Again they laughed and started addressing each other directly and discussing their marital relationship. Once or twice they mentioned the mother-in-law. Each time they did, I either got to my feet to stand between them or made a move to do so. This reminded them of how they used her, and it became a joke throughout their therapy.

In this exercise I was emphasizing that the parents brought the mother-in-law in as a distance regulator. My action showed that the mother-in-law, even thoughts of her, could be as powerful an intrusion into their life as Cindy could be in the flesh. Again they had to experience the reality that a couple can "get rid of" a third party only through mutual agreement. Anything short of this allows the third party to turn toward the member of the couple who is wavering. I symbolically took on the role of distance regulator to the couple but then demonstrated that I could be dismissed from that role through a shared decision. This nonverbal technique is experientially powerful; the problem for me is to avoid laughing as a way of diffusing the tension.

Although the Joneses were no longer talking about the mother-in-law in the sessions, Dai's mother herself became more actively intrusive in the marriage. She asked Dai to stay with her. In her usual style, Evelyn said that she would never allow her mother-in-law to get her hands on him. Dai wanted, as always, to go. Using a genogram, I discovered that Dai's brother had to go to Australia to get away from their mother. I pointed out to Evelyn what a wonderful job she had been doing for her husband over the last 16 years; she had been fighting all of her husband's battles with his mother for him. This had enabled him to be separate from his mother without having to encounter any conflict with her. If Evelyn had not done this for him, he might have had to fight his mother in the way his brother had done. Dawning awareness appeared in Evelyn's eyes.

I then suggested that Dai had an important piece of work to do with his mother, and that Evelyn should make sure that he went to live with his mother for at least a month on his own. The look of horror on Dai's face was instantaneous and somewhat comical. Evelyn and I finally agreed that perhaps a long weekend would be more practical. Dai reported that his wife no longer nagged him after this session. He went for a weekend only once during the therapy, and he became more and more explicit about not wanting to be with his mother. This paradoxical approach exploded the myth that Evelyn would lose her husband to her mother-in-law if they got together even briefly.

In the ensuing contract to work on the marital relationship, Dai continually tried to play the therapist to his wife, causing a distancing effect on their relationship because it always made Evelyn angry, and she would then push him away. I balanced this maneuver by asking Evelyn to be Cindy's "therapist." This had the combined effect of raising Evelyn's status, increasing the generational boundaries between herself and her daughter and creating a boundary between Cindy and her father. Dai had been using his "therapist's" role to be inappropriately intrusive into his attractive daughter's social life. At times during the rest of the treatment, I worked with Evelyn on what was happening to Cindy. Slowly, however, I shifted this emphasis to their joint parenting of Cindy, who was now doing very well at school.

Dealing with Fears of Loss

An effect of my making an alliance with Evelyn was that Dai became exposed to the idea that he might have some troubles of his own. His wife remembered that he had gone to pieces after each of their moves. I followed the theme of illness and discovered that Dai had an acute panic attack during one journey when he was driving away from home. He thought he had a heart attack. The theme of illness was explored through a genogram, and it emerged that his father had died suddenly of a coronary during a trip he took when he was roughly the same age that Dai was now. His aunt had also died of a coronary in middle age. Dai felt he had the shadow of death hanging over him.

Upon exploring Evelyn's genogram (see Figure 10.1) it became obvious that she also had very real reasons for anxiety about separations. She had been removed from her home by her grandmother at the age of 1 because of neglect by her parents. Evelyn's grandmother

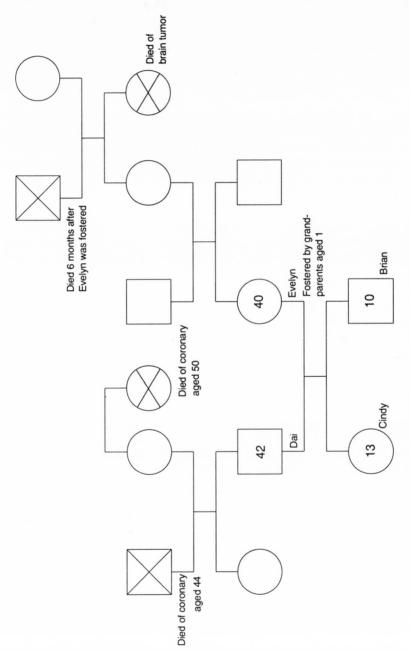

FIGURE 10.1. Jones family genogram.

Died 6 months after
Evelyn was fostered

Died of
brain tumor

Died of coronary
aged 50

Evelyn
Fostered by grand-
parents aged 1

Brian

Cindy

Dai

Died of coronary
aged 44

195

had a double reason for holding onto her as another "daughter." First, she had lost a daughter with a brain tumor, and, second, her husband had died 6 months after Evelyn's arrival in the household. Evelyn and her grandmother had been inseparable. At the age of 5, however, Evelyn was wrenched away from her grandmother and sent to boarding school by her parents. She was said to have cried nonstop for 3 days. The source of Evelyn's fear of someone coming (e.g., mother-in-law) and wrecking her family relationships was now clear. Her other need, however, to have someone available to come and rescue her when the relationship became unsatisfactory was also clear. She remarked that as a young woman she had had many boyfriends who did not have intrusive mothers, but she had finally married a man with a mother who could be relied upon to interfere.

Bringing the Approach–Avoidance Conflict into the Session

In one session the couple was asked to act out, without words, some typical interactions between them. Evelyn stood still facing her husband as he approached her, opening his arms when he got closer as if to hug her. Evelyn then put her hands up to keep him at a slight distance. Dai dropped his hands to his side in resignation and walked toward the door as if to leave; before reaching the door, however, he turned back and walked toward his wife once more. The whole cycle was then repeated. After this cycle had been repeated about 10 times with an increasing sense of frustration, I asked the couple whether they would like to enact the cycle in a way they would both prefer. After a series of tentative efforts, they finally managed to embrace each other. I stood by silently and allowed the tension to rise. Finally they had to pull away again from each other. I asked what it was they were afraid of in their intimate contact. They said that they did not know, but that they would like some help with their sexual relationship, which was unsatisfactory.

In this experiential exercise, the tension in the approach–avoidance conflict was raised to an almost intolerable level. The fears of loss had been explored earlier; now was the time to explore anxieties about intimacy. I offered the couple a contract of six sessions to work on their sexual dysfunction.

Therapy of Sexual Dysfunction—Resolving Fears of Intimacy

I explored the origins of their sexual problems. The couple had been engaged for 4 years and had avoided full intercourse before marriage. They had usually indulged in mutually exciting, heavy petting in

Dai's mother's house. Their shared anxiety was that his mother would find the semen-stained handkerchiefs. It seemed as if they were already using images of his mother to inhibit their sexuality. They once again described the mother-in-law's interference in the wedding. When there is a genuine story of the failure of parents to "give" their children away in the marriage ceremony, the therapist can fruitfully role-play a ritual marriage in which he plays the person on each side of the family who was believed to have disapproved of the marriage. In role-play, he or she gives blessing to the union instead of cursing the marriage. Couples report surprising relief from this experience. In the case of the Joneses, however, I felt that the disapproval was a myth, and so this was not done.

On the first night of their honeymoon, Dai had ejaculated prematurely. This created increasing anxiety between the partners, but they were unable to talk about it. Evelyn reported that she then read an article that advised wives to reduce foreplay to a minimum to enable their husbands to last longer. Dai was amazed when he heard about this article: His wife had never told him about it prior to this session. This technique worked to some extent, and his anxiety about premature ejaculation receded somewhat. However, he now labeled her as frigid and "mechanical." Toward the end of the honeymoon, the couple found some pretext to return to Dai's mother's house. In this account the myth that Dai's mother had caused all the trouble was finally exploded. I reframed Evelyn's acceptance of the label "frigid" as her way of protecting her husband from his anxiety. It also appeared that at times she would achieve an orgasm without foreplay, and so I further relabeled her as being "supersexual." She could reach a climax quickly and with very little stimulation.

Evelyn was also afraid of being hurt by her husband's hands. He was enormously strong and admitted to gripping her powerfully, either when he was nearing orgasm or when he was angry with her. At the end of the first session, I instructed the couple not to have intercourse and said that if they were having trouble following my instructions, they were to invoke the image of the mother-in-law, which they all knew would effectively stop any sex. This instruction was designed either to give the couple an experience of having some control over the "mother-in-law" imagery by actively conjuring it up, or to work paradoxically, but inhibiting the image.

In the next session the couple was asked to use their hands to mime their relationship. Hands had been used to express the difficulties in the marriage, and thus provided a suitable medium for change. Evelyn held her hand stiff and upright with the palm facing her husband. He approached with his hand, but just before they touched, his wife withdrew her hand, lowering it at the same time. His hand then came over the top, but at this point Evelyn gave it a little slap and pushed it away. Dai immediately withdrew his hand back to his body, and then started the process again. This cycle was repeated again and again until they became bored with it. I suggested they try something else. They could not think of anything. "How about sideways?" I suggested. This initiated a whole new dance with Evelyn's hand teasing and inviting her husband to follow her. He interpreted it as withdrawal, but I relabeled it "flirtation." After some time Dai's hand was allowed to come forward and rest on his wife's hand. When asked how he felt, he answered, "Stuck." I suggested that he might be frightened of being stuck inside his wife. He denied this initially but then recalled his memories as a child of being told about the vaginal muscles strangling the penis. I said, "No wonder you wanted to be in and out as quickly as possible, and you, Evelyn, were very intuitive in knowing that you should be mechanical, showing him that your vaginal muscles would not become excited enough to do that to him." Evelyn mentioned that sometimes intercourse hurt her. Following this theme, she admitted that she had a terrifying fear of being broken into by a penis, "as if a membrane would be broken through."

Their shared fears of sex as a potentially damaging act were explored, and ways of making it a safer activity were worked out. In the next session Dai expressed the idea that orgasm should be a mutually experienced ecstasy in which they should understand each other perfectly. I suggested that instead they might have a joint fear that in the mutual excitement of intercourse they would be totally submerged and lost in each other—swallowed up in fact—at the same time they felt wildly out of control, something terrifying to each. This comment seemed to make a lot of sense to the couple.

Dai was given instructions not to talk during intercourse. Up to this point I had been agreeing with him that they needed to be able to discuss their sexuality, whereas Evelyn flatly refused even to mention sex. I had failed to spot that Dai used his "therapist" voice to terminate intimacy in foreplay. A "therapist" in bed is as good an inhibitor as a mother-in-law. At the next session they came in happily reporting exciting and mutually satisfactory intercourse three times during the week. I suggested that things were improving too fast and that they should not expect exciting intercourse as frequently as this. There was a month because of illness and holiday breaks before the final and last session.

When they came back, they reported that Evelyn had been depressed for 2 weeks but had then returned to a sexually satisfying relationship. I related the depression to the end of the sessions. I returned to the original wedding legend in order to reedit it. In the retelling of the story, it emerged that Evelyn had herself paid for the whole reception in order to save her parents money. To protect their pride, she had not told Dai's parents about who was paying. They could see now that from Dai's mother's viewpoint, her intrusion into the reception had been a disagreement between her and Evelyn's parents about how ceremonies should be conducted. It was not an intrusion of a mother-in-law into her daughter-in-law's relationship. The other side of the coin now had to be explored, however. If the mother-in-law was no longer in the way, then nothing was in the way of the fantasy that they could now have a perfect, satisfying, ecstatic, sexual relationship without any difficulties. In practice they had a middle-aged marriage in which they could not expect the same frequency of intercourse as a young couple. The heavy petting had been about three times a week before marriage. They could not expect that frequency now.

Toward the end of the session, Dai said that one thing was certain—his wife would make a much better mother-in-law to their children than his mother had seemed to be. The intergenerational cycle, it is hoped, had been broken. At the 6-month follow-up the family reported continuing improvement.

Positive Framing of Parenting Scripts

When a therapist meets a family there is no way in which the therapist can avoid communicating his or her attitude to how the parents are looking after their children. Everyone will be on tenterhooks to see. Even a careful attempt to be neutral about it will be construed in one way or another by the family. If not positive, it is likely to be experienced as critical. The therapist needs to consider how and what to communicate. I would argue that this is one of the most crucial issues that will decide whether or not the therapist is helpful.

I have observed more important shifts in family functioning arising from praising the family's struggle to manage better than from any other intervention. This is especially important for parenting skills. The family therapist who criticizes, overtly or covertly, what a parent is doing in front of their children, or partner for that matter, undermines that parent's sense of being able to be a good parent, and what is worse denigrates his or her efforts in front of the other members of the family. In contrast, when other members come to understand that the parents' admittedly odd way of parenting reflects a struggle to do a better job than their own parents did, then they are more likely to be able to appreciate these parenting practices. They can respect the parents' efforts rather than merely trying to combat them and seeing the parents as being deliberately destructive or perverse. To positively frame the parents' intentions, the therapist must also be able to respect their struggle. It is also easier for the therapist to avoid criticizing if it is possible to understand, from the parents' past, their current struggle. Respect for the capacity to struggle to find solutions is, in itself, a powerfully enabling attitude, as most people coming for help suffer from low self-esteem. To be treated with respect ushers in the idea that they could succeed. The catch is that no one can artificially manufacture respect. Any underlying disrespect is usually immediately picked up by clients, however well it is hidden. After all, many of our clients have become experts at picking up dislike or criticism. Adequate systemic understanding of the family's dilemmas provides one of the best ways of avoiding blaming one particular person or one particular action. As Stanton, Todd, and Associates (1982) like to convey to the family, "everything that everybody does is for good reason and is understandable." This applies to even the most "destructive" of their behaviors. Such therapeutic moves have been called "ascribing noble intentions" or "noble aspirations."

It is important not to underestimate the pull exerted on the therapist to join the blaming, critical culture of the family. Sometimes parents are so openly horrible to each other in a way that is exasperating. The therapist is then driven to want to point out how horrible each parent has been. If the therapist succumbs to this impulse, he or she will disappear without trace into the family system. In one family, when struggling to avoid this, I came up with the notion that "blaming is what is to blame." Gleefully they blamed each other for blaming, thus making the point that if the core plot of the script that the therapist uses—in this case blaming—is the same as the one he is trying to get the family to change, then the pattern becomes reinforced instead. A more useful strategy with parents deeply entrenched in highlighting each other's deficiencies is to use a courtroom metaphor. I say that each is so keen to get it exactly right for their child that they have prepared as detailed a case as possible and presented it to me, the judge, in the hope that I can make such a good verdict that it will solve their child's problems. Often there is enough resonance in the metaphor to make everyone laugh, which makes it more difficult to get back into the courtroom scenario. Note that the best of intentions are attributed to both parents. There can, however, also be dangers in conveying positive ideas about clearly destructive attitudes or behaviors. This is especially so in parenting, when abuse may form part of that behavior. I will never be positive in any way about abusive or potentially dangerous behaviors. It is, surprisingly, often possible to be positive about the struggle to avoid such behaviors, or trying to take responsibility for them.

There are various techniques for positively framing behaviors and intentions within the family. This is done by either positively connoting behaviors or attitudes that are currently seen as problematic, or positively labeling those that are aimed at producing, or actually do produce, the desired effect.

POSITIVE CONNOTATION
OF THE PARENTING SCRIPT

Positive connotation (Simon et al., 1985) refers to a family therapist's positive evaluation of behavior which otherwise would be regarded as pathological or "sick." Both replicative and corrective parenting scripts may at times be experienced as problematic. Hence, positive connotation is a particularly suitable technique when exploring the parenting style of the previous generation.

One mother in a single-parent household had been brought up in a very violent family. Her son was now out of control, and she was using quite terrifying threats of violence to try to discipline him. She was clear that she wanted to manage better than her parents did with her, and she wanted to avoid hitting him. I was able to positively label her struggle to do better than her parents did, but then went on to point out that she was being loyal to her parents by her threats of violence, something her parents did to her, even if she never carried them out. She was quite put out by the suggestion that she could be in any way positive about her parents, although she could see what I was saying. This made her even more determined to find an alternative way of bringing up her children which did not echo her past. By positively connoting the struggle to avoid behaviors that she already knew to be problematic—such as her lack of sanctions, on the one hand, and terrible threats, on the other—she was able to increase her resolve to change. The important issue is that connotations are made in the context of comparing what was happening now with the past. Any implied criticism is of past generations. However, to avoid merely scapegoating the grandparents instead of the parents, it is important to explore the grandparents' own upbringing. It is then possible to positively connote, in turn, the grandparents' struggle to bring up their own children in the best way they could. This work can be done either with the grandparents present or through a genogram.

I remain very impressed with how positively connoting loyalty to a grandparent through a replicative script can allow someone to let it go. The parent is often aware of the desire to avoid repeating something unpleasant that was done to him or her in childhood. The distress it caused may remain in the memory. Identifying with a parent's behavior is, however, a much more automatic process, usually occurring outside awareness. This is especially so when identifying with the aggressor, where the purpose is to escape from the distress of being a victim by using the "theater of the mind" to disappear into the aggressor's body instead. Being made aware of the loyalty involved in taking the side of the abusing parent's that this identification involves can provide acknowledgment of important aspects of the relationship previously hidden by fury with that parent. Up until this point, the parent in therapy was unaware that the corrective script may have carried the stigma of disloyalty. Once this revelation occurs, the parent can choose whether or not he or she would want to remain loyal in such a destructive way.

POSITIVE CONNOTATION OF CHOICE OF PARTNER FOR ROLE IN PARENTING SCRIPT

It is often possible to see how a partner is selected who is able to fulfill a role in the transgenerational parenting scripts. One approach (discussed in Chapter 3) is to select someone who can replicate those roles from the past which are felt to be undesirable (e.g., a disciplinarian style), which frees one to be more protective and gentle. This enables one to keep a corrective vow not to be the disciplinarian in bringing up one's own children, while asking the partner to replicate the role loyal to one's own family. This can also work the other way around. One can, for example, select a partner who can be firm in contrast to one's own parents who were never able to establish authority. The partner then enacts your corrective script for you.

Positively connoting a choice of partner can be directed at either partner. First, a parent can be congratulated for having chosen someone who could either correct or replicate aspects of one's own family. The chosen partner can be praised for the service that he or she is performing for the other in doing this. Usually it is possible to point out the same process in the reverse direction. The partners can then be seen to be providing a mutual service to one another. Each enables the other to do things differently from their past or, by repeating aspects of the partner's past, enables him or her to remain loyal to the traditions of their family of origin.

As with all corrective and replicative scripts that are both always potentially present, there is always a tension between the two. Sometimes one script will predominate, sometimes the other. This means that partners may originally be chosen on the basis of having similar intentions. For instance, one woman chose an easygoing young man to father her children in contrast to her tyrannically strict father. However, his easygoing nature turned out to be a corrective script to his own strict parenting. It was so wonderful for each of them to find someone so refreshingly determined to create a relaxed easygoing family—"so different than my parents." However, his other side emerged later; the affable young man suddenly became a disciplinarian parent at times. To her horror, the woman realized she had married her father after all. She became very opposed to her partner's discipline. Now he represented her replicative script, which enabled her to keep her corrective, permissive self intact as a counterpart role. In turn, he became increasingly aware of how the children needed discipline because she would set no limits. It was then possible to define the behavior between the partners that maintained the split. When the children misbehaved, episodes or scenarios resulted in which each parent could define themself: On the one hand, she saw herself as warm and loving to the children "whatever they do"; on the other, he saw himself as caring by being firm. In this family it was important to trace the unfolding process and give appropriate positive connotations of each phase, as well as to understand the previous generations' struggle, which had been to provide order out of chaos through discipline. Eventually they came to see that their current roles were complementary, and they made a good team.

Partners might, in part anyway, be chosen on the basis of each operating the same kind of split. In this case a split between authoritarian and permissive discipline allows each to play roles on either the same side of the split or on opposite sides of the split. This enables them to adopt either replicative or corrective behavior at different phases in the relationship. Each can then hope to be able to adopt the more comfortable role.

The same can happen in other arenas. When, for instance, there have been several partners in a series of relationships, it is not uncommon to find that new partners are chosen on the basis of appearing to be "opposites" of the previous partners. In this way, a disciplinarian may be followed by a lax/permissive partner and so on. Opposite sides of the split can occasionally operate around subsequent children. One father was overstrict with his first son. Horrified by this, he became overpermissive with his next son. His wife had done the opposite: She was close and special to the first boy and furious with her husband at not being firm enough with the second. Each family's pattern has to be unraveled and positive connotation applied to the struggle to do better in the next attempt. Of course, families are not usually as neatly arranged as those above, but it is surprising how this way of exploring the difference between past and present can make sense of some of the parenting patterns.

POSITIVE LABELING OF PARENTING SKILLS

The therapist can affirm parenting skills that are shown to be effective. This is in contrast to positive connotation which relates, as we have seen, to those parts of parenting which can be seen as creating problems. Simon et al., (1985) define labeling as "the overt or covert attribution of characteristics, intentions and roles to the members of a social system"(p.10). The general rule that whatever is focused on is likely to be reinforced, while whatever is ignored will fade is a useful one. Competent aspects of family behavior can be noted and labeled. The dysfunctional behaviors can be acknowledged, but the focus remains on the strengths—what is valuable is reinforced. Concentrating on the dysfunctional behavior may have the effect of reinforcing those behaviors instead. However, I see this as having implications beyond the laws of reinforcement. Individual therapists may feel that positive labeling is a dangerous activity because it is simple reassurance. This may be true of individual psychotherapy. In family therapy, however, it often seems to enable the family to acknowledge their problematic behavior. It is easier for parents to talk about those painful issues for which they were expecting criticism if they discover that instead their parenting skills are being supported in front of their partners and their children.

Positive labeling can be one step toward providing a secure family base—a setting conducive to discussing what is going wrong without fear of being undermined. The next step is to acknowledge that some aspects of the parenting, for example, hitting the child, are not helping or are even dangerous. A family experiencing the therapist who has provided a positive frame is much more likely to say for themselves "but it has not worked." For families who have difficulty acknowledging their problems, it is better for them to take responsibility for their behavior than for therapists to confront them with what is dysfunctional. A positive frame can also be given to disclosing harsh realities: "I admire your honesty in sharing that with me."

Perhaps the simplest and the most widely used positive labeling is to observe that the parents have brought their children up to be lively, quick-witted, assertive, outspoken, or just "great kids." These adjectives obviously have to fit in with what the therapist has observed. A challenging child, for instance, often has several of these attributes, while at the same time being characterized as a pain. Parents are, of course, affirmed by the success of their children. In the past they may have been exposed to other people saying something positive merely out of politeness, without actually meaning it. More likely, they will have been criticized for how the children have behaved. Positive labeling when convincing may also be of considerable importance to children who have been the butt of much criticism. Seeing their parents show the pride in them that surprisingly often follows such praise can be crucial in starting a more benign cycle of interaction. It is also very important that therapists always acknowledge the child's part in any change: "I see that you chose to do it in a new way."

Positive labeling is most useful, however, when it is applied to changes that happen in parenting styles during therapy. This can be done by labeling successful strategies that have been used between sessions. This issue has been touched on in previous chapters, but to recap: By asking what is new, in contrast to the usual way of doing things, it is possible to see that behaviors, even if they might compare unfavorably with "the norm," are nevertheless a marked improvement over what has happened previously. By exploring the sequence of events in the episodes that occurred between sessions, it is often possible to see how the new form of behavior has produced a new outcome. As seeing is believing, parents can accept what they may start to call their new script and come to identify themselves as parents who can do things differently and more effectively. Even when the old problem is redramatized in therapy at a later stage, it is usually possible to point out that the family now feels secure enough to attempt to tackle the problem for which they first came. It is usually possible even with what appears to be a catastrophic event, to witness the new methods that they have adopted for dealing with the situation.

New behaviors that are effective and emerge during a session can also be labeled in the same way. If this can be done convincingly, it may be the most potent of all positive affirmations. The labeling must make sense, so that parents can try to use the same approach again. For instance, "I notice that he settled very quickly when the two of you started to discuss together how to manage the situation, and you (*to child*) noticed that and decided to calm down." Or, "Did you notice how he did exactly what you asked him when you said it firmly and while you were looking at him? You (*to child*) could see that she meant it so it made sense to stop."

TEAM MESSAGES

Positive affirmation can also come from team messages. These messages carry a different weight than those of a therapist alone. The family therapist becomes an ordinary person in the eyes of the family and can become somewhat demystified. The unseen group, however, has its own mystique. Its pronouncements emerge from an unseen discussion which takes on particular significance. A number of uses of the team message is discussed by Peggy Papp (1980) who likened it to a Greek chorus.

The use of a reflecting team (Andersen, 1987) in which the team debate is carried out in front of the family who are watching through a one-way screen has a different impact. The family has the advantage of hearing the discussion about their own processes, which may enable them to reflect on their own processes. By the family not being part of the discussion, the group maintains its authority but, being exposed to view, loses its mystique. The family is then less likely to feel judged or distanced by the message.

The reflecting team can also take both sides of any dilemma created by replicative and corrective scripts. The team may choose to split up and debate the dilemmas among themselves in front of the family (Papp, 1983). This allows for a counterpointing between the positive and the negative aspects of what is happening. For example, one member of a team portrayed the pessimistic side of things, admitting that he was seeing only the black side. He found himself worrying about whether the parents would stay together or not. Later, this transpired into a crucial turning point in the therapy. The father said it was the first time he really had to take what was happening seriously. Until then he had seen the family's problems only as his wife's problem. As one team member pointed out on the optimistic side, it gave him hope that something could be done.

In all positive affirmation of parenting, it is important to avoid being patronizing or insincere. The important rule of thumb is to say only what one genuinely feels. That will communicate itself. This requires therapists to avoid becoming preoccupied with pathology and to become interested in coping strategies and resilience, and to have faith in the family's capacity to find solutions.

A CASE ILLUSTRATION: THE WATSON FAMILY

Positive affirmation of parenting scripts has to be understood in the context of the whole approach to the family rather than seen as a series of separate interventions. For this reason I will present here a complete case study, focusing on the issues of positive connotation and positive labeling. I will include many of my interventions verbatim to illustrate usage. The Watson family was referred by the school because Sam, aged 8, was getting along poorly with his peers and was being difficult at home. He got along better with adults and appeared to look down on his peers. This was seriously interfering with his relationships at school. Sam's father, Joshua, was a 42-year-old engineer who worked in a naval shipyard. Freda, his 29-year-old wife, had been a secretary before the children were born but was now a housewife. There was a younger son, John, aged 6, and a baby girl, Rose, age 1.

First Session: Sam Tears Up the Hierarchy

At the beginning of the first session Sam established himself center stage. He talked like a little adult and dominated the proceedings, speaking for everyone. For instance, when I asked John what his age was, Sam replied for him and proceeded to do the same for Rose. I allowed Sam to continue in this vein and then commented to Sam, "So you are a good talker." Freda confirmed this saying, "Sometimes it is very useful, sometimes it is wonderful. The other day we walked into a household full of 17- and 18-year-olds we didn't know, and he just took over the conversation." She was clearly proud of this. Father looked on and nodded in agreement. In this first minute or two of the session I learned that Sam was encouraged to be center stage by his family.

Sam told me that he always rode in the front seat of the car. Freda explained that he fought with his brother. She then had to sit in the backseat to split them up. I said to Sam, "You would not want to change then as that would mean giving up the front seat!" I was beginning to find Sam irritating and felt an impulse to bring him down a peg or two, but refrained from that because I was interested to see if the parents would do anything to oust him from the central role. I asked them what they would like to see changed in the family, and mother said she would like a little more obedience. Father agreed— rather tentatively, however. Sam told me that he was bullied at school and that they told him he was smelly and nasty. I thought to myself, "At least the other children are trying to put him in his place!" Sam continued to describe the other children teasing him, and it was very clear that his pride was desperately hurt by their attitude. Judging by the parents' support for Sam's elevated sense of his own importance, I could see that I had to be careful not to challenge Sam too early. I might lose their support.

I was now interested in how the family managed its irritation, so I asked how each member would express anger and who had the "loudest shout." Sam immediately pointed to his father, so I knew that despite Joshua's rather laid-back approach in the session that he could make his presence felt. A discussion followed about how long each member of the family could go before exploding with anger. Sam's fuse was reported to be short. A little later I talked to John, the second child, for a while. I noticed that Sam put his hand up to regain my attention. I ignored it. Sam became more and more irritated, jumped up and down in his seat, and held his hand up and banged it against the wall behind him. I continued to ignore him, but after a while I commented that Sam, despite what they say, did seem to have a long fuse. He was able to wait to give his younger brother a turn even if he found it difficult.

Sam finally had his say. He said, "I think if you have a child from a family who are all in different levels it is not so nice. I think it would be much nicer for the family if they were all the same level. I think if somebody said, 'Get your shoes, Sam, we are going to the park,' I think that shouldn't happen. We all should be at the same level." I again commented that Sam seemed to want to be grown-up. Father began to challenge Sam a little by saying that if he were grown-up, then at least he would get his shoes on quicker. Sam then went over to sit next to his mother and snuggled up to her rather like a little boy would. In contrast to this, his mother put her arm around his shoulder as if they were a couple sitting together.

Sam then went off to draw a picture. When the picture was finished, he tried to gain my attention again by putting up his hand, but I again insisted on waiting until I had finished talking to his father. Joshua was telling me about his work as an engineer and how they have been refitting ships. Eventually, I turned to Sam and said approvingly, "You really can wait! You were really longing to tell me something, weren't you! *(laughter)*" He then lifted up his drawing to show the family and myself. He told us, the audience, "You know, I was talking about people bossing each other around." He pointed to the picture. It was a chart, which showed two grown-ups at the top, with three children right down at the bottom of the chart. He explained that the two adults were his parents, and the three children were himself, his brother, and his sister. He then went on to explain that he would much prefer it to be like another chart that he showed us on which he had drawn all members of the family on the same line. I said to Sam, "So you think everybody should be bossing everyone around." Here I am deliberately introducing some dissonance into Sam's egalitarian worldview. Interestingly, Freda corrected me by pointing out that he did not mean that. She was clearly very good at positively affirming Sam's view of himself as an equal. Father did not challenge his wife's support of Sam. I then said, "I guess that there must be some part of Mum and Dad that agrees with you. They would like you to be mature." Freda said, "Yes we are very proud of that, but at other times he can be quite rude." "What!" Sam said indignantly turning on his mother. Freda then proceeded to tell me about a recent occasion when he had been cheeky with some friends.

Parents usually have reasons for treating their children as adults.

It is important to acknowledge the respect with which they treat their children before challenging the power of the parentified child. I find that parents will resist my challenges if I do not express first my respect for their respect of the children.

Having found that the anticipated criticism did not arrive, the parents were then free to tell me about the problems. If I had been drawn into expressing my intense irritation with Sam openly, as no doubt many others had done in the past, his parents might well have supported and protected him. I was able to contain my exasperation sufficiently to slow down the increase in my challenging of his exalted position in the family.

I moved on to briefly explore the transgenerational context of this attitude. I asked Sam if he knew whether his father had been treated as an adult at his age. Sam did not know. I partly asked him because I knew he would probably not be able to answer the question, whereas his father would. It framed the issue as one of children being treated as adults by their parents. I turned to the father and asked him whether his family was more like the hierarchical one on Sam's chart, or more like the egalitarian one. Joshua said that it had been hierarchical, but added that he was nevertheless allowed to put forward his own opinions. I asked him whether he remembered wishing his parents would treat him as more of a grown-up. I was looking for a corrective script. Joshua thought and said, "No." I pursued this issue further by asking Sam whether his grandparents would have allowed his father to be cheeky. Sam said his grandfather was strict and would not allow anybody to be cheeky, although his grandmother was a bit more easygoing. Joshua added, "As far as I can remember we never misbehaved." Mother laughingly said that she thought that her generation was, on the whole, much better behaved than the current one that is encouraged to be more articulate, which was good in some respects but not others. She remarked, "We never misbehaved." The transgenerational dimensions were only glimpsed at in this brief exploration, but I knew that I should return to this theme in a later session.

After this discussion, Sam proceeded to ceremoniously tear his hierarchical chart into small pieces. His father looked surprised and asked him what he was doing. Sam said that he was "tearing up the horrible one." Father laughed at this. Sam escalated the tension somewhat by tossing all the pieces of paper up into the air so that they fell all over the floor. Father rather mildly said, "Hey, come on, pick it up." I commented, "So in this situation you are superreasonable with him." Mother said, "Yes, we try to be as reasonable as we can." I commented that Sam was treated with a great deal of respect most of the time and given center stage. Mother said that it was not always good for him.

At this point I had a discussion with the observing group. Immediately after the break, Sam took out a banana and peeled it. I asked the parents whether they wanted him to eat it now. Freda said she preferred that he did not. Sam whined and complained, but his mother came over and took the banana away from him, politely asking him to give it to her and insisting until he did. I said that I had wondered whether they would insist on what they wanted, but they had and so succeeded. I told them that I thought this had occurred because the parents were working together. Once Sam was settled I continued. I said, "The team was impressed with how lively and what fun the kids were in this family. The grown-ups can sit and enjoy them even if they can be exasperating. We were also impressed that Sam could show them the problem so clearly. He would like to be grown-up with equal rights. But that is not like family life. That is the issue." Sam interrupted, asking about the microphones. I turned to him and said, "I am just talking to your parents at the moment," and turned back to his parents. The parents now shared more openly their worries about the situation and how bad it was for Sam and for the rest of the family. I added, "We feel that you are very wise to be coming in at the moment because you have come at a time when you can change things. The way I see it, Sam has not yet gone through the stages that most 5- or 6-year-olds go through. When you are 5 or 6, you sometimes think that you can be in charge of the world, just like John (the 6-year-old), who I expect can feel like that sometimes. Then when you become 7 or 8, you discover that cannot be so, and you settle down to become an ordinary 7- or 8-year-old. So Sam has somehow got stuck with being like a 5-year-old. I see him as being more like a younger child, still holding on to the notion that he can be in charge. Your task is to help him to take that next step. It is important for you to do that because Sam will find it frightening to be treated as if he were in charge of the world. It is nice and exciting, but it is also scary. He finds that he can tell his Mum or his Dad off. But I am pleased to see that you can, and do, stand up to him. I think it is a little bit difficult for Sam to take that step of becoming an ordinary 7-, 8-, or 9-year-old because you are a little bit unsure whether you have a right to say no." Mother interjected, "I am more unsure." And she went on to explain that she was often left wondering whether to make an issue of something or, if it was not important enough, to leave it. I said, "Perhaps this would be the thing that we could work on together: when to take a firm line or when to let things be." I turned to Sam and said to him, "Your parents really enjoy you being so mature at times and they like to be able to talk things over with you." (Sam looked pleased.) Mother quickly came in and said, "When he goes over the top, I even have to resort to smacking him now." I added "I think you know as a family that you need to put your foot down. When Sam becomes an ordinary 8-year-old, this will improve his relationship with the other children at school. I guess it is because he behaves as if he is older and superior to the others that they tease and bully him. I think you know all these things, but you remain a bit unsure about whether you must insist on that happening. You have a problem deciding between bringing the children up by being reasonable or by being firm at times. We were struck by the fact that you had the greatest success when both of you were together in telling Sam, 'No! You must not do that, you must wait.'"

In this feedback I placed the problem firmly within a developmental process which had somehow been delayed and hence could be expected to proceed normally, even if a bit late. I spelled out the dangers fairly clearly, but I also affirmed the family's strengths, while specifying the particular strategy that helped them to regain their authority—that is, working as a team to check Sam.

Second Session: Positive Labeling of Small Changes

It was clear right from the beginning that Sam was in a rebellious mood. He wandered around the room. His father and mother both asked him to sit down, which he eventually did, but he complained, "I don't like being bossed about." I positively labeled their parenting skill by saying, "I noticed that when you two were together and were firm with Sam, he did sit down and then settled, despite the fact that he was in a bad mood before that." I then asked my routine question, "So what has been happening?" They described how Sam had been acting very difficult. I asked them to describe one particular event. Mother described how Sam had been in a foul mood on Monday evening, and nothing she suggested made any difference. Eventually Sam had come up with the idea that he should move some potted plants down to the other end of the garden. At first Mother was appalled by this idea, knowing what chaos would ensue. However, she agreed to allow him to do so as long as he would agree to clear up the mess. Sam had seemed to enjoy this task and ended up sharing the clearing up with his mother. Although he had asked for and had been given what was really an adult's decision and task (old script)—the decision as to where the plants should be placed—it was important for me to identify the new element in the episode. I said, "So insisting that Sam cleared up some of his mess enabled Sam to get on with doing the task."

In exploring a between-session episode, I always try to find out what other members of the family were doing during that time. So I asked how the father was involved in this. On that particular evening, and indeed most evenings, it turned out that the father was at work until after the children had gone to bed. Mother complained, saying that, unfortunately, because of her husband's current work situation, he was not there when she really wanted him. I commented, "So what you want is a husband to be there for you at that moment, but you (*turning to Sam*) are not going to be like a husband to your mum, because you are just an 8-year-old, upset after having a difficult time at school." In this way I positively connoted Sam's difficult behavior as a way of avoiding being married to mother.

The parents then discussed together how things were somewhat better at home because they had been talking to one another and working together more since the first session. This indicated to me that they had become better prepared to confront Sam's behavior together.

Clarifying Who Is in Charge in the Session

When a child is out of control, I always assume that there is a dispute over authority between the parents, and that it is unclear as to who carries the authority for what. This makes it doubly important that the authority issues are clear within the therapy session. I have responsibility for managing the therapeutic situation and have to use my authority to establish conditions in which therapy can be conducted. For instance, I demand that the children should take part in certain activities in which they are needed, and that the children must be settled if they are making it impossible to discuss something. The parents, however, are responsible for the children's behavior and ensuring that it fits in with what is acceptable to them.

At this point of the session Sam got up and wandered off to the window and started to sing in an irritating way. I decided to draw the genogram at this point because it would provide a clear and understandable reason why he should be involved in the process, and it would give the parents a clear task of settling him down so that he could contribute. I normally draw the genogram in the third or fourth session, but I did it at this point in order to provide a family task. I asked the parents to get Sam to come and sit down because I wanted to draw a family tree. Sam was rude and said he had had enough of family trees. Eventually mother forcibly made Sam sit down. He went back to the window again almost straightaway. Father told him to come back in a very polite way; mother went over and brought him back again. She had to hold Sam down in his seat. I thanked her for fetching him back. Sam started making a loud screeching noise and both parents told him to shut up. Then mother asked him, "Who will do the writing then?" He settled momentarily as it was clear that she was offering him the role of drawing the family tree. I countered this by saying, "I will do that because that is the way I like to do it." Here I was modeling some authority. Sam quickly settled. I said to the parents, "I think that Sam has been showing that you need to be in charge of him, and you have been showing me that you can be." I told them that I was interested in what the children knew about the family. However, when I asked Sam something, he made a rude farting noise at me. Both his parents immediately told him not to be rude. I said to them, "Yes, it is important that you decide what is the right behavior in here." Sam went back to the window. I said, "I need Sam to be here to do the family tree." Mother brought him back while Sam squealed. I noticed that the parents took action without consulting with each other, and so I mentioned that it was important that Sam saw that his parents worked together on this. Mother now firmly put Sam in the seat between both parents so that they could both control him.

Father increasingly became involved in disciplining the children and at one time took on the task of retrieving Sam whenever he left the group.

When I got to mother's father on the genogram and asked about how he disciplined her, she said, "Once father smacked me and I was mortified. It was the worst thing that ever happened." I asked her whether that left her feeling that she did not want to smack her own children, and she said, "Yes, it is the modern view that smacking is a bad thing, but I came to reach a point when I realized it was not working, not being firm." I commented, "So Sam made you realize that you needed to be firmer." Here I affirmed both Sam's communication and her understanding in a way that positively labels being firm. The parents had been struggling to improvise a new discipline script. I asked the parents to come on their own in the last session. After a structural session I find it useful to review with the parents what happened.

Third Session: Exploring Losses in the Parents' Past

When I asked the parents what had been happening, they told me that Sam had settled down further and gave the example of him being quite content to stay in the backseat of the car for a whole long journey. I asked them what they had done differently to help this to happen. They agreed that their supporting each other made the difference.

Themes of loss were explored with the help of the genogram on each side of the family. I will describe the work that was focused on positively connoting how the grandparents' generation had "struggled" with loss, and how the present family tried to help now by fulfilling those lost hopes, and by replacing unmourned figures. (See Figure 11.1.)

Freda was the eldest child in her family. She had a younger sister. The next child to follow was a boy who was stillborn at 7 months. This had a profound impact on Freda's mother, Ethel, who became depressed and withdrawn. Ethel became pregnant as soon as she could following this loss. She then had a religious experience during the labor of that pregnancy which produced a son. This happened while she had been left on her own for a long time. I said that Ethel must have had a great need to believe that there was a god protecting her while she was feeling so frightened in the light of the last pregnancy. Ethel's son, now apparently blessed, not surprisingly became a "blue-eyed boy." Nevertheless, she remained depressed and withdrawn, preoccupied with her religious convictions. She did not seem to be interested in the older children. Freda and her sister had to turn to each other for comfort, as their father was a very distant person. It became clear, from the way they described the relationship, that the two children had to look after and protect their mother. I said I thought that it was not surprising then that Freda enjoyed Sam being older than his years and able to be her companion at times. He was also someone who might look after her when she felt upset.

When Freda's parents knew that Freda was pregnant, they wanted her to have a boy. Sam was the light of his grandmother's life. She treated Sam as very special. The grandparents focused all their attention on him. When the family arrived for a visit they never asked Freda about herself. They played with Sam instead. His grandmother cooked Sam special meals which were often better than those she served the rest of the family. I said that I thought that Sam had been another replacement baby for the stillborn boy, as well as for Freda's own miscarriage which preceded Sam. He now had to be protected to make sure he survived.

Joshua's father had worked on the shop floor of a factory. When Joshua had became a company manager, his father was proud but ambivalent about his success. Joshua's mother was an only child who had come to Britain in 1938, at age 18. Her parents, who were Polish Jews, had been caught up in the war before they could join her. They both died in concentration camps, as did the rest of that family. She responded to the tragedies by completely cutting herself off from her

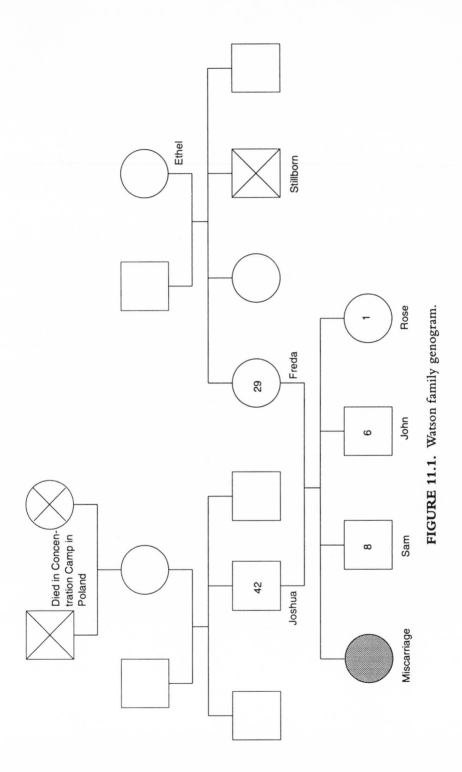

FIGURE 11.1. Watson family genogram.

past. She became Christian and spoke perfect English. When she went home to Poland with Joshua, when he was 20, he was amazed to discover that she was almost unable to speak Polish. She also seemed to cut out most of her emotions and caring instincts. She was a disciplinarian, and she and her husband used to argue and shout at each other. I commented on the service that Freda performed for Joshua by being a gentle, caring parent; so different from his own mother.

Of the three siblings, Joshua seemed to have been the one delegated to explore the Polish connection and to discover whether any family remained. I said I thought that Joshua had chosen to be a delegate for both of his parents: For his father it was to satisfy thwarted work ambitions; for his mother it was to explore her origins and to keep in touch with her past. Perhaps Sam was, in turn, now a delegate for his father, who had never been able to fully express his rebellion against his own father (Sam's grandfather)—or mother, for that matter. So when Sam tore up the "authoritarian" family hierarchy and scattered the pieces to the four winds, this may have been exciting for Joshua. The first grandchild, Sam, I suggested, had become the life and soul of the party as he represented so much for so many people in this family. Replacements for a dead child have to be alive and kicking. No wonder it was difficult to move on from the "King of the Castle" character to being an ordinary child who could get on with the task of growing up.

Fourth Session: Using the Mirror to Give Sam Feedback

The whole family came to this session. Sam complained bitterly about being bullied and teased at school, but could not see that he had any part to play in this. He was distressed as well as angry. I went over to sit next to Sam. I felt he would need my supportive presence to be able to face up to what was happening. I said to him, "Your parents now have the task, which is perhaps the most important they will ever have, of helping you to discover what it is that you do that makes you bullied, rather than any of the other children. They can, in this way, rescue you from always being the one to be bullied." This is an example of positively labeling a future task.

I suggested to the parents that they could help by pointing out to Sam when he does something that irritates them, because it may also irritate his peers at school. Strategically I planned that this would help them to stop rewarding his exasperating behavior. The home truths that they might offer Sam were put within the positive frame of help. I then used the one-way screen as a mirror to help him work on it himself within the session. He had once been bullied when he looked angry, so I suggested that he should get angry so that he could see what he looked like in the mirror. I suggested that he could, with his knowledge, change his appearance. I was trying to channel his omnipotent controlling energy toward his own behavior. Sam joined in the spirit of the exercise by stamping his feet and becoming red in the face. He did indeed look ridiculous. I encouraged him to do it even more, pressing him toward even greater rage and anger. I was able to praise him for being able to do that for me, thus giving a positive connotation to his capacity to look ridiculous. Sam's resistance to authority, which was mobilized by this strategy, helped to make him not want to look angry again.

Father Is Angry: Parents Regain Control

I then gave the parents the task of helping Sam to see how he provoked people. I helped them to act as a team. They found this difficult, but at the end of the session, while the children were clearing up, Freda said that she wished Joshua would really speak out. By this time both Sam and John were racing around the room, throwing paper darts and creating havoc. John threw something that hit his father. Quite suddenly, father became very angry and shouted at the children to stop. There was a stunned silence, and both children immediately complied. This voice was entirely different from the one I had heard before, and it made me realize how unconvincing father's previous, apparently firm statements were in comparison to how firm he was being now. This seemed to be an important turning point in regaining some control.

Fifth Session: Progress

I saw the parents on their own. Joshua was able to say how angry he was about how the children messed him around. However, there had been no major upsets since the last session. The father had in fact been helping Sam by giving him advice on how to handle his peers at school, while the mother had been suggesting that he accept his teacher's authority and stop challenging her. I said, "So both of you are doing a lot of good work with him to help him to use reasoning, so that he can escape from being bullied." Freda went on to tell me that she had got him to look at his face in the mirror, and he now laughs when he makes a face. He had also made two friends, one of whom was a boy who used to bully him. I said I thought that was a brilliant strategy to make friends with the bully. He had also been chosen to represent his class in athletics. This had never happened before, and he was absolutely delighted. I listed the changes that had happened and praised Joshua and Freda for helping him to achieve that. They now told me that John had become the problem. I said that I was not worried about that because now Sam would not be stuck in the position of being their only problem. If they could manage with Sam, who is older, then they would manage with John.

Last Four Sessions: Sam as Distance Regulator

I saw the whole family twice, and the parents on their own twice, before finishing. In the next family session, Sam complained that I had "pulled the plug" on his situation in the family. The structural family therapy continued to try to help his parents stop Sam from playing "King of the Castle," and encourage him to become an ordinary 8-year-old instead. John's behavior was also settling. In this session it was noted that mother laughed when Sam lashed out at his father. The next two parental sessions focused on two themes: first, on how Sam expressed many things for each of them, which they had been unable to express for themselves, like expressing Freda's anger with Joshua; second, on how Sam behaved as a distance regulator in all family relationships. He linked his mother to her parents because they wanted to see him, but he was such an embarrassment to his father's disciplinarian parents that they kept away. This suited Joshua who preferred to remain at some distance from his parents. Sam was also a key figure in the distance between his parents. He could drive a wedge between them by getting close to his mother and loving her, and protecting her from his father's exasperation. But he could also drive them to distraction so that they finally got together to manage him. It was possible to give positive connotations to the service he performed for his parents. He decided that this was not much fun anymore, and he turned more toward his newfound friends at school.

The work then focused on how the parents could relate better. They did not want to discuss their marriage, and so the work remained at the level of coparenting. In the last family session, some of the improvements had been maintained, while there were also difficult times. The parents debated whether or not they needed to continue therapy. I pointed out that Sam was also a distance regulator between the family and myself and that if his behavior continued to improve, then his parents might choose not to come back, but he, Sam, could choose to bring the family back to see me by behaving improperly. As Sam was feeling that I had pulled the plug on his power within the family, he would hopefully use his considerable energies to avoid coming back to the clinic. They did not come back.

Follow-Up

Two years later when I saw the family for follow-up, Sam had remained settled, although John was now having somewhat similar difficulties, although less serious, and his parents were coping with them. He was now the same age as Sam had been when they had first come.

I wondered whether it had been a mistake to use Sam's determination to defeat me and leave therapy in order to win the battle against his own out-of-control behavior. That may have succeeded, but it shortened therapy. Whatever the difficulties of being an 8-year-old in this family were, they had not been resolved. However, a longer timespan for therapy may not have solved anything. This is one of those imponderables.

REEDITING SCRIPTS IN CHANGING CIRCUMSTANCES

Scripts in Formation of a New Family

Babies are inducted into the family script in three main ways. First, there are patterns of interaction that are set up around the care of the baby and in response to the baby. Second, there is the transgenerational influence which comes through the parents' experience of having been parented themselves (already discussed in relationship to attachments in Chapter 6), but more directly through the grandparents and extended family's current relationship to the family. Finally, there are the meanings that the parents give to what is going on and their hopes and expectations about the baby's future, all of which are influenced by the above. A new pattern emerges from exchanges across these three interfaces, which produces a new family script. In this chapter, I will trace this process as it occurs in a normal family at each of these levels and then discuss some problems that can arise.

INTERFACES STUDY GROUP

I am lucky enough to be part of an ongoing international research group meeting in Lausanne, Switzerland (World Association of Infant Mental Health Study Group), that has been studying the interfaces between intrapsychic, interactional, and transgenerational domains of family life. These three elements also represent the basic components necessary for *interactional awareness* (discussed in Chapter 2).

The aim of the project was to take a family with a new baby and study how patterns evolve over the first year. The research group consisted of nine people.[1] The participants covered the following skills:

[1]Elizabeth Fivas-Depeursinge, Lausanne; Daniel Stern, Geneva; Dieter Bürgin, Basel; John Byng-Hall, London; Antoinette Corboz-Warnery, Lausanne; Martine Lamour, Paris; Serge Lebovici, Paris; an anonymous family.

child development, family interaction research, psychoanalysis, parent–child psychotherapy, family and marital systems theory, and family therapy. Both parents from the family being studied were included in the group. They were involved as participant–observer colleagues, who fed back to the researchers their own views of what was being said or written. The central theme chosen for the project was to study how triads can move from two relating together with the third observing (two plus one) to all three relating together as a threesome. Each of the research workers viewed this important process from his or her own perspective. The preliminary findings of the project have been published (Fivas-Depeursinge et al., 1994).

The group chose to use the Lausanne Triadic Play procedure, which has been used in research into triadic interaction (Corboz-Warnery et al., 1993) in which a mother and father play together with their first baby. A nonclinic family was selected from a research project which was comparing clinic and nonclinic families (Coboz-Warnery et al., 1993).

The Lausanne Triadic Play procedure involves a mother, a father, and their baby, who sits in a chair in front of the parents. The chair can be oriented toward either parent or to a point equidistant between the two. The family is asked to enact the following scenario consisting of four different scenes: (1) father plays with the baby while mother watches; (2) mother then plays with the baby while father watches; (3) all three play together as a threesome; and, finally, (4) the parents talk to each other and ignore the baby. In other words, each pair had a turn to play together, with one episode of all three playing together. The transition from scene (2), mother playing with the baby, to scene (3), with all three playing together, was explored in detail using videotape. This procedure is repeated throughout the first year at 3, 5, 8, and 12 months, which enables comparisons across time to be made, in order to see how much continuity or change there is in the pattern. In this study, the most attention was paid to the triadic play at 3 and 12 months.

A STUDY OF A NORMAL FAMILY

In this chapter, I will be using one family to illustrate and explore how family scripts are written for the family. The perspective presented will be my own, while incorporating some of the relevant perspectives coming from the team. This family provides an example of some of the factors that may be operating in a normal family that enable it to make transitions to threesome interaction.

The shift from two, plus one, to a threesome involves disengagement from the twosome before reengaging in the threesome. This shift can evoke fears of being left out as well as the pleasurable anticipation of all three being together. Once established, maintainence of the threesome can be facilitated by each person keeping all three members in mind continuously, making sure that each feels valued and noticed and hence enjoys staying in the threesome. The first baby provides an opportunity to coevolve a new threesome family pattern through the interplay of each parent's past triadification scripts, and in response to the baby's emerging personality.

The whole process is potentially difficult. One temptation is to cling to the partner rather than to disengage from the twosome, or, when reengaging in the threesome, to try to capture one of the others for oneself in order to avoid being left out. This is especially tempting for those with an ambivalent/enmeshed style of relating. For the avoidant person, however, it is tempting to avoid reengaging in a threesome and to remain more of a bystander. These are some of the dilemmas and difficulties that everyone faces as he or she goes through life, either in these brief episodes of engaging in a threesome or when confronting life cycle changes, such as disengaging from one's own parents and then engaging in a new family.

THE WEISS FAMILY

The Weiss family was multilingual and multicultural: Father was Swiss-German; mother was Russian, having emigrated to Switzerland with her family in her teens. The family now lived in the French part of Switzerland. Hans was a 35-year-old lecturer in soil science and Anya was a 32-year-old geneticist.

Description at Level of Interaction: At 3 Months

The transition to the threesome went as follows. Just before the transition, mother had been playing an enjoyable game with a lot of mutual excitement, in which she touched with her finger all points of Peter's face in turn: nose, mouth, eyes, chin, etc., while singing a Russian song about a perfectly formed baby. At the height of the excitement the baby turned his head away as if he had had enough, and father, noticing this, suggested that they make the transition to the threesome. Mother then withdrew; she leaned back, turned away to one side, put her hand on her forehead, and looked down; fleetingly she looked a little fed up. In short, she clearly and decisively marked the end of her turn and displayed that she was happy it was over. This slight disaffection was so brief that it was only noted on the video-tape—and was in stark contrast to her general enjoyment of the process. Father then called her to come back into the play, whereupon she leaned toward the baby and reengaged the baby's gaze. Then followed a slow dance in which father repeatedly and gently tried to gain the baby's attention, but despite his efforts mother and baby maintained most of the eye contact. During this time mother talked to the baby in Russian, which father cannot understand. He attempted to guess in German what his wife was saying, and then made a positive comment about what his wife was doing with the baby. After this, she helped to make the play symmetrical by playing with one of the baby's hands while suggesting that her husband play with the other one. She also called out the father's name in her conversation with the baby, as if encouraging him to notice his father. The dyad was now finally symmetrical, with the baby taking notice of both parents and glancing from one to the other.

The nonverbal pattern of interaction was studied by Elizabeth Fivas-Depeursinge and Antoinette Corboz-Warnery using the same format as their long-term triadic play research (Corboz-Warnery et al., 1993). They explored how bodily posture, gaze direction, and affect—as revealed through facial expression—were organized in a systemic way between all three participants (Sacco et al., 1993). This revealed that the steps involved were coordinated and orderly—in other words, the dance was choreographed. The changes in gaze direction preceded shifts in bodily posture, as if the parents were choreographing the direction of future changes. There was a partial disengagement and partial reengagement just prior to the full disengagement and reengagement as a threesome. This little preliminary step in the dance seemed to act as a forerunner to or rehearsal of what was to come. Just before both the partial disengagement and the full disengagement, there was noted to be an intense triadic engagement at every level, that is, trunk orientation, mutual gaze, and shared affect. This may have been choreographed by the parents as a way of announcing that the eventual aim was to come together as a threesome and/or as a sign of togetherness before separating, thus leaving no one feeling that they were likely to be left out following the disengagement. The full disengagement was marked by each individual being disconnected from the others at all three levels (this was when the mother withdrew and oriented herself away from the play). This disconnection may have also helped each parent to reset the script in his or her mind's eye to include all three family members and to allow for synchronization of the next scene in the script (see Kendon, 1990).

Analysis of the same transition at 5, 8, and 12 months showed similar structures, suggesting that it became scripted.

The Intrapsychic Level of Description: Memories and Personal Meanings Attributed to the Transition

This dimension was investigated by Daniel Stern using a "microinterview" (Bennett et al., 1992), which involves the parents watching videotape of the transition to a threesome. Stern selected individual actions taken by each parent and asked them to remember what they were thinking or feeling at the time and why they did what they did. He also inquired as to what their actions reminded them of now. He asked Anya about the time that she disengaged and looked tired. On viewing this, she was reminded that she had had to look after her younger siblings, which she resented, and how she had felt relieved when it was finished and somebody else would take over. When asked about the decisiveness with which she withdrew from the play, she said that that was her style. When she did it, she did it; when she stopped doing it, she stopped. She associated this with her father's style of decision making. She could see her father in the way she looked away from the proceedings when she withdrew.

Stern, having identified Anya's role as demarcator of family interaction, went on to identify two roles that Hans played. First that of framer, in which he kept an overall eye on the situation and made sure that what was going on fit within the frame of the research task. Second that of diplomat, in which Hans tuned into Peter and Anya's state of mind and coordinated each of their activities so that they fit into the transition dictated by the research. Hans's role could be described in the following way: His actions were mostly focused on reading Anya's and the baby's signals and taking appropriate action. He watched very carefully. He only leaned forward when both the baby and Anya had disengaged, and it was right for him to be involved; quietly and unobtrusively, he then managed the transition. First he suggested that they move to the next stage, then he moved the chair and called Anya back to join in the threesome when she had disengaged. He then showed diplomacy in the way he slowly became more and more involved with the baby. He never competed with his wife, causing no disruption to Anya's enjoyment of the baby, which had continued after her reengagement. Instead, Hans signalled to Anya that he was not yet part of the triad by fantasizing about what she was saying in Russian to Peter. He then made a positive comment about what was going on between Anya and Peter. This could be seen as a signal that he valued what was going on in the dyad and would not be competing with her once he was in the threesome. She then rewarded this by actively inviting him. Her strategy for doing so was by sharing a game. Each parent held a hand and swung around. Father then gave the game meaning by saying, "You like that. It's funny, rowing, swimming, rowing together, swimming around." Thus, it seemed that father played the diplomat/framer, role monitoring and facilitating the whole scenario, while mother provided a demarcation role, marking the beginnings and endings. It could be argued that this allocation of roles was a by-product of the context in which Hans was the observer to the dyadic play at the point of transition, so he would naturally take on the role of framer and organizer. However, it became clear throughout the research that the roles were characteristic of each parent across various contexts, including shared meals that the research team had with the family. The same roles repeated again across the triadic play at 5, 8 and 12 months.

The Threesome as a Learning Context for the Baby

During the whole period, the transition and then the triadic play, the parents were very sensitive to Peter's cues and it could be seen that the baby dictated the pace and the direction in large measure. For instance, in the "perfect-face game" he helped to maintain it by being excited, but it then became too intense and he looked away. However, when the threesome phase had got under way, he was happy to continue his exchanges with his mother. His father's slow wooing of his son was delicately balanced against Peter's obvious enjoyment of continuing the play with his mother. The parents provided a frame, both in length of time and in the setting, for their baby to make the transition to the threesome in his own time. They avoided competing, although it might have been construed that Anya maintained the baby's attention for longer than she needed because she was enjoying it so much. The lack of rivalry enabled a mutual enjoyment by the threesome. This enjoyment would be a likely factor in encouraging further attempts to have a shared experience. Elizabeth Fivas-Depeursinge (1991) discussed how the time frame of attention that parents provide is usually longer than what the child actually uses. This allows the child to explore the space in his or her own time. For instance, Peter was able at times to just watch his parents collaborating in the way they played with him. He was able to be audience to his parents' relationship as well as moving on a stage by choosing to engage and disengage in the threesome. As his cognitive capacities develop, and if this process is repeated over time, it will provide him with a basic script for collaborative triads and for achieving interactional awareness. This could very well be important to him in his future life.

Transgenerational Influences
Babyhood Stories

I interviewed the Weiss parents in order to explore legends told by their parents about the time when they were very young. Hans reported a story about his first birthday. There was a birthday cake with one candle on it. The photo that was taken also helped to ensure the repetition of the story. "My father was trying to make a picture, while I was blowing out the candles, and I was having quite some problems. (*laughter*) It must have been very funny. I am told that with a little bit of help I succeeded. (*laughter*)" I asked, "How does it make you feel when you are told this story?" Hans replied, "It is nothing special, just told to be funny, but it makes me feel that I was smaller, and that I had been a baby." Anya had two stories to tell. The first was about when she was 2 years old and had been sick. "My father was crying for me. I had fever and diarrhea and they thought that I was going to die. But I wiped his tears and said, 'Don't cry.' He told me that this was the first time he had heard me really talk—it was the first time I had spoken a sentence and so he knew that I was a real person." The second story was about a New Year's picnic, which was a tradition in her country. Anya recounted, "When they wanted to go home they looked for me, but I wasn't there. They looked everywhere, behind this tree, behind that tree, but I wasn't anywhere. They got worried, but then they decided that the rest of the family should go home. As they came home they saw me walking toward the house. Father was astonished. How could a 3-, 4-, or 5-year-old find the way home?" I asked, "So what was the message in the story do you think?" Anya replied, "That I might be intelligent. (*Laughs.*)" I inquired, "Do you think that these two stories were about being older than your years?" Anya exclaimed, "Oh, yes, very much!"

It was interesting that these two stories were about age. The message to father was about being little, whereas Anya's was about being older than her years. The injunction to Hans was you are little (so stay at home?). To Anya the message was grow up quickly (so that you can help look after others?). The significance of these two stories became clear later.

Identities: Following the Script or Choosing a New One?

I asked Hans and Anya what they imagined their parents had hoped that they would grow up to be when they were babies. To stimulate the imagination about this context, I suggested, as I asked each parent about each grandparent, that the parent of the same sex as the grandparent under discussion should pick up the baby and hold him. So when I asked father about what his mother hoped for him, Anya picked Peter up and put him on her lap. Hans said that he thought that his mother just wanted him to stay around and that she got pleasure from him being around the house with her. Hans made some cradling movements with his arms to show how he felt his mother would like him to have been in her arms. Hans, understanding of his mother's wish to have him around, had stayed at home until he was 28, although he would have preferred to have left earlier. He chose to be different from his father by becoming a scientist. His father, on the other hand, had hopes for his career. His father was a businessman in a famous Swiss company and had wanted Hans to join the company as well. But, when I explored this a little further, it turned out that, although an academic, Hans also did a lot of consulting with major firms about the land on which they were planning to construct their factories. Anya said that she thought Hans's father was pleased that he was involved in the business end of science. I commented that Hans had made a brilliant compromise between needing to be different from his father (choosing to be a scientist) and wanting to be similar (focusing on the business side of the science). I asked him whom he identified with and he was very clear that he identified with his father. He told me that his father was also diplomatic.

Anya said that her parents had wanted a boy first, because a firstborn son was much treasured in her culture. Anya was identified with her father, who, as we have heard, had a clear-cut decisive style. Her mother had, however, wanted her to look after her younger siblings. When I asked about whether she had felt uneasy about being a girl, she told me, "No, I am quite happy to be like I am." She went on to explain that it was her maternal grandmother who made her feel "good in her own skin." Her maternal identity seems to have been with this grandmother. However, she clearly rejected her mother's wish for her to be a mother to her younger siblings. She resented being treated as older then her years and she told me that she would tell her mother outright that she did not like the babies and did not want to look after them. We could see how Anya's withdrawal and looking momentarily tired and fed up in the triadic play coded a lot of information about one aspect of looking after children. If she was told to look after children—as she had been by the researchers—then she was scripted to be ambivalent. On the other hand, if she herself chose to look after a child, then she could identify with her grandmother who chose to look after her and loved to do it.

Disengaging from Families of Origin and Engaging in this Family

I explored how Anya and Hans had disengaged from their families to see if it would yield information about disengaging processes appearing within the triadic play. As we have seen, Hans delayed leaving home because he did not want to upset his mother. As a 20-year-old he had left home to go to university, but that was different; leaving for school, he explained, was not him saying to his mother that he preferred to be somewhere else other than with her. That step had to wait until he was 28. His attitude toward leaving home was revealed in a story he told about his sister who was younger than him, but left before he did. At the age of 22 she met and then married a man who worked on motorboats. Although Hans had liked his new brother-in-law, he said that his parents were devastated. He was not the type of person that they had hoped their daughter would marry. During this period Hans had worked hard to heal the rift in the family. He felt that he was his sister's last link with the family. He first talked to his sister in an attempt to explain their mother's feelings about her, and then he went and talked to his mother about his sister's feelings. In this way he tried to maintain the link. He labeled this process as diplomacy. I added the definition of "shuttle diplomacy," which he accepted with a laugh. He said that he also uses this technique in other situations. For instance, he explained Anya to his mother and his mother to Anya. Anya said that it was often done in the subtlest way so that the diplomacy was not even noticed. There were also examples of this translating role in the session. He would quietly make some comments to clarify things for other people or translate across from one language to another.

Anya, in turn, helped Hans to differentiate from his family by making clear demarcating statements about the transition from being a son in his last family to being a husband in this family. Anya described how Hans was good friends with his father. When he talked to his father, however, he did not include her in their conversation. Anya said, "Hans does well when he stays with me and doesn't go to his father leaving me with his mother. He is not just the son in his family and I am not just the daughter. I am also treated like his mother's shadow in his family. They think that I am there to bring him up. But I am his wife, not his mother! (*indignant and emphatic*)" Note the passing reference to her hatred for the parentified role. Being asked to "mother" her husband reminds her of having to look after her siblings.

Anya went on to explain the role of the baby in the transition. "Before the baby his family treated him as if he still belonged to them. The baby is important. Now I can say, 'The baby needs me.' I don't have to stay and listen to the family stories. Instead, I can say, 'This family [the new nuclear family] is now more important!'"

Demarcation within the Session

After talking to Hans, I said that I now wanted to talk to Anya. She gave the baby to him and then suggested that he sit somewhere else, saying, "I think that's better. (*moving around to be next to me*) Now there is no barrier! (*laughter*)" Here is another example of framing and demarcating. I provided the frame by saying it was time for me to talk to her, but she demarcated it very clearly by moving her husband aside and positioning herself for the next dialogue. It is also interesting that I have somehow replicated in the interview what she complained of earlier: her husband talking to her father and leaving her out. As I had been talking to her husband for a long time about his family, she now emphasized that it was her turn.

Culture and Gender: Anya Moves Away from Her Family

In this family, but for Anya in particular, gender issues were so tied up with culture that I will treat the two issues together. She said that since the baby her parents had not been able to understand her. She explained that they had decided that Peter could not be between two cultures. He had to grow up in this one. Anya explained that she started thinking in German as a way of identifying herself as belonging to the new culture, but also as a way of seeing the culture from the baby's point of view. She had thus been thinking in German while with her father. She had to then translate her thoughts back into Russian. As a result, her father could not understand her any more. This created a distance between them. The distance between herself and her mother, however, had started much earlier when her mother had wanted her to look after the younger siblings. When she complained to her mother, which she did with vigor, her mother explained to her that when she was Anya's age she had to look after children. She herself was married at the age of 14. Hans explained, "In our culture, however, a woman is a personality. At least she can discuss things. In Anya's culture women do not even have an opinion.

You would have to discuss her opinion with me!" (He appeared unaware that he was replicating what he was complaining about when he explained Anya to me.)

Hopes for the Future: Corrective and Replicative Scripts

Hans and Anya discussed together which elements of their culture they would like to preserve and which they would like to reverse. Anya felt that the German/Swiss culture had no "heart." She explained that what she meant by "heart" was being sympathetic to other people's feelings, being open to everybody. She wanted to bring Peter up with a Russian "heart" and to know about other people's suffering. Hans, however, wanted to avoid the problems he had with his own mother by helping to prepare Peter for friends and a wife, etc. He felt that his mother had restricted his group of friends and kept him in the family.

Anya said, "Hans's mother thinks he is perfect. Now I also have a son and I also think he is perfect! But I will try not to be the same as she did to him," Hans, however, reported, "Anya talks about the future to the little one, saying, 'You know if you want to get a wife, you are only going to get a nice one, a really beautiful one. I am looking out for that.' (*laughter*)" Hans told this story in a way that showed that he would counter any such control over Peter from Anya. That would be his corrective script.

I asked Anya what she thought was the more important lesson of being a parent: How her mother mothered her, or how she mothered her younger siblings? Anya was very clear about this. She said, "It was how my grandmother was to me. What my grandmother gave to me was that she told me, 'Look, you are great. You are beautiful, intelligent,' and all that. When I was sad I came to her. She stroked my hair and she gave me a hug. I could sit on her lap, and it was wonderful because I had a safe place." This is one of the best descriptions of a secure base that I have heard from anyone. We spent the last part of the session talking about how she could provide the same thing for Peter.

Interview At 1 Year

Triadic Play

The triadic play at 1 year was very different because Peter had just learned how to walk and wanted to get down out of the chair and wander around. He was fractious and difficult throughout the procedure. Anya managed surprisingly well to calm him during her play period by putting herself right next to him. She leaned forward putting her head on his lap, calling to him, and turning her head this way and that way, so that eventually he started playing with her hair. With this, he settled occasionally, but when it came to the time for the threesome play he became more desperate. He leaned right out of his chair. When he did this, Anya called out urgently—"Hans, Hans!"—for help.

At the time of transition, Anya judged that the threesome play was not going to work until Peter settled. In her own style she firmly picked up the baby, lifting him out of his chair. She thus demarcated an exit from the research procedure. She then proceeded to try to settle Peter, carrying him around the room, jogging him up and down on her knee, singing to him, feeding him, and seeing whether he needed his diaper changed. During this, she orientated Peter toward his father as much as she could, for instance, holding him facing Hans while he was being fed. Peter still did not settle. She handed him to his father who put him on his knee facing his mother. Peter, however, started grizzling again when on his father's knee. Anya took him onto her knee facing his father while Hans leaned forward catching his attention and cooing to him. It was clear that there was a shared threesome script, or choreograph, in which the child's posture was oriented toward the other parent whenever he was being held, in an attempt to facilitate the engagement with the left-out parent. This would set the stage for establishing the threesome play.

Both parents cooed in a song together, thus creating symmetry in sound. Peter put his hand onto his own nose, at which point Hans created a game by putting his fingers on his own nose, imitating Peter, and then onto Peter's nose. Peter responded by reaching out and grabbing his father's nose. Quiet descended at this point, and the threesome were having an enjoyable game. Anya remained part of the game by leaning forward and turning to face Peter, who could then see her and his father, while mother held him. The threesome was established at gaze level. After this, they decided to end the threesome play. Anya put Peter down and he wandered off. Once again the threesome togetherness had preceded a successful disengagement.

The two transitions to threesomes—one at 3 months, the other at 1 year—showed the importance of body posture and orientation which set the stage for the gaze orientation which, in turn, set the stage for threesome play. When triadic body orientation was not possible because the baby was held by one parent, the trunk was twisted around so that the gaze could be triadic. The whole dance was choreographed by the parents' shared mental representation of a triad in space.

Family Interview: The Previous Generations' Ways of Creating Threesomes

The aim on this occasion was to explore the couple's experience of triads in their families of origin. I started by explaining to them that I was interested in their childhood experiences of being with one parent when the other came in to make a threesome. I told them that I was going to replay the videotape of the threesome play from beginning to end. I asked them to imagine that they had discovered a home video of themselves when they were infants. While they were watching I asked them to put themselves in the place of the baby and to imagine their parents in their places, to go back one generation in their imagination. After the replay was finished, I asked them for their images. Anya found it impossible to recall any times in which both her parents were caring for her together. Instead, she produced a vivid memory of her 2-year-old brother when he was ill with polio. She remembered seeing her mother taking him off the toilet and discovering that his legs went floppy. Her mother told him to stand up and then got increasingly angry, saying that he must be able to stand when he said he could not. After a while she realized it was true, "her world fell in." She became very upset and ran to the phone to ring her father for help. This image may have been provoked by the way she had called Hans in the triadic play when the baby nearly fell over. My disability with polio, I assume, also contributed to the selection of this memory.

Subsequently Anya recalled occasions when her parents were together, but only when she had been left out, not as a threesome. First of all, she remembered sitting in the backseat of the car and pretending to be asleep while listening to her parents talking together. I asked her how she felt about this and she replied, "It's the way it should be." She then went on to talk about how she had been curious about what her mother and father did in bed. She saw what happened when her parents did not realize she was there when she was about age 9. After she found out what happened her curiosity was satisfied. I asked her if she had wanted to go and look again, but she said, "No, I did not want to be in there with my parents. I did not want to be in that position." I asked her again for memories of her parents being together and both enjoying her. This led instead to memories of her grandmother and her father being together, of grandmother and paternal uncle, and of grandmother and a friend of grandmother's. Each of these dyads seemed to enjoy the threesome with her. When I asked about whether her mother would be included in this list, she commented that her parents disagreed over her, especially about the issue of her being asked to look after the younger siblings. That was how she tended to remember their triadic interaction. When asked who she identified with in these disagreements, she told me it was with her father. I inquired whether that had made her feel bad, but she said, "No, because my mother was always against me." There were no torn loyalties here. She continued, "And this was not so unpleasant because my grandmother was always for me."

Hans remembered being actively pushed out by his father when his mother and father were together. I asked about his mother's feelings about this and he said that she would rather break with the other adult than leave her son out. He remembered one seaside scene in which his parents had wanted to go for a walk on the beach on their own, but he insisted on going with them by trying to capture his mother and exclude his father. Eventually his father sat in a chair while he and his mother took a walk together. He remembered feeling very stupid afterward, sensing that he should not have done this: "I should have been more diplomatic." Although there were several more times when this happened, he remembers this as being the first time that he realized that it was the wrong thing to do. He described the experience as finding out that there were rules against certain things happening. I asked him who set the rules and he said it was always his father who stated them. Later, however, he had realized that his mother also upheld the rules, but that she went to his father to support her; in other words, some of the rules came from her. I asked him if he had also watched his parents in bed. He seemed somewhat shocked by this question and said, "I would not dream of it."

Clarifying Differences in Scripts from Family of Origin

I asked them what they would like to continue in this family and what they would like to do differently from their parents. Both immediately focused on how to resolve differences in the current family's rules. Hans was stricter than Anya liked to be, especially about where Peter sat. I asked what Hans felt about how Peter was now sitting, between his parents and very close to Anya and so Hans could not get in. Hans joked that that was against the family rules, linking my question to the previous discussion about his family. He then moved the discussion to a more general level by saying that what he found difficult was when Anya took Peter out of the set of rules and "did her own thing." He felt that overall rules were useful for children. Anya then described a problem scenario in which Hans said that Peter must sit where he was told, but Peter objected. Anya then reinforced the father's instruction and Peter got even more upset. At that moment

Anya wanted to back down, whereas Hans threatened to smack Peter. During this description they were joking about it together, but there was also an underlying sense that what they were describing was important to resolve. It is interesting that the problem scenario in which parents are in disagreement about a child is similar to Anya's family problem. How can they avoid replicating that?

The couple went on to discuss how they differed about this issue. Anya was against what she saw as brutality, whereas Hans felt it was merely firmness and keeping to rules. They clarified the different meanings they gave to the situation. Anya thought that they should have rules about when they should stick to the rules and when they should be a bit more playful in certain areas. Hans was thoughtful. He said that what was preoccupying him was an issue with his parents: Although father set the rules, he realized that his mother was just as strict, and so they were more together than he had realized. To illustrate this, he described how in the seaside scene, in which Hans had walked with his mother, his father had afterward quietly made a reconciliation with him.

It was fascinating to see how both parents moved to a higher level of abstraction, or meta rules, in an attempt to deal with the contradiction between their beliefs about discipline. Anya suggested adjusting the rules about the rules to differentiate those areas where discipline was needed from those where they could improvise. Hans grasped the idea that despite roles appearing to be opposed on the surface, they may in fact be shared at another level and so are not necessarily signs of disagreement. This diplomatic solution was the one he was hoping to achieve in his current family while maintaining the common ground of agreed rules. At this point in the session Peter, who had wandered out of the room earlier, rushed back into the room and ran into his mother's arms. Anya held her arms out wide so that he had to come to her and could not get to his father. Father did not seem to be perturbed by this. Hans put his hand on Peter's head as he sat on his mother's lap. Peter then turned around to look at his father. I asked whether he had been upset that his son had gone to his wife and not to him. He said, "No, because I heard Peter calling for his mother outside so that this is what I expected." Hans knew about his child's need for his mother when distressed and was confident that he could stay in the picture despite being apparently excluded. Hans's own father had accepted his need to be with his mother but reconnected later in the seaside scene.

It was now 5 minutes from the end of the session and I was aware that these people were sitting with a family therapist, and I felt a need to say something about my impressions. I announced that we were going to stop in a moment. I then told my own story. "What happens in new families is that each parent has a different set of rules (*illustrating this by holding my hands wide apart*) and the two have to work out how to connect the two sets of rules (*indicating with my hands how complicated and difficult this was, by bringing my hands together but with the fingers getting in the way and mismatching, and then trying again and again to get the match more comfortable*). The other thing that happens is that each person thinks the other is 'way out' (*holding one hand centrally while moving the other hand way out to one side*), while the other one thinks the other person is also way out. (*I then reverse the direction of my hands—both parents laugh in recognition of the situation.*) But actually, if you are thinking about your past family you know that you yourself have moved a long distance toward your partner's way of doing things. So Hans, when compared with his family of origin, would be much less strict. . . ." Anya interrupted and added, "And much more accepting" (*nodding her head and agreeing vigorously*). I said to Anya, "And you were probably moving. . . ." Anya interrupted, "Toward some rules." Hans agreed (*both parents nodding in agreement and smiling*): "Ya, ya, ya." At this moment there was a pause and it felt more like a threesome that I had joined.

Hans then said, "We are intellectual people and we can discuss how these things happen and why they happen." Anya then emphasized that this was a real problem at the moment. "We get into conflict about it" (*indicating as such with her hands mimicking my way of showing conflict*). I said, "So you are telling me that you now have a way of thinking these things through and discussing it." Hans agreed, saying, "Yes, we are working out when we should stick to the rules, and when we should relax." Anya agreed and seemed a bit more happy about it. I said, "So now you have found a way of working out how each of you needs to accommodate the rules so that you can be together" (*bringing my hands together to show this process of eventually coming together while describing it*). Both parents nodded in agreement. But Anya then said, "We have not found a solution to this problem yet." I said, "This is family life—it goes on and on." Anya said, "It may be easier later, but at the moment it is difficult because you have to deal with things as they come." I said, "But you have a mechanism in which you can talk things through and actually change the rules." Hans added, "and adapt them." Anya (*nodding*) said, "Yes, but we cannot live while we are . . . " (*showing her two hands coming together in considerable conflict*). I commented, "So when it gets to that level (*now mimicking her conflict with my hands*), then you know that you have to do something about it." I then pointed to my head and said, "Because you are both intelligent people, you can then think it through and discuss it." Anya stated, "I cannot live when we have too much conflict" (*lifting her hand and indicating a limit*). I added, "So that's what tells you that you have to do something about it. That's great!" Anya finished, "It takes time." She smiled, finally relaxing and enjoying the baby.

In the last 5 minutes of my time with them, this family demonstrated that it knew about its most important conflict, and that it had devised strategies for resolving it, one of which was using me as a temporary attachment figure. But they remained realistic about what a struggle this would be. This is one of the most crucial aspects of a secure family base in which conflicts can be openly brought to the surface, then acknowledged, and finally attempts made to deal with them. It is also the point that I hope to reach with my clinic families at the end of treatment. It is interesting that in this 5 minutes the parents' roles remained characteristic. Anya demarcated the problem very clearly and would not let it be ignored, while Hans provided a frame in which the negotiation could happen. In my role as "quasi" therapist I provided a story and imagery to go with it, which normalized what was happening to them. They were able to relate to it and use it. My talking style is more like Hans's, in that it provided a conceptual frame in which, I hoped, each could appreciate the other's position better. My nonverbal style, however, mostly through the way I use my hands, is more like Anya's. I demarcate differences, indicating trouble spots and ways of resolving the difficulties. It is interesting that Anya persisted with her demarcation of the problem until I took it sufficiently seriously to explore with her the signs of when something must be done about it. She worried that the two men might enjoy the intellectual exercise of discussing it, but would then deny the need to do anything. She used my hand language to demarcate her own limits beyond which she could not survive. My clear acknowledgment of this and validation of the use of her tolerance levels as a barometer for taking action enabled her to relax. I had perhaps acted as a transgenerational marker of what had to be taken seriously. By saying "That's great!" when Anya indicated her limit, I was like a "father" indicating to the son that his wife's limits are to be valued.

In terms of transgenerational scripts, Anya's determination to resolve disagreement between parents over a child was her corrective script. The couple had shared a transgenerational script in Anya's statement in the first interview about Hans doing well when he comes to her, rather than staying talking to his father. This could be seen as Anya's corrective script to the gulf between her parents. It was also

Hans's corrective script for avoiding the cross-generational coalition that he experienced in his family. This was mediated by Peter's birth. They were now using the new family to write new scripts.

DISCUSSION

The Place of Threesomes in Family Life

The transition to a threesome is arguably one of the most important developmental achievements for families. Some families rarely achieve this state and instead predominately use dyadic interaction, while other families keep at a distance, even keeping away from dyadic interaction. In some families the pattern may script certain relationships as being close, others as distant, but never equidistant.

The unique contribution of the struggle to achieve a threesome interaction is to provide a stage on which it is possible for a child to have an experience of other people, say, parents, being able to keep him or her in their minds at the same time as keeping each other in mind. In other words, each parent thinking about another person (e.g., the other parent) does not mean they have forgotten the child. It is also a setting in which the effect of relationship on relationships (Emde, 1988) can be observed and explored. What happens if the parents' relationship is so intense, either very close or preoccupied by conflict, that the child is left out? What are the results of capturing one parent and keeping the other parent out, etc.? The reciprocal of this experience that two parents can relate to each other while still keeping the child in mind is the discovery that the child can keep the parents and their relationship with each other in his or her mind. Once this is achieved, other people can be added to the threesome, and group interaction can be envisaged, with each member of the group capable of keeping everyone in mind. This is one of the steps toward interactional awareness, in which the emotional consequences of the interaction for everyone in the family can be visualized. The child can imagine how each will be feeling about what is happening, as well as have some sense of his or her own responses.

The Weiss family illustrated that the nonverbal components of a threesome interaction seem to be choreographed, that is, there is a shared model of what to do. This appears to be directed toward providing an approximately symmetrical experience in which each can see the other two equally well. In the 3-month triadic play, body posture sets the scene in which the heads can be turned to allow shared eye-to-eye contact with the baby and, hence, vice versa. What is even more fascinating is that in the triadic play at 1 year the same principles held true even when the artificial symmetry provided by the chair was broken by mother holding the baby on her lap. The threesome's eye contact was made possible despite this. Symmetry was also achieved in both play sessions through other modalities: in movement (in the shared swinging of the baby's arms in the swimming game at 3 months) and by singing a song that went back and forth between the parents. Another important feature of the choreography was the switch of orientation of the baby's attention and gaze to include the newcomer entering the threesome. This was achieved by the parents collaborating: father bidding for attention, while mother invited the baby to notice his father by calling his name. But the timing of his joining in the threesome was left to the baby. At 3 months Peter was allowed to finish his "dance" with mother before symmetry was achieved. At 1 year, however, he had to be settled by his parents before it happened.

The parents setting the stage initially for the baby to follow later provides an example of the developmental hierarchy of time frames. Elizabeth Fivas-Depeursinge (1991) discussed this in terms of parent–child dyads. By providing a longer interactional time frame than the child needs, the parents provide a context in which the child can learn. It provides the hierarchy inherent in a teacher–student relationship. In the threesome, the parents provide a longer time frame by orienting their bodies and gaze for a longer period than the baby actually uses in the threesome play. The longer time frame also allows the baby to explore the experience of initiating the transition from one state to another; how to choose to enter a threesome, or to leave it.

Clearly the baby is not yet ready to engage in full interactional awareness until he has developed the capacity for metacognitive monitoring. The regular experience of threesome or group interaction is one setting where he or she can learn to do it. This raises the question of where in everyday family life threesomes or "moresomes" occur. The pleasure of joining together in a threesome with a loved baby would seem likely to motivate these moments during babyhood and young childhood. The family circle may also convene at other times when all family members can see each other. The classic example is the family meal around a table; although this has steadily given ground to serial snacks in front of different television sets. Many family rituals also involve circles, such as drinking toasts when every member of the family may touch glasses, establishing the symmetrically interconnected nature of the family. This may also include toasting absent members of the family or telephoning the absent member on special occasions, say, Christmas. Everyone in the family circle is kept in mind. However this form of inclusive interaction most frequently occurs in the many informal contexts in which the family or subgroups meet in a way that allows for a group exchange.

The threesome or "moresome" experience goes one step beyond the development stage (described in Chapter 2) in which the child learns to switch back and forth between being in the audience to going on stage and back again. He or she can learn to be simultaneously in both positions. Each is being processed in parallel, although the center of attention may switch from one position to the other. The continuity and congruence between the two is not broken, creating a coherent story in which all members of the cast contribute to the unfolding plot. It is then possible to gain the perspective of circular causality. What happens is no longer perceived as being caused by those "out there," or by only one person. Everyone is involved in what happens and each is aware of the interaction. It is from this frame that new shared expectations—in other words, new scripts—can most readily emerge from improvized interaction. Of course, what I am describing is an ideal end point. Many individuals or families do not reach or maintain this perspective.

Threesomes: Scripts for Security in Families and Groups

If the overall context is one of caring, then the threesome can help to provide the foundations for a shared mental representation of the secure family base; that is, the expectation that everyone has a place in the family circle and that no one undermines other people's caring relationships or competes against others for care. Of course, a secure family base may involve many intimate dyadic exchanges, encouraged and supported by the rest of the family while everyone can confidently wait their turn. Whatever new elements are hatched within a dyad are anticipated to contribute to the whole family, not to impoverish those not involved.

If, however, a family finds it difficult to disengage from dyads and reengage in threesomes—or as a group—then the message is that it is hard to keep more than one person equally in mind at the same time. For those feeling insecure about relationships in a group setting, anxiety may be aroused about being left out and hence forgotten. For those who respond to anxiety in relationships by backing away, as in the avoidant/disengaged person who may assume the other person is rejecting, this may lead to opting out or staying on the periphery. Children in these families may never learn about being part of a group. Those ambivalent/enmeshed individuals who attempt to capture a caregiver in order to ensure being kept in mind become rivalrous with other members of the family. The experience then is of an incessant struggle to be part of an "in-group" because if you do not keep your place, then you will most surely be left in the "out group."

T·H·I·R·T·E·E·N

Grieving Scripts

The title of this chapter is deliberately ambiguous. Two meanings can be read into it—both are relevant. First, there are scripts for grieving, that is, the procedures for mourning—who comforts whom, who manages the situation, and how is the psychological work of grieving to be performed. Second, there is grieving of scripts that have been cut short. Those that are left behind have to give up their hopes and expectations of what would have happened in their relationships with the dead person. In short, they have to grieve the family script for the future and rewrite a script without the deceased.

UNRESOLVED MOURNING AND SECURITY

Parents who have failed to mourn a significant attachment figure, lost in their childhood, are likely to have children who are classified as insecure/disorganized at 1 year (Main et al., 1985). Ainsworth and Eichberg (1991) compared those parents who had bereavements and had resolved their mourning with those who had unresolved mourning. Those who had resolved a loss reported that they had felt very supported by their own family. They had a strong sense of family solidarity with comforting, expression of feelings, and sharing of grief, and/or the individual had taken responsibility for others in the family during the mourning period. Some parents reported that the family had got together over a mourning period and that now "there's a closeness that was never there before."

Parents who had a loss as a child but had resolved their mourning were likely to be rated as autonomous on the Adult Attachment Interview (AAI) and to have securely attached infants. This showed that it was the unresolved mourning that was associated with the disorganized status of the child, and not the fact of having had a bereavement itself. Another interesting finding was that the parents who were rated as "preoccupied" on the AAI, were particularly likely to be associated with the unresolved mourning status. This suggests that adults who are unable to let go of a dead attachment figure were those who were also preoccupied with past events and unable to let go of the past. Ainsworth and Eichberg (1991) felt that a major protective factor was the presence of a secure attachment to the remaining parent or another adult member of the family. In summary, it seems that resolution of mourning is more likely if the family provides a secure base.

THE AIMS OF WORK WITH A GRIEVING FAMILY

The central aim of working with a family who has lost a member is to help the family to manage their own grieving (Byng-Hall, 1991a). The therapist aims to help the family to become a secure base from which the family members can be mutually supportive and able to share their grief. A successful session with a bereaved family might start with the family sitting and talking to the worker, but may end up with each member of the family putting their arms around one another and talking among themselves. If the therapist becomes involved with families soon after a death, it is important to emphasize that this is not therapy, as grieving is a natural process. It is also natural, however, to use people in the community to help families to come to terms with what has happened. The therapist can offer to be that person.

Therapists are more often called in when something has gone wrong with the grieving. Various problems may arise from a failure to take the next appropriate step in a normal grieving process. For instance, there are mechanisms that slow down the full realization of what has happened. Some slowing down, however, may be helpful, in that it prevents the individual members of the family from being overwhelmed. One of these slowing mechanisms is that of the shocked disbelief which can happen on hearing about the death. If this is allowed to go on, however, it can lead to denial of the reality of the death itself or to detachment of the feelings from the event. In families or individuals who have become stuck at the stage of disbelief, it is possible for the therapist to evoke painful memories of the lost person, so that someone in the family starts to cry. Then other members can be encouraged to support that person and consequently move into sharing their own grief. As in other forms of family therapy, the therapist's capacity to provide a temporary secure base will enable the family to feel safe enough to let go of their emotional constraints.

SOME IMPLICATIONS FOR SCRIPTS
IN TRAUMATIC DEATHS

When the death has been particularly unpleasant, for example, witnessing a member of the family being killed, therapists are also more likely to be consulted. In normal circumstances the death scene can be remembered, recalled, or conjured up by those not present, and discussed with the family. The scenario can be seen again and again in the imagination, putting the therapist in the shoes of those involved. In this way the reality can be accepted. In very traumatic losses the individual members of the family may dissociate their experience from aspects of the death scene in order to block the full implications of what has happened. In this situation some individuals may identify with the dead victim as a way of avoiding any separation—they join with the dead person instead. They might also identify with the aggressor if somebody has killed a member of the family; this enables them to avoid imagining what it would have been like to be the victim. Or they may identify with a wished-for rescuer (a potential attachment figure?) conjured up in the imagination as a way of coping with a terrifying situation. This rescuing role may also represent what the observer felt he or she should have done and bitterly regrets not doing. There is then a danger that these identifications can become set and roles become permanently scripted. To identify with the victim is clearly dangerous and can lead to feeling "dead" inside or to self-destructive behavior. Identifying with the aggressor is obviously problematic. But to become a compulsive protector, or caregiver, may also be restrictive because it prescribes a lifetime of repeated rescue attempts.

Another strategy that the family as a whole may use is to script one of the members of the family as a replacement for a dead person, in which case the full implications of the loss of the dead person do not have to be faced immediately. The image of the lost member is kept alive through the presence of the replacement in the family. Also, the role that the dead person played may be transferred inappropriately to the chosen replacement. I discovered the power of this phenomenon after my father died. At the first meal after his death, I found myself sitting in his seat, being treated like him, and also behaving like him. This was a two-way process in which my place setting had been laid at his seat, but I also accepted the role by sitting there. Once I realized what was happening, I was able to talk about it and sit somewhere else the next time.

GRIEVING FOR UNFULFILLED FAMILY SCRIPTS

Those who are left behind have the problem of how to deal with the script for the future of the family, which had been built around the fact that all of the family members would be alive to take part in family life. We are not always aware how powerful this script for the future is and how it will continue to unfold in the mind over many years. Reminders of the deceased will often confront us with what we imagined would have been happening if the person had lived. Perhaps the most poignant example of this is that of parents who lose a child and then are reminded again and again by children of the same age who grow up and reach a new developmental phase. This resonates painfully with their past hopes and expectations for the child's future. Anniversaries of the death or the person's birthday may also bring the old script into a painful clash with reality. In addition to there being an unconscious clock ticking away there is the problem that many unresolved issues are left unresolved after a death. This is especially true of untimely deaths of young people, or unexpected deaths. In deaths that are expected there might have been opportunities for forgiving each other or for making up for one's own past mistakes. Cultural beliefs about what happens to the dead person after death can facilitate the resolution of some of these legacies which, if left unfolding in the back of the mind, can haunt those left behind with powerful images that provoke guilt or anger.

CULTURAL SCRIPTS ABOUT THE AFTERLIFE

Many cultures provide sets of beliefs about what happens to people after they die that allow for some unfolding of the scripts, and hence afford opportunities for making peace with the deceased. One of the crucial issues is whether or not an exchange can be envisaged between the dead and the living person, in which the dead person can acknowledge or forgive something the living person does. Without this, there is less sense that the living person can make up for any past problems with the dead person, and so death may leave the individual with a sense of personal regret or feeling that he or she is owed something by the dead person. This opens up the danger of the legacy being settled through the next generation, perhaps through those who were scripted as replacements for the dead person. Many cultures do, however, provide ways and means for settling old issues through performing rituals or funeral rights, etc.

It is important for the therapist to find out what the family's own views about "afterlife" are and not to impose his or her own view. It is crucial to avoid labeling any particular belief as representing failed mourning. For instance, belief that one can contact the dead may be culturally appropriate or it may represent a denial of the loss. Having been brought up in Africa but in a very British culture, I was interested to find out what African cultural beliefs were. I had been aware of African beliefs about spirits, which were often felt to inhabit boulders, trees, or special places in the countryside. My sister and I used to play in a particular part of the garden in which we created a whole community of spirits which we called "Plumsey men"; who were never perceived as either black African or white British, but who had a life of their own. These people became so real to us that when we moved to a different farm it created something of a crisis to which my parents, who were sensitive to our need for a pretend world, then staged a "move" of the Plumsey men to an interesting boulder near to the new house. Interestingly, neither of us could really believe in the idea that the Plumsey men had moved, and so the game died out. Looking back on it I think this play may have represented, for me anyway, imagery that came from both cultures. Plums can be either black or red (the color of Europeans in Africa). They may also have represented the African "spirits" that inhabited such places.

My sister and I were also aware of other communities of people in the adults' minds. Our parents seemed to be preoccupied with the people they were talking about "back home," in England, whom we had never met. Even more mysterious were the images in the Africans' heads. The images from each set of adults was, however, of "real" worlds. However, Plumsey men were real enough to have their own home, and not to be part of pretend play with dolls, which can be recreated anywhere by the context marker of "children's play." My sister and I have often wondered why this experience had been so intense and real for us.

Having not been within the African culture itself, I was unsure as to how spirits related to dead ancestors. Professor Archie Smith, Jr.,[1] a black American family therapist who is also a theologian, had just visited Kenya; he observed me working with the family I am about to describe.

The idea of the "living dead" is present in many African societies and is described by John Mbiti (1975) of Kenya who studied views of death and afterlife across the African continent. The following ac-

[1] I am indebted to him for helping me to explore some of the African cultural beliefs about the afterlife.

count is a generalized summary of what is very complex and varied. The living dead live on in memory for up to five generations following the death. After that point it is likely that the last person who remembers the dead person, say, a grandmother who can remember her own grandparents, will have died themselves. After the last memory dies, the living dead lose their human form and become dead. In some African societies these living dead are present in the ground or stones where they were buried, or in some African societies—as in many Western cultures—they pass up into the sky.

How then do the remaining family members and the living dead transact? At times the living dead visit. Someone will announce, "I met 'so and so' today." But there is a barrier between the living and the dead. The dead cannot rejoin the living. Visitations by the living dead are often not welcomed with enthusiasm—they often spell trouble. The living dead's revenge for past wrongdoings doing can lead to illness or misfortune. Some sort of ritual or sacrifice may have to be made to make up for past misdemeanors or for the failure to give a correct "burial." On the positive side, the living dead can intercede with "God" on the behalf of the living. In other words, there is scope for settling both the debts and the credits left over from the severed relationship.

The dead person can also be partially reincarnated, in which case another member of the family can be seen to have some of the characteristics of the lost person. Sometimes names are used to identify this link. This is like the a replacement script. What is interesting to me is not only how different cultures have contrasting beliefs but also by how much they overlap, illustrating the universality of human experience. There is some shared human wisdom about how to manage the experience of death.

I will illustrate this overlap by describing some brief work with an Irish Catholic family, using the lens of the living dead. As we know from Monica McGoldrick's (McGoldrick et al. , 1991) writing, the Irish have a particularly rich view of the spiritual world. But even if I know something of the culture, I needed to know this particular family's interpretation of cultural beliefs.

THERAPEUTIC IMPLICATIONS

At the beginning of therapy, following a bereavement, I routinely ask where the dead person is right now. I learned to do this early in my career. When visiting the home of a Greek mother whose 15-year-old son had been killed, I suddenly became aware that, incongruously, there was loud adolescent-style music being played despite mother being the only one at home. I asked where the boy was, and she pointed to the bench next to me.

A Case Example: The Casey Family

The father, Patrick, had been killed in a traffic accident 18 months before and the priest had suggested that the family should be referred to the clinic. Mary, the mother (aged 29), was now wanting to face some family issues and was not sure whether she had told her two sons, James (aged 5) and John (aged 3), the right thing about their father. The parents had not been married, but Mary considered that they were as good as husband and wife. James was currently being aggressive and difficult.

First Session: Where Is Daddy?

Mary came with her two children. James immediately communicated his preoccupation with illness by finding a doll whose head had come off. He tried desperately to put it back on again. When I asked why he had come, he was thoughtful. Then he started to bang his own head with the palm of his hands in the region of his ear. His mother said that perhaps he thought that he was coming to have his ears treated. (I discovered later that his mother had originally told him that his father had died after tripping and banging his head.) She explained to James that they came to talk about the boy's father. Within a few minutes of the beginning of the session, I was deep in conversation with James about where his father was. When I asked where he was, James pointed upward and explained that the angels had come down and taken him up. With further probing I found that James thought that his father was almost alive, being looked after by God who was like a doctor and would make him better so that his father could come back. He went to the phone to ring upstairs to his Dad. He had clearly come to "God's" hospital to collect his father. James had probably also identified with his dead father as his banging of his own head indicated.

Mary then told me how Patrick was killed. This was apparently the first account the children had heard of his death, although she had told them that he had been killed in a car crash, rather than tripping, a week before the session. The tripping story was important for the children, as falling over and hitting your head is not a very convincing image of death. Children themselves are always tripping and recovering quickly. I became interested in finding out how much of James's view of the "living dead" was also part of the family belief system. Or, was his view a sign that he had not accepted the reality of the death? One of the things that Mary repeatedly said to James was that his father was not going to come back, although it was clear that she considered that he was existing somewhere. This brought his father's "presence" more in line with the African idea of the living dead who one knows will not return. Toward the end of the session, although James was saying that his father was not coming back, he started throwing paper darts high into the air, which, he explained, would go on right up to the sun. This suggested that he still had not given up the idea of making direct contact with his father.

James's beliefs only slowly changed during the therapy. In a later session, for instance, he told me that God would make his father better and "make him big, big, big so he can come back," and that he was going to "put a ladder up to heaven." By the end of therapy, however, he said he knew his Dad was not going to come back.

The way I work with small children in families where there has been a catastrophe of some sort is to help the adult members of the family to decide on a shared story for the children. The story must be basically true and must fit with the adult's own beliefs, so that as the children grow older and ask more questions of each of the adults about what happened, they will get the same consistent and coherent account from everyone. The story has to include the basic plot, but it does not have to include all the subplots and details. These can be added later when the children reach an appropriate age. A shared story was told in a later session.

Second Session: The Story of Father's Death

Mary came on her own to the second session. She was able to share with me those details that she found difficult to share with her children. Five months before Patrick died, the couple had separated and Mary had returned home to her mother with the children. Patrick, however, was around so much during the day that Mary never had to explain to the children that they had separated. Five weeks before he died, Patrick told Mary that he was dating another woman, but 2 day's before the crash, he came home and made love to her, while telling her that she was the only person for him and that this other woman meant nothing to him. She believed him, as she had always held onto the view that they were really meant for each other and would finally resolve their difficulties. Two days later, Patrick's brother rang her up to tell her that Patrick had been in a serious car accident in which his new fiancée had been killed outright. Patrick died 2 weeks later, never having regained consciousness. They had been driving to her parents' home in Birmingham to introduce him to her parents as her fiancée.

An interfamily battle ensued for his body. Patrick's family did not want Mary or the children to come to the funeral. Mary went, however, but without the children. The inscription on the headstone read: "Patrick remembered by his father, mother and brother, now reunited with his beloved Theresa." Theresa was the fiancée who had died. Mary was shattered and her family was furious. How would she ever take the children to their father's grave and expose them to that? The next day the police arrived to accuse her of stealing the headstone which had disappeared. Mary offered to give them a list of a hundred people, which included her extended family and her numerous friends, all of whom, she told the police, would love to claim to have taken the headstone. One of Mary's difficulties was to decide whether or not to tell the children about Theresa. She felt there was a danger that Patrick's family would tell them about it. She wanted it to come from her lips, but whenever she tried to tell them, she found she could not. I said that I thought her lips had been wise and that until she herself had come to terms with what had happened they would only hear her distress. It was clear that the two children were at risk of being involved in the intergalactic battle between these two Irish families who lived in an extensive Irish community a few streets away from each other. It is interesting that the way this story was told organized my perception of this apparently outrageous behavior on his family's part. It took time for me to establish a perspective from their point of view, which was that their son had become involved in an unmarried relationship—something disapproved of by their family—which had then broken down. Suddenly, through the accident, they had learned about a new relationship, but with marriage in prospect this time. This new relationship was in the process of seeking a blessing by the couples' families when the tragedy happened. The funeral then provided the perfect opportunity to complete that tragically curtailed wedding by uniting the couple in heaven. Both Patrick's and Theresa's families could thus give their blessing to the relationship. An ex-girlfriend and her children would clearly blight that ritual.

Third Session: Exploring Past Grieving Scripts

Grandmother Martha and mother came to the third session. In order to get a picture of past grieving scripts which might still operate today I drew a genogram. I asked Martha about her family and the deaths in the family. (See Figure 13.1.) The first one she described

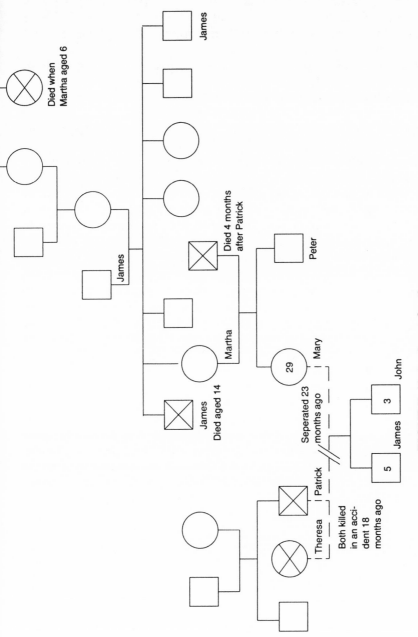

FIGURE 13.1. Casey family genogram.

Died when
Martha aged 6

James

James
Died aged 14

Martha

Died 4 months
after Patrick

Peter

29 | Mary

Seperated 23
months ago

Theresa | Patrick

Both killed
in an acci-
dent 18
months ago

5 | 3
James | John

253

was her great aunt (you will notice that this represents the five generations of the living dead). She had been very old, but she had been like a second mother to her. While her great aunt was dying, Martha, aged 6, crept into bed with her, gave her a cuddle, and said, "I will miss you at tea in the morning." Martha explained that everybody just accepted death in those days and this was much better. She described how they used to keep the bodies at home for 2 days and then the body would go straight from the home to the cemetery. "Now they just take you out of the home and put you in a fridge; you don't get a chance to grieve." I asked her what she had been told by her parents about where people go when they are dead. She replied, "We were told they go to heaven, which was a wonderful place, everyone enjoying themselves. It was definitely the place to be. We were a bit puzzled when the grown-ups cried when someone died!"

The next death she described was that of James, her eldest brother who was named after his father. He had died at the age of 14. A year later, during the potato-picking season, their mother had heard potatoes being thrown into the bucket outside and looked out and saw that it was James. When the family was questioned, it became clear that they believed that indeed James had been there. This was not merely the common experience of "seeing" the dead person only to realize painfully that it was in fact someone else. But it should be noted that as with the living dead the family did not call out and invite him in. In other words, the irreversible barrier of death was accepted. His mother never got over James's death. She also idealized him by saying that he was too good for this earth and had been taken straight to heaven. His only visit back to earth, after all, had been as a good eldest son coming home to help with the potato harvest. She had said to the family soon after the death, "I will give you another James," and indeed the next baby that was born was called James. So part of the grieving script in this family, especially for untimely deaths, included the possibility of a visitation of the living dead and the use of a replacement to lessen the sense of loss. We know that a replacement may cause problems for the mourning process. It was also tempting to consider such a vivid experience of the living dead, almost as if he was still alive, contributing to the fact that mother failed to grieve her eldest son. But this is an idea held securely within this family and within its culture. I was careful to be respectful of the visitation experience. However, the knowledge that there might be a visitation anytime certainly gave vitality to the unfolding, unfinished drama in the family's minds.

Each grieving script can be modified or confirmed by subsequent deaths. James's maternal grandfather died a few months after

Patrick. James had started calling this grandfather "Dad" after Patrick's death, but following grandfather's death he started calling his uncle Peter "Daddy." The 3-year-old John called his elder brother James "Dad." Replacement was being used by both children and presumably supported by the adults who could have refused to allow it to happen.

Fourth Session: James as Replacement Father

Mother, grandmother, and the two children then came for a session. James came into the room first. He was walking with a curious stiff-legged gait. Mary commented on how he looked like a little old man. Later in the session when his grandmother was crying he got up onto her lap and embraced her just like an adult would. James had become his grandmother's constant companion and comforter. The "little old man" was James's identification with his grandfather. Again, this identification was supported by the family. I asked later about whether he took after his father. The two adults were very quick to say that he was just like his father: he looked like his father, he talked like his father, and his temperament was like that of his father. Having explored the positive aspects of that identification, I said that perhaps being a stand-in for his father was also difficult. Mary admitted that she had flown into rages with James and hit him at times. She recognized that this was part of the period when she was working through her intense anger with Patrick. This was an example of how the stand-in, or replacement, can be traumatized by becoming a player in an unfinished drama.

I now worked on some of the authority problems in the family. Part of the difficulty of scripting a child in a dead adult's role is that children are imbued with enormous power. James had been aggressively controlling the adults and had been very disobedient, like his father. I now worked with the family structurally in order to help the adults to regain authority and help grandmother and mother sort out their complex authority relationships. Grandmother owned the house, but Mary had parental responsibility. They started to collaborate on who was to decide what, and James started to settle down. He began acting like a little boy again.

Fifth Session: Mary Lets Patrick Go

Mary told me that she had started dating another man. We had a discussion about the sense of Patrick being present at times, and she had anticipated that she would feel very awkward when she was with her new boyfriend. However, to her surprise it had not been like that. Although she was aware of Patrick's "presence," it was as if he did not object to her new relationship and she said to me, "I want to let go of Patrick. . . . I want to say goodbye and let him get on with his own life and me with mine." I explored with Mary what she meant when she used the present tense in wanting Patrick to get on with his own life. She said that she had consciously intended to say it that way. For her the living dead existed in a very real world. It seemed that 2 years after the death, Mary had finally given up her ideal happy family scenario and allowed the divorce scenario to run its course. In her imagination they had been able to agree to a mutual separation, with neither now objecting to the other dating.

When doing grieving work I often use techniques that evoke the image of the dead person, such as suggesting that the grieving person go to the grave and say what they would like to have said to the dead person. There was little need to do this with Mary as she had these conversations with her dead partner automatically. For instance, when she was driving she would find herself screaming at him for having driven dangerously, and enraged at him for betraying her and their lovely children.

Last Session: Mary Gets On with Her Life

At the last session Mary came without James because he had told her that he was fine and did not want to come. He knew his Dad was not going to come back and that was fine. I think he had also discovered that I was not "God" and could not cure his father. Mary had taken a temporary job and had also gone with both children to the grave. She said that the next thing that she planned to do was to sort out the headstone with Patrick's sister. She wanted the names of the boys put on it. As she put it, "Patrick will always be part of my life because of the boys." She did not mind about her name not being there. Mary had not yet told James about Theresa, but I said I was confident that she would know when the right time had come. We discussed the need for him to know one day in order to validate his experience of his parents having separated and of their many arguments. At the moment there was a discrepancy between James's actual experience of his parents' relationship—his episodic memory—and the idealized relationship that the adults told him about, now held in his semantic memory. John, although he did not remember his father, needed to have the same story as his brother.

The final step in laying old dramas to rest depends on a sense of having no more legacies of guilt or resentment toward the dead. But the reciprocal image of the dead person also being at peace in his or her mind is necessary, otherwise a restless search for ways of making restitution starts up again. Forgiveness, in other words, needs to be experienced as being in both directions. The laws of mutuality do not stop with death. The living dead imagery can allow that to happen. The term "to *co*-memorate" the dead encapsulates a fundamental wisdom. What is needed is the capacity to remember the dead person and at the same time know that he or she remembers you. The mental representation of an attachment figure who makes one feel secure is of someone who "keeps you in mind." The co-memory can be a source of security after the death of a loved one. Attachments go on even after death.

Epilogue

At follow-up I learned that Martin had asked his mother what had happened when his father had been killed, and whether there had been anyone else in the car. Mary had surprised herself by being quite natural in the way she told him the whole story. In turn Martin had accepted it in a natural manner. She said it was easy. The family was getting on with its life, and Patrick no longer loomed large in their minds. Her relationship had not lasted, but she had learned that she could look forward to having another one at some point. She told me that her time would come—probably when the children were a little older.

F·O·U·R·T·E·E·N

Disrupted Scripts:
Family Breakup
and Disability

There are many other losses to mourn as well as that of a death. This chapter will discuss two of these: a parent leaving home and chronic illness or disability. The general principles of grieving, however, are similar to those of a family member dying. The old script has to be grieved, given up, and a new one accepted. The grieving has to be shared. These forms of loss are often more complicated and, in some ways, more difficult, than those following a death. First, the losses are often less clearcut. They may not happen at one particular moment in time. Second, the future is even less certain. It can be much easier to find ways of denying the significance of the loss, with a greater danger of trying to carry on as before in increasingly difficult circumstances. The family may fail to adapt and find itself unable to cope with the reality of what is facing them.

The degree of security of the family base will also affect what happens. With a secure base, it is likely there will be a capacity to face the difficulties and explore ways of coping while supporting each other's distress. Ambivalent/enmeshed families are likely to become extremely anxious and preoccupied with what has happened, finding it very difficult to come to terms with loss. The avoidant/disengaged families are likely to behave as if they do not care or it does not matter, and by denying the importance of the situation they are less likely to face up to the consequences, or to help their vulnerable children. The script for dealing with the situation is, as always, likely to be based on the experience of previous losses and hence is likely to be a mix of replicative and corrective scripts. When the situation is

258

outside previous experience, however (e.g., an accident leaving a member of the family in a wheelchair), old scripts are unlikely to be sufficiently applicable to the new circumstance. An innovative script is then needed.

MAKING SOME SENSE OF PARENTS SEPARATING

Separation is usually heralded by problems appearing in the parents' relationship. There may have been arguments, or even brief separations, before the final break. In many ways this gives everybody warning but leaves many unsettled issues in the air. Ambivalent/Enmeshed relationships may take a long time to break down and usually remain unresolved over many years afterward, with attempts to settle old scores either through the children and the lawyers, or to keep the old ambivalent exchanges going through letter, telephone, and face-to-face arguments. Avoidant/disengaged relationships, on the other hand, may end abruptly; sometimes without any warning, even to the partner. Another phenomenon is "crazy hate" replacing "crazy love": Bonding and attachments created by the intensity of quite irrational passionate love, blind to all difficulties, may require an equally blind hatred to break the bond and leave each partner thankful that they have got away from such an awful person. In other words, romantic couples may avoid the mixed feelings of their relationship, both at the beginning in order to join and at the end in order to get separated. The children, of course, are not so often witness to their parents' crazy love, but see only the quite extraordinary hatred that can occur at the separation. I find, however, that children often understand this when it is explained to them. In one family I explained to an 8-year-old girl, "You know, Mum and Dad decided that they could not live with each other any more— you remember how they always used to disagree with each other when they both lived at home—so that was a sensible decision. But it was very, very difficult for them as they used to love each other so much. So now they have to get very, very cross with each other so that they don't want to be with each other any more. This is their way of making it easier to stick to their sensible decision not to live together any more. They know that they fight too much when they are together." The girl's mother told me afterward that hearing this explanation helped her to realize—for the very first time—why she had felt so angry with her ex-husband. Putting things in words that children can understand is often also a good way of helping adults.

Glimpses of the Uncertain Journey Ahead

Following the separation there are commonly three main expectations, often held in different levels of awareness:

1. The parents will come together again despite everything.
2. The family will become a single-parent household and remain so.
3. Either or both parents will find new partners.

The family is not only grappling with feelings about torn-up old scripts and dashed expectations but they are also dealing with all these ideas that are jumbled up together with the pain of the loss and the guilt of what has happened. All this can feel frightening and strange, and it is disturbing to have all these feelings at the same time. The family may feel less insecure if what is happening can be understood to be following pathways common to many families. I often sketch these out to help family members feel oriented again. If I hear that a parent has recently left home for good, then, before finding out the details of what has happened, I will often make the following statement, which is my generalized script for what is likely to happen. Although I have not experienced it myself—this may or may not be a disadvantage—I have seen it happen many times before. This is my statement:

> When Mums and Dads separate I often find that certain things happen. The children almost always have a big, big hope that Mum and Dad will get together again. Surprisingly, they may even feel this when one parent has been violent to the other. They may not even think it is very sensible if they did get together again, but deep inside that is what they hope.

Even if children deny this wish, it is important to state it. Later, if the wish surfaces neither the parent nor the child is then surprised. Sometimes, however, children can openly agree that this is what they hope. Their parents may be very surprised to hear this, and so will make their intention much clearer to the children in future.

> Children also often think that perhaps they did something to make their Daddy or Mum go away, or think that they should have done something to get Mum and Dad together to be friends, so that nobody had to leave. They often feel that it is their fault even when they really know that it was Mum's and Dad's decision. Of course (*to the children*), you may be one of the very few children who don't feel like that.

And then, perhaps a little later in the session, when discussing what might happen next, I say (this is not usually stated in monologue form, but in several statements threaded together within a conversation):

> Sometimes Mums and Dads decide that they are going to live on their own after something like that has happened. But children can sometimes wish that Dad would find another Mum, or Mum find another Dad for them. But then, if they do find someone else, the children often find they don't like it at all, because they themselves have now become very special to their Mum or their Dad. So when the new grown-up becomes very special to Mum or Dad, that can sometimes make children feel very left out. But, you know, it is also very difficult for parents to let the new grown-up person be a proper Mum or Dad, who can tell their children what to do. Sometimes the very last thing, before you know there really is a new family, is when Mum lets the new Dad look after you and tell you what to do in the way he thinks best.

I will then ask the family to describe what sort of stage they have reached in this process. Presenting my story of what happens after a separation, before I hear their details, gives the family, and the children in particular, a sense that what they are going through is an understandable and expected process. Many other people have also been through it, they are not crazy or incompetent or bad. It also gives the family a sense that there can be some light at the end of the tunnel.

When I am working with parents who are in the process of separating, or have separated, I emphasize the need to move toward two households, each with its own script for family life. I anticipate with them how difficult that may be. I weave this story into the conversation with the couple, without the children being present:

> Okay, so you have finally decided that it is best to make separate lives for yourselves. I just want to share some thoughts about what might happen. Although you have prepared yourself well for this occasion by making sure you are so fed up with each other that you are not going to miss each other, it might nevertheless be a much more difficult task than you think. Because the attachment between two people who have known each other a long time does not disappear overnight you may be tempted to keep the link going through other people. Often this can be through lawyers. They could help you to go on fighting for the next 10 or 20 years. Alternatively, you might be tempted to use the children, sending messages through them or extracting information about what goes on in the other family, subtly inviting them to behave

badly in the other family. Children do not like this at all. The problem is that it is not always obvious what you are doing. You may say to yourselves, I just wanted to find out how the other one was getting on, or it can even feel like being caring. I know you want to put the children first in all this. You can choose to do something much more caring, which is to allow each other to be parents in your different ways. This can be very difficult as you have probably, like so many parents, been so used to trying to check each other's parenting and trying to improve it. After you have separated you may find that your standards, say, of discipline or bedtimes become very different. This can lead to problems. If you feel anxious about the degree of difference, as the children themselves are commenting on this and complaining about it, then I suggest that you find a way of talking to each other about it. Try to respect each other's style and move toward a compromise. Whatever you do, do not use the children as pawns in this struggle. Finally, I predict, the most difficult thing you will come up against is when your ex-spouse finds a new partner. You will find it extremely hard to allow this partner to be a parent to your own children. It will be hard enough allowing your own new partner to have parental responsibility for the children, but it is much more difficult to allow your spouse's partner to have a say in what happens. This, of course, is made even more difficult too, if either of you is blaming the new partner for breaking up your marriage.

If you can choose to do it by negotiation, obviously in your own particular style, then the rewards will be great. Best of all, the children can look forward to visiting each household. They don't have to worry that enjoying going to the other home is being disloyal. There are rewards for each of you. You can get along with your own lives while the children are with the other partner. Do not constantly worry about what is happening there. It is also not impossible, but not always guaranteed either, that you might even become friends eventually. That may need to be delayed, however, because of the anxieties about the pull of the old attachments which are still there and which you have so thoroughly buried. The children, however, will certainly not have buried that hope so deep. When they can see you being friendly with the old partner, then they will know that you are not being rivalrous, and they will secretly try to get the old marriage going again. When, and if, you do become friends again, each of you needs to make it clear to the kids what is going on.

These two lengthy statements—one with the children there and one with the parents only—are strung together here for the sake of clarity. In practice, of course, they came in bits and pieces as part of the dialogue of therapy. Having the therapist's story about family breakup, single parenthood, and perhaps a new family helps to make sure that all the basic steps are discussed by the end of the work together. I see the statements as part of a preview of what might happen. On the other hand, this is also like the therapist's script for the family which may, or may not, have much influence on the course of events. It may, however, provide the family with an anchor when things are being blown off course. The feature that draws parents back on course is its shared goal that everything that happens has to be in the children's best interest.

The preview then defines a number of steps that need to be taken, with difficulties that should be anticipated and possible plans to overcome them. It also indicates alternative pathways and the possible consequences of each. However, it is vital that the therapist's story is tentative; this will allow the family their own potentially inventive pathways. All sorts of novel solutions and new family structures may be created in the complicated dance that follows a breakup.

Putting aside the debate about the damage that divorce can cause, after the pain subsides children may find that they have a far wider potential range of relationships, with new grandparents, uncles, aunts, family, friends etc, as well as a new set of siblings. Whether or not these will be fruitful may depend on how the previous family script is mourned and let go, and how the adults allow and facilitate children to stay in contact with both sides of the old family. It also includes how they help them to engage with these new members without feeling disloyal to the original families.

Exploring Scripts from Previous Marital Breakdown

I explore the old scripts that the family bring to this new situation. Sometimes one or other of the partners have separated—sometimes several times—before this current separation. I will explore with them something of how they experienced previous separations and what they have learned from it. These experiences can be compared in terms of replicative or corrective scripts. Often each partner is trying to avoid the worst of what had happened in the previous breakup. This corrective script is to be welcomed, although the tendency to repeat has to be given due acknowledgment. Not infrequently a partner thinks he or she has chosen someone very different, only to discover that the "dance away" is very similar. It may be that this realization will provide a glimpse of his or her own part in the dance. The separated parent may then be faced with the fear that all future partners also will leave in the same way. "Why am I so unlikeable?"

Each partner may also be experiencing transgenerational repetition of marital breakdown, having had parents who separated—perhaps also several times. This provides probably an even more important exploration of replicative or corrective scripts. Here parents can be invited to remember how it had been as children, and to think of what they would have liked their parents to have done differently in those circumstances. Some of this work is best done with the parents on their own, but some can usefully be done with the children who can then understand their parents' determination to do things that may appear quite crazy, but make sense if understood in terms of trying to avoid their own painful past experiences of their parents' divorcing.

As it is so common and so powerful, one important postseparation script that should always be sought is the replacement of the absent parent by one of the children. It not only keeps the absent parent "at home," but, unfortunately, it can also be a way of keeping the battling relationship alive. A common scenario is of a single parent, say, a mother who fights with her aggressive "son/husband." When this happens, and when grandparents themselves are divorced, one can quite frequently find evidence that this phenomenon happened in the previous generation. In other words, the replacement phenomenon is itself a replicative script. Once this is pointed out, parents can then easily see what is happening.

CHRONIC ILLNESS AND DISABLEMENT

As I am disabled myself, I have been particularly interested in this problem and how it affects families. I was a very fit young man of 18 going to read agriculture at Cambridge when I was struck down by polio. This affected both my legs and my trunk, with initial fears that I would be wheelchair bound, but later I made sufficient recovery to walk first with the aid of crutches and then with a cane. I learned something about grieving the loss of my athletic self and rescripting my future around a different plot. Long periods in hospital allowed me to become an observer of ward life, and I found myself switching my identity from that of farmer, like my father, to that of doctor. This led to medicine. The training was just feasible for me to complete as a disabled person. Agriculture was not.

Later I learned something of the impact of disability on other members of my family. When my sons started to grow up, I watched each of them, in turn, climb the stairs one step at a time, just as I climbed it. I became aware of the issue confronting them, which was how to identify with me as a person rather than with the illness. While for me the reciprocal task was how not to identify myself with the disability, but as myself now having to cope with one of life's problems—that of disability. Most of the time I do not think of myself as disabled, except when having to move around or manage potential limitations. My family of procreation, however, only knew me after I was disabled. Later, as a child psychiatrist, I became interested in those families where a new illness or disability created a loss for the family and a need for them to readjust. I have now worked with many families who have a disabled member, either a parent or a child. I will focus here on families with a parent who became disabled through either illness or accident.

Problems in Adapting to the Disability

Every family has a "temporary illness" script which dictates what to do when someone is ill. Who takes on the functions of the sick person until they are well again? Who looks after the sick person? How is this organized? Common illnesses such as flu provide an excellent opportunity for families to work this out. Children can suddenly find themselves being asked to take on caring roles: they can fetch and carry, bring drinks, take messages, and generally cheer the sick parent up. Or they share caring roles with siblings. This is a useful rehearsal for later life.

Problems can come, however, when the illness becomes chronic, and the family needs to accept the fact that the ill person is not going to get better. Some disabilities happen suddenly, after an accident, for instance. In this situation the illness script can come into action when the patient arrives home, with the longer-term adjustments coming later. As with all losses, a number of things can happen, one of which is denial of the seriousness of the illness and/or of the implications of the loss of function that the illness or disability imposes. This is more likely to happen if adequate grieving is not done for the lost function. Grieving, of course, has to include replanning of life, in which roles are taken over by somebody else, or adjustments to the lifestyle. The danger is that the "temporary illness" script becomes a permanent state of affairs if the loss is not accepted. The temporary caring arrangements may then become permanent while long-term goals, based on assumed recovery, are maintained. This may mean that children are tied into long-term "parentified" roles, or partners have to continue with just as many jobs as they were doing before, merely adding to them all the extra caring that is needed. The children may find themselves drawn into inappropriate roles. They can become the disabled parent's arms and legs—fetching and carrying and performing all the physical tasks previously performed by the parent. Children can also take on the disabled parent's lost ambitions. For example, certain children strive to become athletic and active, with the disabled parent taking fanatical interest in that aspect of the child's life. Sometimes this is beyond the natural abilities of the child. A child might start to express the feelings of the disabled parent or those of the parent who might now feel trapped by their disabled partner. A child may give vent to the anger, frustration, and depression which are his or her family's as well as his or her own.

Children become caretakers of their parents in a very real way. Disability can lead to a breakup of marriage and partnerships, often leaving a child looking after the disabled member. Society also capitalizes on the impulse that children have to care for their sick parents. There are thousands of very young children looking after totally disabled parents. Even 6- and 7-year-olds can be left looking after parents in wheelchairs. As caretakers children are sometimes involved in physically intimate relationships with the disabled parent. In one family the 11-year-old girl had been nursing her depressed, disabled stepfather. This involved changing his wet trousers and putting on his shoes. Her mother could not stand this task and so spent all her time out at work, or doing things out of the home in the evenings. The step-father started sexually abusing the girl. The child caretaker also became a substitute partner for the able-bodied parent. The resulting role reversal can further upset the authority structures of the family, which has already been rocked by the disability of one of the parents.

I have noticed particular types of problems that children exhibit in these families. Running away is a favorite. This expresses everybody's wish: the disabled person's wish to get up and run, the partner who would love to escape, or the children who would want to run away from the awfulness of the situation. The fact that the child actually acts this out, however, often attracts enormous anger and scapegoating. In one family in which the father had a spinal injury, the eldest daughter became ultragood and stayed to look after her father; her mother got depressed and became ineffectual, while the younger daughter ran away from home which enraged everyone, especially her father. Another symptom is that of doing dangerous or exciting things which enliven the family and get them out of their depression. This is often done by provoking the depressed parent's anger. Children who are parentified are, as with all parentified children, likely to have regressive symptoms as well, such as bed-wetting or learning problems thus reminding the adults that they are still children.

A disabled parent may try to counter the feeling of vulnerability by becoming very controlling, shouting at everyone, giving them orders and trying to dominate the situation. The disabled person can become like a puppeteer trying to make the family do what he or she can no longer do. In this way the disabled parent may become a tyrant, using his or her tongue as a lethal weapon. The original position of dominance in the preillness power balance can thus be maintained, or even exaggerated, compensating for a desperate sense of loss of power and vulnerability. The opposite extreme is for a disabled person to retreat into a passive position, feeling they can contribute nothing and not believing they could do, or achieve, anything at all. Self-esteem can reach rock bottom. The marriage can suffer from a change of roles. After all, the marital relationship may well have been originally built around each being able to play particular roles in the marital script. If this involves counterpart roles such as "he is strong, she is vulnerable," or "she cares, he provides," etc., then the very core of the relationship is undermined. The disability can also affect the mechanics of the sexuality of the couple, which often needs some specialized help.

The transactional style of the family will also influence what happens. Disengaged families can fail to meet each other's needs. The illness can lead to a greater distancing rather than an increase in caring. Ambivalent enmeshed families can, on the other hand, use the illness to control and to trap family members so that they are constantly having to look after the sick person, being made to feel guilty because they have never done enough. The illness then becomes just one more way of coercing members of the family to stay connected. It joins the repertoire of behaviors used as an attachment strategy in an insecure/ambivalent attachment. The danger then is that the illness behavior will be maintained. It is very difficult to give up, and the disabled person's struggle to fend for him- or herself and become more autonomous may be sabotaged.

It would be a great mistake, however, to see disability as always producing these sets of dour circumstances. A family can become more loving, closer, and achieve great feats of empathy and care. Families may come out emotionally strengthened rather than weakened by the illness. If the family provided a secure base before the illness struck, this outcome is more likely, and the security can continue afterward, perhaps with the disabled parent using his or her relative immobility to become a good listener—someone who is more readily available than either parent was before the illness. An interesting question arises: Can a family therapist harness the impulse to care to good ends? I aim to increase the security in an otherwise insecure family. The disability can provide an increase in the security of family relationships, with benefits for the future generations.

A Case Example: The Lucca Family

The Lucca family was Italian, but had lived in Britain for two generations. The father, Georgio, was in a wheelchair, having had multiple
sclerosis diagnosed 3 years before. He had felt suicidal following his
recent rapid deterioration. Francesca, the 6-year-old daughter, had
been doing poorly at school and wetting the bed; she had also been
extremely angry and abusive toward her father. Giuseppe, aged 3, had
been creating difficulties, the most troubling of which was playing
with matches and lighting fires. Both the children had been running
out into the street and the parents were terrified that they would be
run over. Not surprisingly, Maria, the mother, had reached the end
of her tether and felt she could no longer cope. I saw this family with
a colleague, Anna Dartington. Disabled families are often too much
of a trigger family for me, and although I bring special insights to the
family's situation, I also need special support from a colleague. So I
usually try to find a cotherapist or see these families with a team.

   In the first session, Georgio sat slumped in his wheelchair, depressed and angry. He was full of complaints about everybody treating him in a patronizing way, as if he was "a fourth-class citizen." He
had been a tennis coach before the illness struck him, so that disability attacked his very core. We noticed that Georgio was also sarcastic
about himself, and so we suggested that the real problem might be
that he was treating himself as a fourth-class citizen, while also acknowledging his experience that disabled people can be patronized.
We could also understand that Francesca's abusive behavior was really
echoing what father thought about himself. We explored Francesca's
symptom and its consequences. She would be horrible to her father,
saying nasty things about him, and also coming up and hitting him
on the face when he could not lift his arms to defend himself. We
asked how Georgio responded to this and he said that he threatened
to get up and beat her up. He also became very angry and shouted at
her. We could all now understand that Francesca's "symptom" managed to get her father out of his despair into a lively anger. Also, he
implied that he was going to suddenly become well again; well enough
to get out of his chair and come and hit her. No wonder she went on
doing it. She was indeed the only one in the family who could mo-
bilize her father, who in his threats to come over and hit her was also
expressing his own hopes of recovery.

   Multiple sclerosis is an extremely difficult illness to come to terms
with because of both its relapsing course and the possibility of remissions. Sadly, Georgio had no remissions up to now, but he was ever
hopeful of this and put off accepting permanent disability. The two

children's running away also made sense when we heard that Georgio would threaten to run after them and catch them. In the sessions both children would run wild around the room, and all the adults would become riveted by what was going on. They certainly brought life and excitement into the situation. On one occasion, Giuseppe took a particular interest in my cane, and at another point he rushed up to me and kicked me in the shins. I said to him that I thought he was very cross with legs that did not work properly, and he was very cross that Daddy had legs that did not work properly. Apparently he had been kicking strangers on the shins as well. We said we thought that Giuseppe was being cross for everybody about legs that did not work.

We helped Georgio to see that although he had lost his ability to express himself physically, he still had his voice. He complained often about not being able to offer his children anything, but we pointed out that he could offer words. He was a wonderful storyteller in normal circumstances, and so he gradually started taking on the role of telling stories and reading to the children. He went further than this by writing stories and entering them for competitions. He also wrote songs, some of which were accepted and played by bands. His self-esteem started to flood back again. We spent a lot of time talking to Maria about her predicament. She was devoted to Georgio and did everything for him; yet she was longing to have a life of her own. She was an artist and started experimenting with illustrating children's books and planned to develop that skill which she saw eventually leading to an occupation compatible with looking after Georgio. Some of the work with the couple and with the family was routine family therapy, helping them to work out parenting issues and on improving the parents' own relationship.

When the winter came, Georgio got a chest infection and nearly died. He was admitted to hospital where they kept him alive on an intravenous drip. He became suicidally depressed, and in the small hours of one morning he somehow rustled up enough strength to pull the intravenous out. Luckily the nurse noticed this and he was rescued. Having come out of his depression the work resumed, and the relationships within the family generally improved enormously. Before one session, Anna and I remarked on the fact that we had never discussed that one day Georgio would die and that this may not be so far away. We acknowledged that it had been too difficult a topic for us. As it happened, one of the children's pets had died a few days before, and somewhat to our amazement Georgio himself, without any prompting from us, talked about how he would die one day and was able to discuss this in a calm and natural way with his children. Perhaps our shared discussion of the topic of death may have enabled us to give cues that we could now stand the topic when it came up around the rabbit's death. Georgio, of course, lived with the shadow of death and yearned for it at times. It was our taboo, not his or that of his family.

Despite the improvement in relationships in the family, Francesca's learning problems at school persisted. It was clear that she was still very upset by her own abusive behavior toward her father, although this had disappeared. She was now preoccupied with what she had done in the past. We organized some individual psychotherapy for her, in which she worked out some of her feelings about her father. Some of her drawings were of a man with a huge head and an enormous mouth shouting, symbolic of just how frightened she was of her father's angry, powerful words. After 2 years the family seemed happier and Francesca was doing well at school. They decided that they did not need to come anymore. Georgio was grateful, saying that he was so pleased that he had not managed to kill himself and that we had helped him to have a better relationship with his children before he died. He knew this would make a big difference to them in the future. That is what he really wanted. They would be able to remember him with warmth.

Epilogue

This family provides a good ending to the book. Ultimately the work is to help families with difficulties to cope better in the future. It is hoped that this will affect not only the period following the end of therapy but also the developmental pathways over the long-term future, both of this family and of the next generation. We will have to wait a long time for evidence of the transgenerational effects of family therapy. Also, how many 30-year research projects are funded?

In the meantime we have to imagine future scenarios. Without the reconciliation between Georgio and Francesca, how would Francesca treat a future partner? Her script had been that men have to be provoked into action. What transgenerational parenting scripts would she use? Would she replicate a mother who could not expect anything of the father? Or, would she correct the experience and find a physically powerful partner on whom she would rely? It is hard to envisage either scenario having seen Francesca and her father behaving together in an affectionate way. Georgio could now give her care by being there emotionally. He was, in some ways, more available as an attachment figure for her after the illness than before. It seems likely that she might look for a partner who could provide this for their children. A secure family base seems more likely than before.

What about Giuseppe? What sort of man might he have grown into? What sort of identity would he assume? A counteridentity of a rough and tough man who kicked people?

Both children now had an experience of a father they could be proud of and of a mother who was quite extraordinarily resourceful. They would take to their future marriages the idea that even the most intolerable difficulties can be overcome if partners support each other. Families can solve their problems.

This is probably idealizing the therapy. Likely as not, families will take many of the scars from the experience as well. Therapists, however, need the gift of hope from their families. That is why we do the work.

References

Achermann, J., Dinneen, E., & Stevenson-Hinde, J. (1991). Clearing up at 2.5 years. *British Journal of Developmental Psychology*, *9*, 365–376.

Adams, K. S. (1982). Loss, suicide and attachment. In C. M. Parkes & J. Stevenson-Hinde (Eds.), *The place of attachment in human behaviour*. London: Tavistock.

Ainsworth, M. D. S. (1967). *Infancy in Uganda: Infant care and growth of attachment*. Baltimore: John Hopkins Press.

Ainsworth, M. D. S. (1991). Attachments and other affectional bonds across the life cycle. In C. M. Parkes, J. Stevenson-Hinde, & P. Marris (Eds.), *Attachment across the life cycle*. London & New York: Tavistock/Routledge.

Ainsworth, M. D. S., Blehar, R. M. C., Waters, E., & Wall, S. (1978). *Patterns of attachment: A psychological study of the strange situation*. Hillsdale, NJ: Erlbaum.

Ainsworth, M. D. S., & Eichberg, C. (1991). Effects on infant–mother attachment of mother's unresolved loss of an attachment figure, or other traumatic experience. In C. M. Parkes, J. Stevenson-Hinde, & P. Marris (Eds.), *Attachment across the life cycle*. London & New York: Tavistock/Routledge.

Andersen, T. (1987). The reflecting team: Dialogue and meta-dialogue in clinical work. *Family Process*. *26*(4), 415–428.

Anderson, J. W. (1972). Attachment behavior out of doors. In B. Jones (Ed.), *Ethological studies of child behavior*. Cambridge: Cambridge University Press.

Bagarozzi, D. A., & Anderson, S. A. (1989). *Personal, marital, and family myths: Theoretical formulations and clinical strategies*. New York & London: W. W. Norton.

Barnes, G. G. (1983). A difference that makes a difference; brief interventions in family pattern (1). *Journal of Family Therapy*, *5*(1), 37–52.

Baron-Cohen, S., Tager-Flusberg, H., & Cohen, D. J. (Eds.). (1993). *Understanding other minds: Perspectives from autism*. Oxford: Oxford University Press.

Bell, J. E. (1951). *Family group therapy* (Public Health Monograph No. 64). Washington, DC: U.S. Department of Health, Education and Welfare.

Belsky J., & Nezworski, T. (1988). *Clinical implications of attachment*. Hillsdale, NJ & London: Erlbaum.

Belsky, J., Rovine, M. & Fish, M. (1989). The developing family system. In M. R. Gunnar, & E. Thelen, (Eds.), *Minnesota Symposia of Child Psychology: Vol. 22. Systems and development*. Hillsdale, NJ & London: Erlbaum.

Belsky, J., & Vondra, J. (1990). Lessons from child abuse; the determinants of parenting. In C. Cicchetti & V. Carlson (Eds.), *Handbook of child maltreatment: Theory and research*. Boston: Cambridge University Press.

Bennett, S., Stern D. N., Lefcourt, I., Haft, W., Nachman, P., Beebe, B., & Massey, C. (1992). *The micro-interview: A technique to access maternal representations*. Paper presented at the Fifth World Congress of the World Association of Infant Psychiatry and Allied Disciplines, Chicago.

Bowlby, J. (1949). The study and reduction of group tensions in the family. *Human Relations, 2*, 123–129.

Bowlby, J. (1953). *Child care and the growth of love*. Middlesex: Harmondsworth.

Bowlby, J. (1969). *Attachment and loss: Vol 1. Attachment* (2nd ed. 1982). London & New York: Hogarth.

Bowlby, J. (1973). *Attachment and loss: Vol. 2. Separation, anxiety and anger*. London & New York: Hogarth.

Bowlby, J. (1979). *The making and breaking of affectional bonds*. London: Tavistock.

Bowlby, J. (1980). *Attachment and loss: Vol. 3. Loss: Sadness and depression*. London & New York: Hogarth.

Bowlby, J. (1988). *A secure base: Clinical applications of attachment theory*. London: Routledge.

Boszormenyi-Nagy, I., & Ulrich, D. N. (1981). Contextual family therapy. In A. S. Gurman & D. P. Kniskern (Eds.), *Handbook of family therapy*. New York: Brunner/Mazel.

Bretherton, I. (1985). Attachment theory: Retrospect and prospect. In I. Bretherton & E. Waters (Eds.), *Growing points of attachment theory and research* (Monographs of the Society for Research in Child Development, Vol. 50, Serial No. 209: Nos. 1–2). Chicago & London: University of Chicago Press.

Bruggen, P., Byng-Hall, J., & Pitt-Aikens, T. (1973). The reason for admission as a focus of work of an adolescent unit. *British Journal of Psychiatry, 122*, 319–329.

Byng-Hall, J. (1973). Family myths used as defence in conjoint family therapy. *British Journal of Psychology, 46*, 239–250.

Byng-Hall, J. (1979). Re-editing family mythology during family therapy. *Journal of Family Therapy. 1*(2), 103–116.

Byng-Hall, J. (1980). The symptom bearer as marital distance regulator: Clinical implications. *Family Process, 19*, 355–365.

Byng-Hall, J. (1982a). Family legends: Their significance for the family therapist. In A. Bentovim, A. Cooklin, & G. Gorell Barnes (Eds.), *Family therapy: Complementary frameworks of theory and practice* (Vol. 2). London: Academic Press.

Byng-Hall, J. (1982b). Grand parents, other relatives, friends and pets. In A. Bentovim, A. Cooklin, & G. Gorell Barnes (Eds.), *Family therapy: Complementary frameworks of theory and practice* (Vol. 2). London: Academic Press.

Byng-Hall, J. (1982c). The use of the earphone in supervision. In R. Whiffen & J. Byng-Hall (Eds.), *Family therapy supervision: Recent developments in practice*. London & New York: Academic Press/Grune & Stratton.

Byng-Hall, J. (1985a). Resolving distance conflicts. In A. Gurman (Ed.), *Casebook of marital therapy*. New York: Guilford Press.

Byng-Hall, J. (1985b). The family script: A useful bridge between theory and practice. *Journal of Family Therapy, 7*, 301–305.

Byng-Hall, J. (1986). Family scripts: A concept which can bridge child psycho-therapy and family therapy thinking. *Journal of Child Psychotherapy, 12*(2), 3–13.

Byng-Hall, J. (1988). Scripts and legends in families and family therapy. *Family Process, 27*(2), 167–180.

Byng-Hall, J. (1990). Attachment theory and family therapy: A clinical view. *Infant Mental Health Journal, 11*(3), 228–236.

Byng-Hall, J. (1991a). Family scripts and loss. In F. Walsh & M. McGoldrick (Eds.), *Living beyond loss: Death in the family*. Norton Press.

Byng-Hall, J. (1991b). The application of attachment theory to understanding and treatment in family therapy. In C. M. Parkes, & J. Stevenson-Hinde (Eds.), *The place of attachment in human behaviour*. London: Tavistock.

Byng-Hall, J. (1991c). An appreciation of John Bowlby: His significance for family therapy. *Journal of Family Therapy, 13*(1), 5–16.

Byng-Hall, J. (1995). Creating a family science base: Some implications of attachment theory for family therapy. *Family Process, 34*(1), 45–58.

Byng-Hall, J., & Bruggen, P. (1974). Family admission decisions as a therapeutic tool. *Family Process, 13*, 443–459.

Byng-Hall, J., de Carteret, J., & Whiffen, R. (1982). Evolution of supervision: An overview. In R. Whiffen & J. Byng-Hall (Eds.), *Family therapy supervision: Recent developments in practice*. London & New York: Academic Press/Grune & Stratton.

Byng-Hall, J., & Stevenson-Hinde, J. (1991). Attachment relationships within a family system. *Infant Mental Health Journal, 12*(3), 187–200.

Cain, A.C., & Fast, I. (1972). Children's disturbed reactions to parent suicide. In A. C. Cain (Ed.), *Survivors of suicide*. Springfield, IL: C. C. Thomas.

Cassidy, J., & Berlin, L. J. (1994). The insecure/ambivalent pattern of attachment: Theory and research. *Child Development., 65*, 971-991.

Cassidy, J., & Marvin, R. (1992). *Attachment organization in preschool children: Coding guidelines*. Seattle: MacArthur Working Group on Attachment.

Chodorow, N. (1978). *The reproduction of mothering: Psychoanalysis and the sociology of gender*. Berkeley: University of California Press.

Corboz-Warnery, A., Fivas-Depeursinge, E., Gertsch-Bettens, C., & Favez, N. (1993). Systemic analysis of triadic father–mother–baby interactions. *Infant Mental Health Journal, 14*, 298–316.

Cotgrove, A.J. (1993). *Attachment theory and the family: A single case study to pilot measures of attachment and change in family therapy*. MSc dissertation in Family Therapy, Tavistock Clinic, London.

Craik, K. (1943). *The nature of explanation*. Cambridge: Cambridge University Press.

Cramer, B. G. (1992). *The importance of being baby: The scripts parents write and the roles babies play*. New York: Addison-Wesley.

Crittenden, P. M. (1988). Relationships at risk. In J. Belsky & T. Nezworsky (Eds.), *Clinical implications of attachment*. Hillsdale, NJ & London: Erlbaum.

Cronen, V. E., Johnson, K. M., & Lannamann, J. W. (1982). Paradoxes, double binds, and reflexive loops: An alternative theoretical perspective. *Family Process, 21*(1), 91–112.

Cronen, V. E., & Pearce, W. B. (1985). Toward an explanation of how the Milan method works: An invitation to a systemic epistemology and the evolution of family systems. In D. Campbell & R. Draper (Eds.), *Applications of systemic family therapy: The Milan approach*. London & New York: Grune & Stratton.

Dicks, H. V. (1967) *Marital tensions: Clinical studies towards a psychological theory of interaction*. New York: Basic Books.

Doane, J. A., & Diamond, D. (1994). *Affect and attachment in the family: A family-based treatment of major psychiatric disorder*. New York: Basic Books.

Doane, J. A., Hill, W. L., & Diamond, D. (1991). A developmental view of therapeutic bonding in the family: Treatment of the disconnected family. *Family Process, 30*(2), 155–176.

Donley, G. D. (1993). Attachment and the emotional unit. *Family Process, 32*(1), 3–20.

Edelman, G. (1987). *Neuronal Darwinism: The theory of neuronal group selection*. New York: Basic Books.

Egeland, B., & Farber, E. A. (1984). Infant–mother attachment: Factors related to its development and changes over time. *Child Development, 55*(3), 753–771.

Emde, R. N. (1988). The effects of relationships in relationships: A developmental approach to clinical intervention. In R. A. Hinde & J. Stevenson-Hinde (Eds.), *Relationships within families*. Oxford: Oxford Science Publications

Ferreira, A. (1963). Family myth and homeostasis. *Archives of General Psychiatry, 9*, 457–463.

Fivas-Depeursinge, E. (1991). Documenting a time-bound, circular view of hierarchies: A microanalysis of parent–infant dyadic interaction. *Family Process, 30*(1), 101–102

Fivas-Depeursinge, E., Stern, D., Burgin, D., Byng-Hall, J., Corboz-Warnery, A., Lamour, M., Lebovici, S., & an Anonymous Family. (1994). The dynamics of interfaces: Seven authors in search of encounters across levels of description of an event involving a mother, father, and baby. *Infant Mental Health Journal, 16*(1), 69–89.

Fonagy, P., Steele, H., & Steele, M. (1991). Maternal representation of attachment during pregnancy predict the organization of infant–mother attachment at one year of age. *Child Development, 62*, 891–905.

Freud, S. (1909). Analysis of a phobia of a five year old boy. *Standard Edition, 10*.

Goldberg, W. A., & Easterbrooks, M. A. (1984). The role of marital quality in toddler development. *Developmental Psychology, 20*, 504–514.

Goldner, V., Penn, P., Sheinberg, M., & Walker, G. (1990). Love and violence: Gender paradoxes in volatile attachments. *Family Process, 29*(4), 343–364.

Greenberg, M. T., & Speltz, M. L. (1988). Attachment and the ontogeny of conduct problems. In J. Belsky & T. Nezworsky (Eds.), *Clinical implications of attachment*. Hillsdale, NJ & London: Erlbaum.

Hazan, C., & Shaver, P. (1987). Romantic love conceptualised as an attachment process. *Journal of Personality and Social Psychology, 52*, 511–524.

Hoffman, L. (1971). Deviation-amplifying processes in natural groups. In J. Haley (Ed.), *Changing families: A family therapy reader*. New York: Grune & Stratton.

Hoffman, L. (1975). Enmeshment and the too richly cross-joined system. *Family Process, 14*(4), 457–468.

Holmes, J. (1993). *John Bowlby and attachment theory*. London & New York: Routledge.

Imber-Black, E., Roberts, J., & Whiting, R. A. (Eds.). (1988). *Rituals in families and family therapy*. New York: W. W. Norton.

Karen, R. (1994). *Becoming attached: Unfolding the mystery of the infant–mother bond and its impact on later life*. New York: Warner Books.

Keeney, B. P. (1991). *Improvisational therapy: A practical guide for creative clinical strategies*. New York: Guilford Press.

Kelvin, P. (1977). Predictability, power, and vulnerability in interpersonal attraction. In S. W. Duck (Ed.), *Theory and practice in interpersonal attraction*. London & New York: Academic Press.

Kendon, A. (1990). Some functions of the face in the kissing round. In A. Kendon (Ed.), *Conducting interaction: Patterns of behaviour in focused encounters*. Cambridge: Cambridge University Press.

Kobak, R. B., & Sceery, A. (1988). Attachment in late adolescence: Working models, affect regulation, and representations of self and others. *Child Development, 59*, 135–146.

Liotti, G. (1991). Insecure attachment and agoraphobia. In C. M. Parkes, J. Stevenson-Hinde, & P. Marris (Eds.), *Attachment across the life cycle*. London & New York: Tavistock/Routledge.

Linnemann, E. (1966). *Parables of Jesus: Introduction and exposition*. London: S.P.C.K.

Loewenstein, S. F., Reder, P., & Clark, A. (1982). The consumer's response: Trainees' discussion of the experience of live supervision. In R. Whiffen & J. Byng-Hall (Eds.), *Family therapy supervision: Recent developments in practice*. London & New York: Academic Press/Grune & Stratton.

Main, M. (1991). Metacognitive knowledge, metacognitive monitoring, and singular (incoherent) vs. multiple (incoherent) models of attachment: Findings and directions for future research. In C. M. Parkes, J. Stevenson-Hinde, & P. Marris (Eds.), *Attachment across the life cycle*. London & New York: Tavistock/Routledge.

Main, M., & Cassidy, J. (1988). Categories of response to reunion with the parent at age 6: Predictable from infant attachment classifications and stable over a 1 month period. *Developmental Psychology, 24*, 415–426.

Main, M., & Goldwyn, R. (1985–1995). *Adult attachment scoring and classification system*. Unpublished manuscript, Department of Psychology, University of California, Berkeley.

Main, M., & Hesse, E. (1990). Parent's unresolved traumatic experiences are related to infant disorganisation attachment status: Is frightened and/or frightening parental behaviour the linking mechanism? In M. T. Greenberg, D. Cicchetti, & E. M. Cummings (Eds.), *Attachment in the preschool years: Theory, research and intervention*. Chicago & London: University of Chicago Press.

Main, M., Kaplan, N., & Cassidy, J. (1985). Security in infancy, childhood, and adulthood: A move to the level of representation. In I. Bretherton & E. Waters (Eds.), *Growing points of attachment theory and research* (Monographs of the Society for Research in Child Development, Vol. 50, Serial No. 209, Nos. 1–2). Chicago: University of Chicago Press.

Main, M., & Solomon, J. (1986). Discovery of a new, insecure/disorganised/disorientated attachment pattern. In T. B. Brazelton & M. Yogman (Eds.), *Affective development in infancy*. Norwood, NJ: Ablex.

Main, M., & Solomon, J. (1990). Procedures for identifying infants as disorganized/ disoriented during the Ainsworth Strange Situation. In M.T. Greenberg, D. Cicchetti, & E. M. Cummings (Eds.), *Attachment in the preschool years: Research and intervention.* Chicago & London: University of Chicago Press.

Main, M., & Weston, D. R. (1982). Avoidance of the attachment figure in infancy: Descriptions and interpretations. In C. M. Parkes & J. Stevenson-Hinde (Eds.), *The place of attachment in human behaviour.* London: Tavistock.

Marvin, R. S., & Stewart, R. B. (1990). A family systems framework for the study of attachment. In M. T. Greenberg, D. Cicchetti, & E. M. Cummings (Eds.), *Attachment in the preschool years: Research and intervention.* Chicago & London: University of Chicago Press.

Matas, L., Arend, R., & Sroufe, L.A. (1978). Continuity of adaptation in the second year: The relationship between quality of attachment and later competence. *Child Development, 49,* 547–556.

Mbiti, J. S. (1975). *Introduction to African religion.* Oxford: Heinemann.

McCormick, N. B. (1987). Sexual scripts: Social and therapeutic implications. *Sexual and Marital Therapy, 2*(1) 3–27.

McDougall, J. (1986). *Theatres of the mind: Illusion and truth on the psychoanalytic stage.* London: Free Association Books.

McGoldrick, M. (1982). Through the looking glass: Supervision of a trainee's "trigger family." In R. Whiffen & J. Byng-Hall (Eds.), *Family therapy supervision: Recent developments in practice.* London & New York: Academic Press/Grune & Stratton.

McGoldrick, M., Almeida, R., Hines, P. M., Garcia-Preto, N., Rosen, E., & Lee, E. (1991). Mourning in different cultures. In F. Walsh & M. McGoldrick (Eds.), *Living beyond loss: Death in the family.* New York: W. W. Norton.

McGoldrick, M., & Gerson, R. (1985). *Genograms in family assessments.* New York & London: W. W. Norton.

Minuchin, P. (1985). Families and individual development: Provocations from the field of family therapy. *Child Development, 56,* 289–302.

Minuchin, S. (1974). *Families and family therapy.* Boston: Harvard University Press; London: Tavistock.

Minuchin, S., & Fishman, H. C. (1981). *Family therapy techniques.* New York & London: Harvard University Press.

Murray, L., & Cooper, P. J. (1994). Clinical applications of attachment theory and research: Changes in infant attachment with brief psychotherapy. In J. Richer (Ed.), *The clinical application of ethology and attachment theory* (Association for Child Psychology and Psychiatry, Occasional Papers No. 9). London:ACPP.

Neisser, U., & Winograd, E. (1988). *Remembering reconsidered: Ecological and traditional approaches to the study of memory: Emory symposia in cognition.* Cambridge & New York: Cambridge University Press.

Nelson, K. (1981). Social cognition in a script framework. In J. H.Flavell & L. Ross (Eds.), *Social cognitive development: Frontiers and possible futures.* Cambridge & New York: Cambridge University Press.

Nelson. K. (1988). The ontogeny of memory for real events. In U. Neisser & E. Winograd (Eds.), *Remembering reconsidered: Ecological and traditional approaches to the study of memory: Emory symposia in cognition.* Cambridge & New York: Cambridge University Press.

Palazzoli, M., Boscolo, L., Cecchin, G., & Prata, G. (1980). Hypothesizing–circularity–neutrality: Three guidelines for the conductor of the session. *Family Process, 19*, 3–12.

Papp, P. (1976). Family choreography. In P. J. Guerin (Ed.), *Family therapy: Theory and practice*. New York: Gardner Press.

Papp, P. (1980). The Greek chorus and other techniques of family therapy. *Family Process, 19*(1), 45–58

Papp, P. (1983). *The process of change*. New York: Guilford Press.

Patrick, M., Hobson, R. P., Castle, D., Howard, R., & Maughan, B. (1994). Personality disorder and the mental representation of early social experience. *Development and Psychopathology, 6*, 375–388.

Patterson, G. R., & Dishion, T. J. (1988). Multilevel family process models: Traits, interactions, and relationships. In R. A. Hinde & J. Stevenson-Hinde (Eds.), *Relationships within families: Mutual influences*. Oxford: Clarendon Press.

Pincus, L., & Dare, C. (1978). *Secrets in the family*. London and Boston: Faber & Faber.

Pistole, M.C. (1994). Adult attachment styles: Some thoughts on closeness–distance struggles. *Family Process, 33*(2), 147–160.

Pochock, D. (1995). Searching for a better story: Harnessing modern and postmodern positions in family therapy. *Journal of Family Therapy,* 17(2), 149–174.

Quinton, D., Rutter, M., & Liddle, C. (1984). Institutional rearing, parenting difficulties and marital support. *Psychological Medicine, 14*, 107–124.

Radke-Yarrow, M. (1991). Attachment patterns in children of depressed mothers. In C. M. Parkes, J. Stevenson-Hinde, & P. Marris (Eds.), *Attachment across the life cycle*. London & New York: Tavistock/Routledge.

Reiss, D. (1981). *The family's construction of reality*. Boston: Harvard University Press.

Ricks, M. H. (1985). The social transition of parental behavior: Attachment across the generations. In I. Bretherton & E. Waters (Eds.), *Growing points of attachment theory and research* (Monographs of the Society for Research in Child Development, Vol. 50, Serial No. 209, Nos. 1–2). Chicago: University of Chicago Press.

Robertson, J. (1952). *A two year old goes to hospital* [Film]. New York: New York Film Library.

Rosen, R. (1979). Old trends and new trends in systems research: Ludwig von Bertalanffy Memorial Lecture. In *General systems research: A science, a methodology, a technology*. Proceedings of the 1979 North American Meeting, Louisville, KY.

Rosenfield, I. (1988). *The invention of memory: A new view of the brain*. New York: Basic Books.

Rubin, K. H., & Lollis, S. P. (1988). Origins and consequences of social withdrawal. In J. Belsky & T. Nezworsky (Eds.), *Clinical implications of attachment*. Hillsdale, NJ & London: Erlbaum.

Rutter, M., Quinton, D., & Liddle, C. (1983). Parenting in two generations: Looking backwards and looking forwards. In N. Madge (Ed.), *Families at risk*. London: Heinemann.

Ryder, R. G., & Bartle, S. (1991). Boundaries as distance regulators in personal relationships. *Family Process, 30*(4), 393–406.

Santayana, G. (1905). *The life of reason* (Vol. 1). New York: Scribner.

280

                                                            References

Sacco, M., Corboz-Warnery, A., & Fivas-Depeursinge, E. (1993). *Comment passe-t-on de deux plus un à troit?: Microanalyse de transitions dans l'interaction père, mère et bébé* (Research Report FRNS No.49). Prilly: Centre d'Etude de la Famille.

Skynner, A. C. R. (1979). Reflections on the family therapist as family scapegoat. *Journal of Family Therapy, 1*, 7–22.

Schank, R. C. (1982). *Dynamic memory: A theory of reminding and learning in computers and people.* Cambridge: Cambridge University Press.

Schank, R. C., & Abelson, R. P. (1977). *Scripts, plans, goals and understanding.* Hillsdale, NJ: Erlbaum.

Scharff, D. E., & Scharff, J. S. (1987). *Object relations family therapy.* Northvale, NJ & London: Jason Aronson.

Simon, F. B., Stierlin, H., & Wynne, L. C. (1985). *The language of family therapy: A systemic vocabulary and source book.* New York: Family Process.

Skolnick, A. (1986). Early attachment and personal relationships. In P. Baltes, D. Featherman, & R. Lerner (Eds.), *Life-span development and behavior* (Vol. 7). Hillsdale, NJ: Erlbaum.

Sroufe, L. A. (1988). The role of infant–caregiver attachment in development. In J. Belsky & T. Nezworsky (Eds.), *Clinical implications of attachment.* Hillsdale, NJ & London: Erlbaum.

Sroufe, L. A. (1989). Relationships and relationship disturbances. In A. Sameroff & R. Emde (Eds.). *Relationship disturbances in early childhood.* Hillsdale, NJ: Erlbaum.

Sroufe, L. A., & Waters, E. (1977). Heart rate as a convergent measure in clinical and developmental research. *Merrill-Palmer Quarterly, 23*, 3–28.

Stanton, M. D., Todd, T. C., & Associates (1982). *The family therapy of drug abuse and addiction.* New York: Guilford Press.

Steiner, C. (1974). *Scripts people live.* New York: Grove Press.

Stern, D. N. (1985). *The interpersonal world of the infant: A view from psychoanalysis and developmental psychology.* New York: Basic Books.

Stevenson-Hinde, J. (1990). Attachment within family systems: An overview. *Infant Mental Health Journal, 11*(3), 218–227.

Stevenson-Hinde, J., & Shouldice, A. (1995). Maternal interactions and self-reports related to attachment classifications at 4.5 years. *Child Development 66*, 583–596.

Toman, W. (1961). *Family constellation: Its effects on personality and social behavior.* New York: Springer.

Tomkins, S. S. (1979). Script theory: Differential magnification of affects. In H.E. Howe, Jr. & R. A. Dienstbier (Eds.), *Nebraska Symposium on Motivation* (Vol. 26). Lincoln: University of Nebraska Press.

Urban, J., Carlson, E., Egeland, B., & Sroufe, L. A. (1991). Patterns of individual adaptation across childhood. *Development and Psychopathology, 3*, 445–460.

Van IJzendoorn, M. H., & Kroonenberg, P. M. (1988). Cross-cultural patterns of attachment: A meta-analysis of the Strange Situation. *Child Development, 59*, 147–156.

Watzlawick, P. (1978). *The language of change: Elements of therapeutic communication.* New York: Basic Books.

Watzlawick, P. (1984). Self-fulfilling prophecies. In P. Watzlawick (Ed.), *The invented reality.* New York & London: W. W. Norton.

Watzlawick, P., Beavin, J. H., & Jackson, D. D. (1967). *Pragmatics of human communi-

cation: A study of interaction patterns, pathologies, and paradoxes. New York: W. W. Norton.

Weiss, R. S. (1982). Attachments in adult life. In C.M. Parkes & J. Stevenson-Hinde (Eds.), *The place of attachment in human behavior.* London: Tavistock.

Winnicott, D.W. (1960). The theory of parent–infant relationship. In M.Kahn (Ed.), *The maturational processes and the facilitating environment: Studies in the theory of emotional development.* (The International Psychoanalytic Library). London: Hogarth.

White, M., & Epston, D. (1989). *Literate means to therapeutic ends.* Adelaide: Dulwich Centre Publications.

Wynne, L.C. (1984). The epigenesis of relational systems: A model for understanding family development. *Family Process, 23*(1), 297–318.

Zucker, K.J., & Green, R. (1992). Psychosexual disorders in children and adolescents. *Journal of Child Psychology and Psychiatry, 33*(1), 107–152.

Index